EXPOSITION ON THE CHRISTIAN FAITH

I0558251

Translated by H. de Romestin, E. de Romestin and H.T.F. Duckworth. From Nicene and Post-Nicene Fathers, Second Series, Vol. 10. Edited by Philip Schaff and Henry Wace. (Buffalo, NY: Christian Literature Publishing Co., 1896.)

Edited by: D.P. Curtin

Library of Congress Cataloging-in-Publication Data

EXPOSITION ON THE CHRISTIAN FAITH

St. Ambrose of Milan

Dalcassian
Publishing
Company
PHILADELPHIA, PA

Preface.

On the eve of setting out for the East, to aid his uncle Valens in repelling a Gothic invasion, Gratian, the Emperor of the West, requested St. Ambrose to write him a treatise in proof of the Divinity of Jesus Christ. Gratian's object in making this request was to secure some sort of preservative against the corrupting influence of Arianism, which at that time (a.d. 378) had gained the upper hand of Orthodoxy in the Eastern provinces of the Empire, owing to its establishment at the Imperial Court. In compliance with Gratian's wish, the Bishop of Milan composed a treatise, which now forms the first two Books of the De Fide. With this work the Emperor was so much pleased that on his return from the East, after the death of Valens at Hadrianople, he wrote to St. Ambrose, begging for a fresh copy of the treatise, and further, for its enlargement by the addition of a discourse on the Divinity of the Holy Spirit. The original treatise was, indeed, enlarged by St. Ambrose in 379, but the additional Books dealt, not with the Divinity of the Holy Spirit, but rather with new objections raised by the Arian teachers, and points which had either been passed over or not fully discussed already. In this way St. Ambrose's Exposition was brought into its present form.

The object of the Exposition is, as has already been indicated, to prove the Divinity of Jesus Christ, and His co-eternity, co-equality, and consubstantiality, as God the Son, with God the Father. This the author does by constant appeal to the Scriptures, both of the Old and of the New Testament, which the Arians had in many cases forced into the mould of false interpretation to make them fit their doctrine.

Besides the title of De Fide, that of De Trinitate was one by which this treatise was largely known in after ages; it is certain, though, that the former was that assigned by St. Ambrose himself.

Prefatory Note.

The notes to the first four books of the De Fide have in some instances been taken over from those in Father Hurter's Edition of the treatise (Innsbruck: Wagner), which has been used in preparing the translation of these books. These notes are distinguished by the letter "H." placed at the end.

The citations from Scripture embodied in the text have been translated as they stood in the original. This will account for any divergence from the renderings in the English Bible and Prayer-book, while any agreement may be set down to reminiscences of the more familiar versions. It was thought best to adopt this treatment of St. Ambrose's citations, inasmuch as the divergences are worth noticing, and indeed, in some cases, the argument rather turns upon them. The references are, throughout, made to chapters and verses in the English Bible, and not to the Vulgate, unless especially stated so to be.

The Prefaces and Summaries of Contents are based on those in Father Hurter's Edition.

St. Ambrose's Exposition of the Christian Faith

Book I.

Prologue.

The author praises Gratian's zeal for instruction in the Faith, and speaks lowly of his own merits. Taught of God Himself, the Emperor stands in no need of human instruction; yet this his devoutness prepares the way to victory. The task appointed to the author is difficult: in the accomplishment whereof he will be guided not so much by reason and argument as by authority, especially that of the Nicene Council.

1. The Queen of the South, as we read in the Book of the Kings, came to hear the wisdom of Solomon. 1 Kings 10:1 Likewise King Hiram sent to Solomon that he might prove him. 1 Kings 5:1 So also your sacred Majesty, following these examples of old time, has decreed to hear my confession of faith. But I am no Solomon, that you should wonder at my wisdom, and your Majesty is not the sovereign of a single people; it is the Augustus, ruler of the whole world, that has commanded the setting forth of the Faith in a book, not for your instruction, but for your approval.

2. For why, august Emperor, should your Majesty learn that Faith which, from your earliest childhood, you have ever devoutly and lovingly kept? Before I formed you in your mother's belly I knew you, says the Scripture, and before you came forth out of the womb I sanctified you. Sanctification, therefore, comes not of tradition, but of inspiration; therefore keep watch over the gifts of God. For that which no man has taught you, God has surely given and inspired.

3. Your sacred Majesty, being about to go forth to war, requires of me a book, expounding the Faith, since your Majesty knows that victories are gained more by faith in the commander, than by valour in the soldiers. For Abraham led into battle three hundred and eighteen men, and brought home the spoils of countless foes; and having, by the power of that which was the sign of our Lord's Cross and Name, overcome the might of five kings and conquering hosts, he both avenged his neighbour and gained victory and the ransom of his brother's son. So also Joshua the Son of Nun, when he could not prevail against the enemy with the might of all his army, Joshua 6:6 overcame by sound of seven sacred trumpets, in the place where he saw and knew the Captain of the heavenly host. For victory, then, your Majesty makes ready, being Christ's loyal servant and defender of the Faith, which you would have me set forth in writing.

4. Truly, I would rather take upon me the duty of exhortation to keep the Faith, than that of disputing thereon; for the former means devout confession, whereas the latter is liable to rash presumption. Howbeit, forasmuch as your Majesty has no need of exhortation, while I may not pray to be excused from the duty of loyalty, I will take in hand a bold enterprise, yet modestly withal, not so much reasoning and disputing concerning the Faith as gathering together a multitude of witness.

5. Of the Acts of Councils, I shall let that one be my chief guide which three hundred and eighteen priests, appointed, as it were, after the judgment of Abraham, made (so to speak) a trophy raised to proclaim their victory over the infidel throughout the world, prevailing by that courage of the Faith, wherein all agreed. Verily, as it seems to me, one may herein see the hand of God, forasmuch as the same number is our authority in the Councils of the Faith, and an example of loyalty in the records of old.

Chapter 1.

The author distinguishes the faith from the errors of Pagans, Jews, and Heretics, and after explaining the significance of the names God and Lord, shows clearly the difference of Persons in Unity of Essence. In dividing the Essence, the Arians not only bring in the doctrine of three Gods, but even overthrow the dominion of the Trinity.

6. Now this is the declaration of our Faith, that we say that God is One, neither dividing His Son from Him, as do the heathen, nor denying, with the Jews, that He was begotten of the Father before all worlds, and afterwards born of the Virgin; nor yet, like Sabellius, confounding the Father with the Word, and so maintaining that Father and Son are one and the same Person; nor again, as does Photinus, holding that the Son first came into existence in the Virgin's womb: nor believing, with Arius, in a number of diverse Powers, and so, like the benighted heathen, making out more than one God. For it is written: Hear, O Israel: the Lord your God is one God.

7. For God and Lord is a name of majesty, a name of power, even as God Himself says: The Lord is My name, Exodus 3:15 and as in another place the prophet declares: The Lord Almighty is His name. God is He, therefore, and Lord, either because His rule is over all, or because He beholds all things, and is feared by all, without difference.

8. If, then, God is One, one is the name, one is the power, of the Trinity. Christ Himself, indeed, says: Go, baptize the nations in the name of the Father, and of the Son, and of the Holy Spirit. Matthew 28:19 In the *name*, mark you, not in the *names*.

9. Moreover, Christ Himself says: I and the Father are One. John 10:30 One, said He, that there be no separation of power and nature; but again, *We are*, that you may recognize Father and Son, forasmuch as the perfect Father is believed to have begotten the perfect Son, Matthew 5:48 and the Father and the Son are One, not by confusion of Person, but by unity of nature.

10. We say, then, that there is one God, not two or three Gods, this being the error into which the impious heresy of the Arians does run with its blasphemies. For it says that there are three Gods, in that it divides the Godhead of the Trinity; whereas the Lord, in saying, Go, baptize the nations in the name of the Father and of the Son and of the Holy Spirit, has shown that the Trinity is of one power. We confess Father, Son, and Spirit, understanding in a perfect Trinity both fullness of Divinity and unity of power.

11. Every kingdom divided against itself shall quickly be overthrown, says the Lord. Now the kingdom of the Trinity is not divided. If, therefore, it is not divided, it is one; for that which is not one is divided. The Arians, however, would have the kingdom of the Trinity to be such as may easily be overthrown, by division against itself. But truly, seeing that it cannot be overthrown, it is plainly undivided. For no unity is divided or rent asunder, and therefore neither age nor corruption has any power over it.

Chapter 2.

The Emperor is exhorted to display zeal in the Faith. Christ's perfect Godhead is shown from the unity of will and working which He has with the Father. The attributes of Divinity are shown to be proper to Christ, Whose various titles prove His essential unity, with distinction of Person. In no other way can the unity of God be maintained.

12. Not every one that says unto Me Lord, Lord, shall enter into the kingdom of heaven, Matthew 7:21 says the Scripture. Faith, therefore, august Sovereign, must not be a mere matter of performance, for it is written, The zeal of your house has devoured me. Let us then with faithful spirit and devout mind call upon Jesus our Lord, let us believe that He is God, to the end that whatever we ask of the Father, we may obtain in His name. For the Father's will is, that He be entreated through the Son, the Son's that the Father be entreated.

13. The grace of His submission makes for agreement [with our teaching], and the acts of His power are not at variance therewith. For whatsoever things the Father does, the same also does the Son, in like manner. The Son both does the same things, and does them in like manner, but it is the Father's will that He be entreated in the matter of what He Himself proposes to do, that you may understand, not that He cannot do it otherwise, but that there is one power displayed. Truly, then, is the Son of God to be adored and worshipped, Who by the power of His Godhead has laid the foundations of the world, and by His submission informed our affections.

14. Therefore we ought to believe that God is good, eternal, perfect, almighty, and true, such as we find Him in the Law and the Prophets, and the rest of the holy Scriptures, for otherwise there is no God. For He Who is God cannot but be good, seeing that fullness of goodness is of the nature of God: nor can God, Who made time, be in time; nor, again, can God be imperfect, for a lesser being is plainly imperfect, seeing that it lacks somewhat whereby it could be made equal to a greater. This, then, is the teaching of our faith— that God is not evil, that with God nothing is impossible, that God exists not in time, that God is beneath no being. If I am in error, let my adversaries prove it.

15. Seeing, then, that Christ is God, He is, by consequence, good and almighty and eternal and perfect and true; for these attributes belong to the essential nature of the Godhead. Let our adversaries, therefore, deny the Divine Nature in Christ — otherwise they cannot refuse to God what is proper to the Divine Nature.

16. Further, that none may fall into error, let a man attend to those signs vouchsafed us by holy Scripture, whereby we may know the Son. He is called the Word, the Son, the Power of God, the Wisdom of God. The Word, because He is without blemish; the Power, because He is perfect; the Son, because He is begotten of the Father; the Wisdom, because He is one with the Father, one in eternity, one in Divinity. Not that the Father is one Person with the Son; between Father and Son is the plain distinction that comes of generation; so that Christ is God of God, Everlasting of Everlasting, Fulness of Fulness.

17. Now these are not mere names, but signs of power manifesting itself in works, for while there is fullness of Godhead in the Father, there is also fullness of Godhead in the Son, not diverse, but one. The Godhead is nothing confused, for it is an unity: nothing manifold, for in it there is no difference.

18. Moreover, if in all them that believed there was, as it is written, one soul and one heart: Acts 4:32 if every one that cleaves to the Lord is one spirit, 1 Corinthians 6:17 as the Apostle has said: if a man and his wife are one flesh: if all we mortal men are, so far as regards our general nature, of one substance: if this is what the Scripture says of created men, that, being many, they are one, who can in no way be compared to Divine Persons, how much more are the Father and the Son one in Divinity, with Whom there is no difference either of substance or of will!

19. For how else shall we say that God is One? Divinity makes plurality, but unity of power debars quantity of number, seeing that unity is not number, but itself is the principle of all numbers.

Chapter 3.

By evidence gathered from Scripture the unity of Father and Son is proved, and firstly, a passage, taken from the Book of Isaiah, is compared with others and expounded in such sort as to show that in the Son there is no diversity from the Father's nature, save only as regards the flesh; whence it follows that the Godhead of both Persons is One. This conclusion is confirmed by the authority of Baruch.

20. Now the oracles of the prophets bear witness what close unity holy Scripture declares to subsist between the Father and the Son as regards their Godhead. For thus says the Lord of Sabaoth: Egypt has laboured, and the commerce of the Ethiopians and Sabeans: mighty men shall come over to you, and shall be your servants, and in your train shall they follow, bound in fetters, and they shall fall down before you, and to you shall they make supplication: for God is in you, and there is no God beside you. For you are God, and we knew it not, O God of Israel.

21. Hear the voice of the prophet: In You, he says, is God, and there is no God beside You. How agrees this with the Arians' teaching? They must deny either the Father's or the Son's Divinity, unless they believe, once for all, unity of the same Divinity.

22. In You, says he, is God — forasmuch as the Father is in the Son. For it is written, The Father, Who abides in Me, Himself speaks, and The works that I do, He Himself also does. John 14:10 And yet again we read that the Son is in the Father, saying, I am in the Father, and the Father in Me. John 14:10 Let the Arians, if they can, make away with this kinship in nature and unity in work.

23. There is, therefore, God in God, but not two Gods; for it is written that there is one God, and there is Lord in Lord, but not two Lords, forasmuch as it is likewise written: Serve not two lords. Matthew 6:24 And the Law says: Hear, O Israel! The Lord your God is one God; Deuteronomy 6:4 moreover, in the same Testament it is written: The Lord rained from the Lord. Genesis 19:24 The Lord, it is said, sent rain from the Lord. So also you may read in Genesis: And God said — and God made, Genesis 1:6-7 and, lower down, And God made man in the image of God; Genesis 1:26-27 yet it was not two gods, but one God, that made [man]. In the one place, then, as in the other, the unity of operation and of name is maintained. For surely, when we read God of God, we do not speak of two Gods.

24. Again, you may read in the forty-fourth psalm how the prophet not only calls the Father God but also proclaims the Son as God, saying: Your throne, O God, is for ever and ever. And further on: God, even your God, has anointed you with the oil of gladness above your fellows. This God Who anoints, and God Who in the flesh is anointed, is the Son of God. For what fellows in His anointing has Christ, except such as are in the flesh? You see, then, that God is by God anointed, but being anointed in taking upon Him the nature of mankind, He is proclaimed the Son of God; yet is the principle of the Law not broken.

25. So again, when you read, The Lord rained from the Lord, acknowledge the unity of Godhead, for unity in operation does not allow of more than one individual God, even as the Lord Himself has shown, saying: Believe Me, that I am in the Father, and the Father in Me: or believe Me for the very works' sake. Here, too, we see that unity of Godhead is signified by unity in operation.

26. The Apostle, careful to prove that there is one Godhead of both Father and Son, and one Lordship, lest we should run into any error, whether of heathen or of Jewish ungodliness, showed us the rule we ought to follow, saying: One God, the Father, from Whom are all things, and we in Him, and one Lord, Jesus Christ, by Whom are all things, and we by Him. For just as, in calling Jesus Christ Lord, he did not deny that the Father was Lord, even so, in saying, One God, the Father, he did not deny true Godhead to the Son, and thus he taught, not that there was more than one God, but that the source of power was one, forasmuch as Godhead consists in Lordship, and Lordship in Godhead, as it is written: Be sure that the Lord, He is God. It is He that has made us, and not we ourselves.

27. In you, therefore, is God, by unity of nature, and there is no God beside You, by reason of personal possession of the Substance, without any reserve or difference.

28. Again, Scripture speaks, in the Book of Jeremiah, of One God, and yet acknowledges both Father and Son. Thus we read: He is our God, and in comparison

with Him none other shall be accounted of. He has discovered all the way of teaching, and given it to Jacob, His servant, and to Israel, His beloved. After these things He appeared upon earth, and conversed with men.

29. The prophet speaks of the Son, for it was the Son Himself Who conversed with men, and this is what he says: He is our God, and in comparison with Him none other shall be accounted of. Why do we call Him in question, of Whom so great a prophet says that no other can be compared with Him? What comparison of another *can* be made, when the Godhead is One? This was the confession of a people set in the midst of dangers; reverencing religion, and therefore unskilled in strife of argument.

30. Come, Holy Spirit, and help Your prophets, in whom You are wont to dwell, in whom we believe. Shall we believe the wise of this world, if we believe not the prophets? But where is the wise man, where is the scribe? When our peasant planted figs, he found that whereof the philosopher knew nothing, for God has chosen the foolish things of this world to confound the strong. Are we to believe the Jews? For God was once known in Jewry. Nay, but they deny that very thing, which is the foundation of our belief, seeing that they know not the Father, who have denied the Son.

Chapter 4.

The Unity of God is necessarily implied in the order of Nature, in the Faith, and in Baptism. The gifts of the Magi declare (1) the Unity of the Godhead; (2) Christ's Godhead and Manhood. The truth of the doctrine of the Trinity in Unity is shown in the Angel walking in the midst of the furnace with Shadrach, Meshach, and Abednego.

31. All nature testifies to the Unity of God, inasmuch as the universe is one. The Faith declares that there is one God, seeing that there is one belief in both the Old and the New Testament. That there is one Spirit, all holy, grace witnesses, because there is one Baptism, in the Name of the Trinity. The prophets proclaim, the apostles hear, the voice of one God. In one God did the Magi believe, and they brought, in adoration, gold, frankincense, and myrrh to Christ's cradle, confessing, by the gift of gold, His Royalty, and with the incense worshipping Him as God. For gold is the sign of kingdom, incense of God, myrrh of burial.

32. What, then, was the meaning of the mystic offerings in the lowly cattle-stalls, save that we should discern in Christ the difference between the Godhead and the flesh? He is seen as man, Philippians 2:7 He is adored as Lord. He lies in swaddling-clothes, but shines amid the stars; the cradle shows His birth, the stars His dominion; it is the flesh that is wrapped in clothes, the Godhead that receives the ministry of angels. Thus the dignity of His natural majesty is not lost, and His true assumption of the flesh is proved.

33. This is our Faith. Thus did God will that He should be known by all, thus believed the three children, Daniel 4:17 and felt not the fire into the midst whereof

they were cast, which destroyed and burnt up unbelievers, Daniel 4:22 while it fell harmless as dew upon the faithful, Hosea 14:5 for whom the flames kindled by others became cold, seeing that the torment had justly lost its power in conflict with faith. For with them there was One in the form of an angel, Daniel 4:28 comforting them, Luke 22:43 to the end that in the number of the Trinity one Supreme Power might be praised. God was praised, the Son of God was seen in God's angel, holy and spiritual grace spoke in the children.

Chapter 5.

The various blasphemies uttered by the Arians against Christ are cited. Before these are replied to, the orthodox are admonished to beware of the captious arguments of philosophers, forasmuch as in these especially did the heretics put their trust.

34. Now let us consider the disputings of the Arians concerning the Son of God.

35. They say that the Son of God is unlike His Father. To say this of a man would be an insult.

36. They say that the Son of God had a beginning in time, whereas He Himself is the source and ordainer of time and all that therein is. We are men, and we would not be limited to time. We began to exist once, and we believe that we shall have a timeless existence. We desire after immortality— how, then, can we deny the eternity of God's Son, Whom God declares to be eternal by nature, not by grace?

37. They say that He was created. But who would reckon an author with his works, and have him seem to be what he has himself made?

38. They deny His goodness. Their blaspheming is its own condemnation, and so cannot hope for pardon.

39. They deny that He is truly Son of God, they deny His omnipotence, in that while they admit that all things are made by the ministry of the Son, they attribute the original source of their being to the power of God. But what is power, save perfection of nature?

40. Furthermore, the Arians deny that in Godhead He is One with the Father. Let them annul the Gospel, then, and silence the voice of Christ. For Christ Himself has said: I and the Father are one. John 10:30 It is not I who say this: Christ has said it. Is He a deceiver, that He should lie? Numbers 23:19 Is He unrighteous, that He should claim to be what He never was? But of these matters we will deal severally, at greater length, in their proper place.

41. Seeing, then, that the heretic says that Christ is unlike His Father, and seeks to maintain this by force of subtle disputation, we must cite the Scripture: Take heed that no man make spoil of you by philosophy and vain deceit, according to the tradition of men, and after the rudiments of this world, not according to Christ; for in Him dwells all the fullness of Godhead in bodily shape.

42. For they store up all the strength of their poisons in dialetical disputation, which by the judgment of philosophers is defined as having no power to establish anything, and aiming only at destruction. But it was not by dialectic that it pleased God to save His people; for the kingdom of God consists in simplicity of faith, not in wordy contention.

Chapter 6.

By way of leading up to his proof that Christ is not different from the Father, St. Ambrose cites the more famous leaders of the Arian party, and explains how little their witness agrees, and shows what defense the Scriptures provide against them.

43. The Arians, then, say that Christ is unlike the Father; we deny it. Nay, indeed, we shrink in dread from the word. Nevertheless I would not that your sacred Majesty should trust to argument and our disputation. Let us enquire of the Scriptures, of apostles, of prophets, of Christ. In a word, let us enquire of the Father, Whose honour these men say they uphold, if the Son be judged inferior to Him. But insult to the Son brings no honour to the good Father. It cannot please the good Father, if the Son be judged inferior, rather than equal, to His Father.

44. I pray your sacred Majesty to suffer me, if for a little while I address myself particularly to these men. But whom shall I choose out to cite? Eunomius? or Arius and Aëtius, his instructors? For there are many names, but one unbelief, constant in wickedness, but in conversation divided against itself; without difference in respect of deceit, but in common enterprise breeding dissent. But wherefore they will not agree together I understand not.

45. The Arians reject the person of Eunomius, but they maintain his unbelief and walk in the ways of his iniquity. They say that he has too generously published the writings of Arius. Truly, a plentiful lavishing of error! They praise him who gave the command, and deny him who executed it! Wherefore they have now fallen apart into several sects. Some follow after Eunomius or Aëtius, others after Palladius or Demophilus and Auxentius, or the inheritors of this form of unbelief. Others, again, follow different teachers. Is Christ, then, divided? 1 Corinthians 1:13 Nay; but those who divide Him from the Father do with their own hands cut themselves asunder.

46. Seeing, therefore, that men who agree not among themselves have all alike conspired against the Church of God, I shall call those whom I have to answer by the common name of heretics. For heresy, like some hydra of fable, has waxed great from its wounds, and, being ofttimes lopped short, has grown afresh, being appointed to find meet destruction in flames of fire. Or, like some dread and monstrous Scylla, divided into many shapes of unbelief, she displays, as a mask to her guile, the pretence of being a Christian sect, but those wretched men whom she finds tossed to and fro in the waves of her unhallowed strait, amid the wreckage of their faith, she, girt with beastly monsters, rends with the cruel fang of her blasphemous doctrine.

47. This monster's cavern, your sacred Majesty, thick laid, as seafaring men do say it is, with hidden lairs, and all the neighbourhood thereof, where the rocks of unbelief echo to the howling of her black dogs, we must pass by with ears in a manner stopped. For it is written: Hedge your ears about with thorns; Sirach 28:28 and again: Beware of dogs, beware of evil workers; Philippians 3:2 and yet again: A man that is an heretic, avoid after the first reproof, knowing that such an one is fallen, and is in sin, being condemned of his own judgment. Titus 3:10-11 So then, like prudent pilots, let us set the sails of our faith for the course wherein we may pass by most safely, and again follow the coasts of the Scriptures.

Chapter 7.

The likeness of Christ to the Father is asserted on the authority of St. Paul, the prophets, and the Gospel, and especially in reliance upon the creation of man in God's image.

48. The Apostle says that Christ is the image of the Father — for he calls Him the image of the invisible God, the first-begotten of all creation. First-begotten, mark you, not first-created, in order that He may be believed to be both begotten, in virtue of His nature, and first in virtue of His eternity. In another place also the Apostle has declared that God made the Son heir of all things, by Whom also He made the worlds, Who is the brightness of His glory, and the express image of His substance. Hebrews 1:2 The Apostle calls Christ the image of the Father, and Arius says that He is unlike the Father. Why, then, is He called an image, if He has no likeness? Men will not have their portraits unlike them, and Arius contends that the Father is unlike the Son, and would have it that the Father has begotten one unlike Himself, as though unable to generate His like.

49. The prophets say: In Your light we shall see light; and again: Wisdom is the brightness of everlasting light, and the spotless mirror of God's majesty, the image of His goodness. Wisdom 7:26 See what great names are declared! Brightness, because in the Son the Father's glory shines clearly: spotless mirror, because the Father is seen in the Son: John 12:45 image of goodness, because it is not one body seen reflected in another, but the whole power [of the Godhead] in the Son. The word image teaches us that there is no difference; expression, that He is the counterpart of the Father's form; and brightness declares His eternity. The image in truth is not that of a bodily countenance, not one made up of colors, nor modelled in wax, but simply derived from God, coming out from the Father, drawn from the fountainhead.

50. By means of this image the Lord showed Philip the Father, saying, Philip, he that sees Me, sees the Father also. How then do you say, Show us the Father? Do you not believe that I am in the Father, and the Father in Me? John 14:9-10 Yes, he who looks upon the Son sees, in portrait, the Father. Mark what manner of portrait is spoken of. It is Truth, Righteousness, the Power of God: not dumb, for it is the Word; not insensible, for it is Wisdom; not vain and foolish, for it is Power; not soulless, for it is the Life; not dead, for it is the Resurrection. You see, then, that while an image is spoken of, the meaning is that it is the Father, Whose image the Son is, seeing that no one can be his own image.

51. More might I set down from the Son's testimony; howbeit, lest He perchance appear to have asserted Himself overmuch, let us enquire of the Father. For the Father said, Let us make man in Our image and likeness. Genesis 1:26 The Father says to the Son in *Our* image and likeness, and you say that the Son of God is unlike the Father.

52. John says, Beloved, we are sons of God, and it does not yet appear what we shall be: we know that if He be revealed, we shall be like Him. 1 John 3:2 O blind madness! O shameless obstinacy! We are men, and, so far as we may, we shall be in the likeness of God: dare we deny that the Son is like God?

53. Therefore the Father has said: Let us make man in Our image and likeness. At the beginning of the universe itself, as I read, the Father and the Son existed, and I see one creation. I hear Him that speaks. I acknowledge Him that does: but it is of one image, one likeness, that I read. This likeness belongs not to diversity but to unity. What, therefore, you claim for yourself, you take from the Son of God, seeing, indeed, that you can not be in the image of God, save by help of the image of God.

Chapter 8.

The likeness of the Son to the Father being proved, it is not hard to prove the Son's eternity, though, indeed, this may be established on the authority of the Prophet Isaiah and St. John the Evangelist, by which authority the heretical leaders are shown to be refuted.

54. It is plain, therefore, that the Son is not unlike the Father, and so we may confess the more readily that He is also eternal, seeing that He Who is like the Eternal must needs be eternal. But if we say that the Father is eternal, and yet deny this of the Son, we say that the Son is unlike the Father, for the temporal differs from the eternal. The Prophet proclaims Him eternal, and the Apostle proclaims Him eternal; the Testaments, Old and New alike, are full of witness to the Son's eternity.

55. Let us take them, then, in their order. In the Old Testament— to cite one out of a multitude of testimonies — it is written: Before Me has there been no other God, and after Me shall there be none. Isaiah 43:10 I will not comment on this place, but ask you straight: Who speaks these words — the Father or the Son? Whichever of the two you say, you will find yourself convinced, or, if a believer, instructed. Who, then, speaks these words, the Father or the Son? If it is the Son, He says, Before Me has there been no other God; if the Father, He says, After Me shall there be none. The One has none before Him, the Other none that comes after; as the Father is known in the Son, so also is the Son known in the Father, for whenever you speak of the Father, you speak also by implication of His Son, seeing that none is his own father; and when you name the Son, you do also acknowledge His Father, inasmuch as none can be his own son. And so neither can the Son exist without the Father, nor the Father without the Son. The Father, therefore, is eternal, and the Son also eternal.

56. In the beginning was the Word, and the Word was with God, and the Word was God. The same was in the beginning with God. Was, mark you, with God. Was—

see, we have was four times over. Where did the blasphemer find it written that He was not. Again, John, in another passage — in his Epistle — speaks of That which was in the beginning. 1 John 1:1 The extension of the was is infinite. Conceive any length of time you will, yet still the Son was.

57. Now in this short passage our fisherman has barred the way of all heresy. For that which was in the beginning is not comprehended in time, is not preceded by any beginning. Let Arius, therefore, hold his peace. Moreover, that which was with God is not confounded and mingled with Him, but is distinguished by the perfection unblemished which it has as the Word abiding with God; and so let Sabellius keep silence. And the Word was God. This Word, therefore, consists not in uttered speech, but in the designation of celestial excellence, so that Photinus' teaching is refuted. Furthermore, by the fact that in the beginning He was with God is proven the indivisible unity of eternal Godhead in Father and Son, to the shame and confusion of Eunomius. Lastly, seeing that all things are said to have been made by Him, He is plainly shown to be author of the Old and of the New Testament alike; so that the Manichæan can find no ground for his assaults. Thus has the good fisherman caught them all in one net, to make them powerless to deceive, albeit unprofitable fish to take.

Chapter 9.

St. Ambrose questions the heretics and exhibits their answer, which is, that the Son existed, indeed, before all time, yet was not co-eternal with the Father, whereat the Saint shows that they represent the Godhead as changeable, and further, that each Person must be believed to be eternal.

58. Tell me, thou heretic — for the surpassing clemency of the Emperor grants me this indulgence of addressing you for a short space, not that I desire to confer with you, or am greedy to hear your arguments, but because I am willing to exhibit them — tell me, I say, whether there was ever a time when God Almighty was not the Father, and yet was God. I say nothing about time, is your answer. Well and subtly objected! For if you bring time into the dispute, you will condemn yourself, seeing that you must acknowledge that there was a time when the Son was not, whereas the Son is the ruler and creator of time. He cannot have begun to exist after His own work. You, therefore, must needs allow Him to be the ruler and maker of His work.

59. I do not say, do you answer, that the Son existed not before time; but when I call Him Son, I declare that His Father existed before Him, for, as you say, father exists before son. But what means this? You deny that time was before the Son, and yet you will have it that something preceded the existence of the Son — some creature of time — and you show certain stages of generation intervening, whereby thou dost give us to understand that the generation from the Father was a process in time. For if He began to be a Father, then, in the first instance, He was God, and afterwards He became a Father. How, then, is God unchangeable? For if He was first God, and then the Father, surely He has undergone change by reason of the added and later act of generation.

60. But may God preserve us from this madness; for it was but to confute the impiety of the heretics that we brought in this question. The devout spirit affirms a generation that is not in time, and so declares Father and Son to be co-eternal, and does not maintain that God has ever suffered change.

61. Let Father and Son, therefore, be associated in worship, even as They are associated in Godhead; let not blasphemy put asunder those whom the close bond of generation has joined together. Let us honour the Son, that we may honour the Father also, as it is written in the Gospel. John 5:23 The Son's eternity is the adornment of the Father's majesty. If the Son has not been from everlasting, then the Father has suffered change; but the Son is from all eternity, therefore has the Father never changed, for He is always unchangeable. And thus we see that they who would deny the Son's eternity would teach that the Father is mutable.

Chapter 10.

Christ's eternity being proved from the Apostle's teaching, St. Ambrose admonishes us that the Divine Generation is not to be thought of after the fashion of human procreation, nor to be too curiously pried into. With the difficulties thence arising he refuses to deal, saying that whatsoever terms, taken from our knowledge of body, are used in speaking of this Divine Generation, must be understood with a spiritual meaning.

62. Hear now another argument, showing clearly the eternity of the Son. The Apostle says that God's Power and Godhead are eternal, and that Christ is the Power of God — for it is written that Christ is the Power of God and the Wisdom of God. If, then, Christ is the Power of God, it follows that, forasmuch as God's Power is eternal, Christ also is eternal.

63. You can not, then, heretic, build up a false doctrine from the custom of human procreation, nor yet gather the wherewithal for such work from our discourse, for we cannot compass the greatness of infinite Godhead, of Whose greatness there is no end, in our straitened speech. If you should seek to give an account of a man's birth, you must needs point to a time. But the Divine Generation is above all things; it reaches far and wide, it rises high above all thought and feeling. For it is written: No man comes to the Father, save by Me. John 14:6 Whatsoever, therefore, thou dost conceive concerning the Father — yea, be it even His eternity— you can not conceive anything concerning Him save by the Son's aid, nor can any understanding ascend to the Father save through the Son. This is My dearly-beloved Son, the Father says. Is mark you — He Who is, what He is, forever. Hence also David is moved to say: O Lord, Your Word abides for ever in heaven, — for what abides fails neither in existence nor in eternity.

64. Do you ask me how He is a Son, if He have not a Father existing before Him? I ask of you, in turn, when, or how, do you think that the Son was begotten. For me the knowledge of the mystery of His generation is more than I can attain to, — the mind fails, the voice is dumb — ay, and not mine alone, but the angels' also. It is above Powers, above Angels, above Cherubim, Seraphim, and all that has feeling and

thought, for it is written: The peace of Christ, which passes all understanding. If the peace of Christ passes all understanding, how can so wondrous a generation but be above all understanding?

65. Do thou, then (like the angels), cover your face with your hands, for it is not given you to look into surpassing mysteries! We are suffered to know that the Son is begotten, not to dispute upon the manner of His begetting. I cannot deny the one; the other I fear to search into, for if Paul says that the words which he heard when caught up into the third heaven might not be uttered, 2 Corinthians 12:2-5 how can we explain the secret of this generation from and of the Father, which we can neither hear nor attain to with our understanding?

66. But if you will constrain me to the rule of human generation, that you may be allowed to say that the Father existed before the Son, then consider whether instances, taken from the generation of earthly creatures, are suitable to show forth the Divine Generation. If we speak according to what is customary among men, you cannot deny that, in man, the changes in the father's existence happen before those in the son's. The father is the first to grow, to enter old age, to grieve, to weep. If, then, the son is after him in time, he is older in experience than the son. If the child comes to be born, the parent escapes not the shame of begetting.

67. Why take such delight in that rack of questioning? You hear the name of the Son of God; abolish it, then, or acknowledge His true nature. You hear speak of the womb — acknowledge the truth of undoubted begetting. Of His heart — know that here is God's word. Of His right hand — confess His power. Of His face — acknowledge His wisdom. These words are not to be understood, when we speak of God, as when we speak of bodies. The generation of the Son is incomprehensible, the Father begets impassibly, and yet of Himself and in ages inconceivably remote has very God begotten very God. The Father loves the Son, John 5:20 and you anxiously examine His Person; the Father is well pleased in Him, you, joining the Jews, look upon Him with an evil eye; the Father knows the Son, and you join the heathen in reviling Him. Luke 23:36-37

Chapter 11.

It cannot be proved from Scripture that the Father existed before the Son, nor yet can arguments taken from human reproduction avail to this end, since they bring in absurdities without end. To dare to affirm that Christ began to exist in the course of time is the height of blasphemy.

68. You ask me whether it is possible that He Who is the Father should not be prior in existence. I ask you to tell me when the Father existed, the Son as yet being not; prove this, gather it from argument or evidence of Scripture. If you lean upon arguments, you have doubtless been taught that God's power is eternal. Again, you have read the Scripture that says: O Israel, if you will hearken unto Me, there shall be no new God in you, neither shall you worship a strange God. The first of these commands betokens [the Son's] eternity, the second His possession of an identical nature, so that we can neither believe Him to have come into existence after the

Father, nor suppose Him the Son of another Divinity. For if He existed not always with the Father, He is a new [God]; if He is not of one Divinity with the Father, He is a strange [God]. But He is not after the Father, for He is not a new God; nor is He a strange God, for He is begotten of the Father, and because, as it is written, He is God above all, blessed forever. Romans 9:5

69. But if the Arians believe Him to be a strange God, why do they worship Him, when it is written: You shall worship no strange God? Else, if they do not worship the Son, let them confess thereto, and the case is at an end — that they deceive no one by their professions of religion. This, then, we see, is the witness of the Scriptures. If you have any others to produce, it will be your business to do so.

70. Let us now go further, and gather the truth in conclusion from arguments. For although arguments usually give place, even to human evidence, still, heretic, argue as you will. Experience teaches us, you say, that the being which generates is prior to that which is generated. I answer: Follow our customary experience through all its departments, and if the rest agree herewith, I oppose not your claim that your point be granted; but if there be no such agreement, how can you claim assent on this one point, when in all the rest you lack support? Seeing, then, that you call for what is customary, it comes about that the Son, when He was begotten of the Father, was a little child. You have seen Him an infant, crying in the cradle. As the years passed, He has gone forward from strength to strength — for if He was weak with the weakness of things begotten, He must also have fallen under the weakness, not only of birth, but of life also.

71. But perchance you run to such a pitch of folly as not to flinch from asserting these things of the Son of God, measuring Him, as you do, by the rule of human infirmity. What, then, if, while you cannot refuse Him the name of God, you are bent to prove Him, by reason of weakness, to be a man? What if, while you examine the Person of the Son, you are calling the Father in question, and while you hastily pass sentence upon the Former, you include the Latter in the same condemnation!

72. If the Divine Generation has been subject to the limits of time — if we suppose this, borrowing from the custom of human generation, then it follows, further, that the Father bare the Son in a bodily womb, and laboured under the burden while ten months sped their courses. But how can generation, as it commonly takes place, be brought about without the help of the other sex? You see that the common order of generation was not the commencement, and you think that the courses of generation, which are ruled by certain necessities whereunto bodies are subject, have always prevailed. You require the customary course, I ask for difference of sex: you demand the supposition of time, I that of order: you enquire into the end, I into the beginning. Now surely it is the end that depends on the beginning, not the beginning on the end.

73. Everything, say you, that is begotten has a beginning, and therefore because the Son is the Son, He has a beginning, and came first into existence within limits of time. Let this be taken as the word of their own mouth; as for myself, I confess that the Son is begotten, but the rest of their declaration makes me shudder. Man, do you

confess God, and diminish His honour by such slander? From this madness may God deliver us.

Chapter 12.

Further objections to the Godhead of the Son are met by the same answer — to wit, that they may equally be urged against the Father also. The Father, then, being in no way confined by time, place, or anything else created, no such limitation is to be imposed upon the Son, Whose marvellous generation is not only of the Father, but of the Virgin also, and therefore, since in His generation of the Father no distinction of sex, or the like, was involved, neither was it in His generation of the Virgin.

74. The next objection is this: If the Son has not those properties which all sons have, He is no Son. May Father, Son, and Holy Spirit pardon me, for I would propound the question in all devoutness. Surely the Father is, and abides for ever: created things, too, are as God has ordained them. Is there any one, then, among these creatures which is not subject to the limitations of place, time, or the fact of having been created, or to some originating cause or creator. Surely, none. What, then? Is there any one of them whereof the Father stands in need? So to say were blasphemy. Cease, then, to apply to the Godhead what is proper only to created existences, or, if you insist upon forcing the comparison, bethink you whither your wickedness leads. God forbid that we should even behold the end thereof.

75. We maintain the answer given by piety. God is Almighty, and therefore God the Father needs none of those things, for in Him there is no changing, nor any place for such help as we need, we whose weakness is supported by means of things of this kind. But He Who is Almighty, plainly He is uncreate, and not confined to any place, and surpasses time. Before God was not anything — nay, even to speak about anything being before God is a grave sin. If, then, you grant that in the nature of God the Father there is nought that implies a being sustained, because He is God, it follows that nothing of this sort can be supposed to exist in the Son of God, nothing that connotes a beginning, or growth, forasmuch as He is very God of very God.

76. Seeing, then, that we find not the customary order prevailing, be content, Arian, to believe in a miraculous generation of the Son. Be content, I say, and if you believe me not, at least have respect unto the voice of God saying, To whom have you esteemed Me to be like? Isaiah 46:5 and again: God is not like a man that He should repent. Numbers 23:19 If, indeed, God works mysteriously, seeing that He does not work any work, or fashion anything, or bring it to completion, by labor of hands, or in any course of days, for He spoke, and they were made; He gave the word and they were created, why should we not believe that He Whom we acknowledge as a Creator, mysteriously working, discerning it in His works, also begot His Son in a mysterious manner? Surely it is fitting that He should be regarded as having begotten the Son in a special and mysterious way. Let Him Who has the grace of majesty unrivalled likewise have the glory of mysterious generation.

77. Not only Christ's generation of the Father, but His birth also of the Virgin, demands our wonder. You say that the former is like the manner wherein we men are conceived. I will show — nay more, I will compel you yourself to confess, that the latter also has no likeness to the manner of our birth. Tell me how it was that He was born of Mary, with what law did His conception in a Virgin's womb agree, how there could be any birth without the seed of a man, how a maiden could become great with child, how she became a mother before experience of such intercourse as is between wives and husbands. There was no [visible] cause — and yet a son was begotten. How, then, came about this birth, under a new law?

78. If, then, the common order of human generation was not found in the case of the Virgin Mary, how can you demand that God the Father should beget in such wise as you were begotten in? Surely the common order is determined by difference of sex; for this is implanted in the nature of our flesh, but where flesh is not, how can you expect to find the infirmity of flesh? No man calls in question one who is better than he is: to believe is enjoined upon you, without permission to question. For it is written, Abraham believed God, and it was accounted to him for righteousness. Genesis 15:6 Language is vain to set forth, not only the generation of the Son, but even the works of God, for it is written: All His works are executed in faithfulness; His works, then, are done in faithfulness, but not His generation? Ay, we call in question that which we see not, we who are bidden to believe rather than enquire of that we see.

Chapter 13.

Discussion of the Divine Generation is continued. St. Ambrose illustrates its method by the same example as that employed by the author of the Epistle to the Hebrews. The duty of believing what is revealed is shown by the example of Nebuchadnezzar and St. Peter. By the vision granted to St. Peter was shown the Son's Eternity and Godhead — the Apostle, then, must be believed in preference to the teachers of philosophy, whose authority was everywhere falling into discredit. The Arians, on the other hand, are shown to be like the heathen.

79. It will be asked: In what sort was the Son begotten? As one who is for ever, as the Word, as the brightness of eternal light, Hebrews 1:3 for brightness takes effect in the instant of its coming into existence. Which example is the Apostle's, not mine. Think not, then, that there was ever a moment of time when God was without wisdom, any more than that there was ever a time when light was without radiance. Judge not, Arian, divine things by human, but believe the divine where you find not the human.

80. The heathen king saw in the fire, together with the three Hebrew children, the form of a fourth, like as of an angel, Daniel 3:25 and because he thought that this angel excelled all angels, he judged Him to be the Son of God, Whom he had not read of, but in Whom he believed. Abraham, also, saw Three, and adored One. Genesis 18:1-3

81. Peter, when he saw Moses and Elias on the mountain, with the Son of God, was not deceived as to their nature and glory. For he enquired, not of them, but of Christ, what he ought to do, inasmuch as though he prepared to do homage to all three, yet he waited for the command of one. But since he ignorantly thought that for three persons three tabernacles should be set up, he was corrected by the sovereign voice of God the Father, saying, This is My dearly beloved Son: hear Him. Matthew 17:5 That is to say: Why do you join your fellow-servants in equality with your Lord? This is My Son. Not Moses is My Son, nor Elias is My Son, but This is My Son. The Apostle was not dull to understand the rebuke; he fell on his face, brought low by the Father's voice and the glorious beauty of the Son, but he was raised up by the Son, Whose wont it is to raise up them that are fallen. Matthew 17:6-8 Then he saw one only, Matthew 17:8 the Son of God alone, for the servants had withdrawn, that He might be seen to be Lord alone, Who alone was entitled Son.

82. What, then, was the purpose of that vision, which signified not that Christ and His servants were equal, but betokened a mystery, save that it should be made plain to us that the Law and the Prophets, in agreement with the Gospel, revealed as eternal the Son of God, Whom they had heralded. When we, therefore, hear of the Son coming forth of the womb, the Word from the heart, let us believe that the Son was not fashioned with hands but begotten of the Father, not the work of a craftsman but the offspring of a parent.

83. He, therefore, Who said, This is My Son, said not, This is a creature of time, nor This being is of My creation, My making, My servant, but This is My Son, Whom you see glorified. This is the God of Abraham, the God of Isaac, the God of Jacob, Who appeared to Moses in the bush, Exodus 3:14 concerning Whom Moses says, He Who is has sent me. It was not the Father Who spoke to Moses in the bush or in the desert, but the Son. It was of this Moses that Stephen said, This is He Who was in the church, in the wilderness, with the Angel. Acts 7:38 This, then, is He Who gave the Law, Who spoke with Moses, saying, I am the God of Abraham, the God of Isaac, the God of Jacob. This, then, is the God of the patriarchs, this is the God of the prophets.

84. It is of the Son, therefore, that we read, your mind understands the reading, let your tongue make confession. Away with arguments, where faith is required; now let dialectic hold her peace, even in the midst of her schools. I ask not what it is that philosophers say, but I would know what they do. They sit desolate in their schools. See the victory of faith over argument. They who dispute subtly are forsaken daily by their fellows; they who with simplicity believe are daily increased. Not philosophers but fishermen, not masters of dialectic but tax-gatherers, now find credence. The one sort, through pleasures and luxuries, have bound the world's burden upon themselves; the other, by fasting and mortification, have cast it off, and so does sorrow now begin to win over more followers than pleasure.

85. Let us now see how far Arians and pagans do differ. The latter call upon gods, who are different in sex and unequal in power; the former affirm a Trinity where there is likewise inequality of power and diversity of Godhead. The pagans assert that their Gods began to exist once upon a time; the Arians lyingly declare that Christ

began to exist in the course of time. Have they not all dyed their impiety in the vats of philosophy? But indeed the pagans do extol that which they worship, the Arians maintain that the Son of God, Who is God, is a creature.

Chapter 14.

That the Son of God is not a created being is proved by the following arguments: (1) That He commanded not that the Gospel should be preached to Himself; (2) that a created being is given over unto vanity; (3) that the Son has created all things; (4) that we read of Him as begotten; and (5) that the difference of generation and adoption has always been understood in those places where both natures — the divine and the human — are declared to co-exist in Him. All of which testimony is confirmed by the Apostle's interpretation.

86. It is now made plain, as I believe, your sacred Majesty, that the Lord Jesus is neither unlike the Father, nor one that began to exist in course of time. We have yet to confute another blasphemy, and to show that the Son of God is not a created being. Herein is the quickening word that we read as our help, for we have heard the passage read where the Lord says: Go into all the world, and preach the Gospel to all creation. Mark 16:15 He Who says all creation excepts nothing. How, then, do they stand who call Christ a creature? If He were a creature, could He have commanded that the Gospel should be preached to Himself? It is not, therefore, a creature, but the Creator, Who commits to His disciples the work of teaching created beings.

87. Christ, then, is no created being; for created beings are, as the Apostle has said, given over to vanity. Romans 8:20 Is Christ given over unto vanity? Again, creation—according to the same Apostle — groans and travails together even until now. What, then? Does Christ take any part in this groaning and travailing — He Who has set us miserable mourners free from death? Creation, says the Apostle, shall be set free from the slavery of corruption. Romans 8:21-22 We see, then, that between creation and its Lord there is a vast difference, for creation is enslaved, but the Lord is the Spirit, and where the Spirit of the Lord is, there is freedom. 2 Corinthians 3:17

88. Who was it that led first into this error, of declaring Him Who created and made all things to be a creature? Did the Lord, I would ask, create Himself? We read that all things were made by Him, and without Him was nothing made. John 1:3 This being so, did He make Himself? We read — and who shall deny?— that in wisdom has God made all things. If so, how can we suppose that wisdom was made in itself?

89. We read that the Son is begotten, inasmuch as the Father says: I brought you forth from the womb before the morning star. We read of the first-born Son, Colossians 1:15 of the only-begotten John 1:14 — first-born, because there is none before Him; only-begotten, because there is none after Him. Again, we read: Who shall declare His generation? Isaiah 53:8 Generation, mark you, not creation. What argument can be brought to meet testimonies so great and mighty as these?

90. Moreover, God's Son discovers the difference between generation and grace when He says: I go up to My Father and your Father, to My God and your God. He did not say, I go up to our Father, but I go up to My Father and your Father. This distinction is the sign of a difference, inasmuch as He Who is Christ's Father is our Creator.

91. Furthermore He said, to My God and your God, because although He and the Father are One, and the Father is His Father by possession of the same nature, while God began to be our Father through the office of the Son, not by virtue of nature, but of grace— still He seems to point us here to the existence in Christ of both natures, Godhead and Manhood — Godhead of His Father, Manhood of His Mother, the former being before all things, the latter derived from the Virgin. For the first, speaking as the Son, He called God His Father, and afterward, speaking as man, named Him as God.

92. Everywhere, indeed, we have witness in the Scriptures to show that Christ, in naming God as His God, does so as man. My God, My God, why have You forsaken Me? And again: From My mother's womb You are My God. In the former place He suffers as a man; in the latter it is a man who is brought forth from his mother's womb. And so when He says, From My mother's womb You are My God, He means that He Who was always His Father is His God from the moment when He was brought forth from His Mother's womb.

93. Seeing, then, that we read in the Gospel, in the Apostle, in the Prophets, of Christ as begotten, how dare the Arians to say that He was created or made? But, indeed, they ought to have bethought them, where they have read of Him as created, where as made. For it has been plainly shown that the Son of God is begotten of God, born of God — let them, then, consider with care where they have read that He was made, seeing that He was not made God, but born as God, the Son of God; afterward, however, He was, according to the flesh, made man of Mary.

94. But when the fullness of time had come, God sent His Son, *made* of a woman, made under the Law. *His* Son, observe, not as one of many, not as His in common with another, but His own, and in saying His Son, the Apostle showed that it is of the Son's nature that His generation is eternal. Him the Apostle has affirmed to have been afterwards made of a woman, in order that the making might be understood not of the Godhead, but of the putting on of a body — made of a woman, then, by taking on of flesh; made under the Law through observance of the Law. Howbeit, the former, the spiritual generation is before the Law was, the latter is after the Law.

Chapter 15.

An explanation of Acts 2:36 and Proverbs 8:22 , which are shown to refer properly to Christ's manhood alone.

95. To no purpose, then, is the heretics' customary citation of the Scripture, that God made Him both Lord and Christ. Let these ignorant persons read the whole passage, and understand it. For thus it is written. God made this Jesus, Whom you crucified,

both Lord and Christ. It was not the Godhead, but the flesh, that was crucified. This, indeed, was possible, because the flesh allowed of being crucified. It follows not, then, that the Son of God is a created being.

96. Let us dispatch, then, that passage also, which they do use to misrepresent — let them learn what is the sense of the words, The Lord created Me. It is not the Father created, but the Lord created Me. The flesh acknowledges its Lord, praise declares the Father: our created nature confesses the first, loves, knows the latter. Who, then, cannot but perceive that these words announce the Incarnation? Thus the Son speaks of Himself as created in respect of that wherein he witnesses to Himself as being man, when He says, Why do you seek to kill Me, a *man*, Who have told you the truth? He speaks of His Manhood, wherein He was crucified, and died, and was buried.

97. Furthermore, there is no doubt but that the writer set down as past that which was to come; for this is the usage of prophecy, that things to come are spoken of as though they were already present or past. For example, in the twenty-first psalm you have read: Fat bulls (of Bashan) have beset me, and again: They parted My garments among them. This the Evangelist shows to have been spoken prophetically of the time of the Passion, for to God the things that are to come are present, and for Him Who foreknows all things, they are as though they were past and over; as it is written, Who has made the things that are to be.

98. It is no wonder that He should declare His place to have been set fast before all worlds, seeing that the Scripture tells us that He was foreordained before the times and ages. The following passage discovers how the words in question present themselves as a true prophecy of the Incarnation: Wisdom has built her a house, and set up seven pillars to support it, and she has slain her victims. She has mingled her wine in the bowl, and made ready her table, and sent her servants, calling men together with a mighty voice of proclamation, saying: 'He who is simple, let him turn in to me.' Do we not see, in the Gospel, that all these things were fulfilled after the Incarnation, in that Christ disclosed the mysteries of the Holy Supper, sent forth His apostles, and cried with a loud voice, saying, If any man thirst, let him come to Me and drink. John 7:37 That which follows, then, answers to that which went before, and we behold the whole story of the Incarnation set forth in brief by prophecy.

99. Many other passages might readily be seen to be prophecies of this sort concerning the Incarnation, but I will not delay over books, lest the treatise appear too wordy

Chapter 16.

The Arians blaspheme Christ, if by the words created and begotten they mean and understand one and the same thing. If, however, they regard the words as distinct in meaning, they must not speak of Him, of Whom they have read that He was begotten, as if He were a created being. This rule is upheld by the witness of St. Paul, who, professing himself a servant of Christ, forbade worship of a created being. God being a substance pure and uncompounded,

there is no created nature in Him; furthermore, the Son is not to be degraded to the level of things created, seeing that in Him the Father is well pleased.

100. Now will I enquire particularly of the Arians, whether they think that begotten and created are one and the same. If they call them the same, then is there no difference between generation and creation. It follows, then, that forasmuch as we also are created, there is between us and Christ and the elements no difference. Thus much, however, great as their madness is, they will not venture to say.

101. Furthermore — to concede that which is no truth, to their folly — I ask them, if there is, as they think, no difference in the words, why do they not call upon Him Whom they worship by the better title? Why do they not avail themselves of the Father's word? Why do they reject the title of honour, and use a dishonouring name?

102. If, however, there is — as I think there is — a distinction between created and begotten, then, when we have read that He is begotten, we shall surely not understand the same by the terms begotten and created. Let them therefore confess Him to be begotten of the Father, born of the Virgin, or let them say how the Son of God can be both begotten and created. A single nature, above all, the Divine Being, rejects strife (within itself).

103. But in any case let our private judgment pass: let us enquire of Paul, who, filled with the Spirit of God, and so foreseeing these questionings, has given sentence against pagans in general and Arians in particular, saying that they were by God's judgment condemned, who served the creature rather than the Creator. Thus, in fact, you may read: God gave them over to the lusts of their own heart, that they might one with another dishonour their bodies, they who changed God's truth into a lie, and worshipped and served the thing created rather than the Creator, Who is God, blessed forever. Romans 1:24-25

104. Thus Paul forbids me to worship a creature, and admonishes me of my duty to serve Christ. It follows, then, that Christ is not a created being. The Apostle calls himself Paul, a servant of Jesus Christ, Romans 1:1 and this good servant, who acknowledges his Lord, will likewise have us not worship that which is created. How, then, could he have been himself a servant of Christ, if he thought that Christ was a created person? Let these heretics, then, cease either to worship Him Whom they call a created being, or to call Him a creature, Whom they feign to worship, lest under color of being worshippers they fall into worse impiety. For a domestic is worse than a foreign foe, and that these men should use the Name of Christ to Christ's dishonour increases their guilt.

105. What better expounder of the Scriptures do we indeed look for than that teacher of the Gentiles, that chosen vessel — chosen from the number of the persecutors? He who had been the persecutor of Christ confesses Him. He had read Solomon more, in any case, than Arius has, and he was well learned in the Law, and so, because he had read, he said not that Christ was created, but that He was begotten. For he had read, He spoke, and they were made: He commanded, and they were created. Was Christ, I ask, made at a word? Was He created at a command?

106. Moreover, *how* can there be any created nature in God? In truth, God is of an uncompounded nature; nothing can be added to Him, and that alone which is Divine has He in His nature; filling all things, yet nowhere Himself confounded with anything; penetrating all things, yet Himself nowhere to be penetrated; present in all His fullness at one and the same moment, in heaven, in earth, in the deepest depth of the sea, to sight invisible, by speech not to be declared, by feeling not to be measured; to be followed by faith, to be adored with devotion; so that whatsoever title excels in depth of spiritual import, in setting forth glory and honour, in exalting power, this you may know to belong of right to God.

107. Since, then, the Father is well pleased in the Son; believe that the Son is worthy of the Father, that He came out from God, as He Himself bears witness, saying: I went out from God, and have come; John 8:42 and again: I went out from God. John 16:27 He Who proceeded and came forth from God can have no attributes but such as are proper to God.

Chapter 17.

That Christ is very God is proved from the fact that He is God's own Son, also from His having been begotten and having come forth from God, and further, from the unity of will and operation subsisting in Father and Son. The witness of the apostles and of the centurion — which St. Ambrose sets over against the Arian teaching — is adduced, together with that of Isaiah and St. John.

108. Hence it is that Christ is not only God, but very God indeed — very God of very God, insomuch that He Himself is the Truth. John 14:6 If, then, we enquire His Name, it is the Truth; if we seek to know His natural rank and dignity, He is so truly the very Son of God, that He is indeed God's *own* Son; as it is written, Who spared not His own Son, but gave Him up for our sakes, Romans 8:32 gave Him up, that is, so far as the flesh was concerned. That He is God's own Son declares His Godhead; that He is very God shows that He is God's own Son; His pitifulness is the earnest of His submission, His sacrifice, of our salvation.

109. Lest, however, men should wrest the Scripture, that God gave Him up, the Apostle himself has said in another place, Galatians 1:3-4 Peace from God the Father, and our Lord Jesus Christ, Who gave Himself for our sins; and again: Ephesians 5:2 Even as Christ has loved us, and given Himself for us. If, then, He both was given up by the Father, and gave Himself up of His own accord, it is plain that the working and the will of Father and Son is one.

110. If, then, we enquire into His natural pre-eminence, we find it to consist in being begotten. To deny that the Son of God is begotten [of God] is to deny that He is God's *own* Son, and to deny Christ to be God's own Son is to class Him with the rest of mankind, as no more a Son than any of the rest. If, however, we enquire into the distinctive property of His generation, it is this, that He came forth from God. For while, in our experience, to come out implies something already existent, and that which is said to come out seems to proceed forth from hidden and inward places, we, though it be presented but in short passages, observe the peculiar attribute of the

Divine Generation, that the Son does not seem to have come forth out of any place, but as God from God, a Son from a Father, nor to have had a beginning in the course of time, having come forth from the Father by being born, as He Himself Who was born said: I came forth from the mouth of the Most High. Sirach 24:3

111. But if the Arians acknowledge not the Son's nature, if they believe not the Scriptures, let them at least believe the mighty works. To whom does the Father say, Let *us* make man? Genesis 1:26 save to Him Whom He knew to be His true Son? In Whom, save in one who was true, could He recognize His Image? The son by adoption is not the same as the true Son; nor would the Son say, I and the Father are one, John 10:30 if He, being Himself not true, were measuring Himself with One Who is true. The Father, therefore, says, Let us make. He Who spoke is true; can He, then, Who made be not true? Shall the honour rendered to Him Who speaks be withheld from Him Who makes?

112. But how, unless the Father knew Him to be His true Son, should He commend to Him His will, for perfect co-operation, and His works, for perfect bringing in out in actuality? Seeing that the Son works the works which the Father does, and that the Son quickens whom He will, as it is written, He is then equal in power and free in respect of His will. And thus is the Unity maintained, forasmuch as God's power consists in that the Godhead is proper to each Person, and freedom lies not in any difference, but in unity of will.

113. The apostles, being storm-tossed in the sea, as soon as they saw the waters leaping up round their Lord's feet, and beheld His fearless footsteps on the water, as He walked amid the raging waves of the sea, and the ship, which was beaten upon by the waves, had rest as soon as Christ entered it, and they saw the waves and the winds obeying Him — then, though as yet they did not believe in their hearts they believed Him to be God's true Son, saying, Truly You are the Son of God. Matthew 14:33

114. To the same effect the confession of the centurion, and others who were with him, when the foundations of the world were shaken at the Lord's Passion, — and this, heretic, you deny. The centurion said, Truly this was the Son of God. Matthew 27:54 Was said the centurion — Was *not* says the Arian. The centurion, then, with bloodstained hands, but devout mind, declares both the truth and the eternity of Christ's generation; and thou, O heretic, deniest its truth, and makest it matter of time! Would that you had imbued your hands rather than your soul! But you, unclean even of hand, and murderous of intent, seekest Christ's death, so far as in you lies, seeing that you think of Him as mean and weak; nay, and this is a worse sin, you, albeit the Godhead can feel no wound, still would do your diligence to slay in Christ, not His Body, but His Glory.

115. We cannot then doubt that He is very God, Whose true Godhead even executioners believed in and devils confessed. Their testimony we require not now, but it is withal greater than your blasphemies. We have called them in to witness, to put you to the blush, while we have also cited the oracles of God, to the end that you should believe.

116. The Lord proclaims by the mouth of Isaiah: In the mouth of them that serve Me shall a new name be called upon, which shall be blessed over all the earth, and they shall bless the true God, and they who swear upon earth shall swear by the true God. Isaiah 65:16 These words, I say, Isaiah spoke when he saw God's Glory, and thus in the Gospel it is plainly said that he saw the Glory of Christ and spoke of Him. John 12:41

117. But hear again what John the Evangelist has written in his Epistle, saying: We know that the Son of God has appeared, and has given us discernment, to know the Father, and to be in His true Son Jesus Christ, our Lord. He is very God, and Life Eternal. 1 John 5:20 John calls Him true Son of God and very God. If, then, He be very God, He is surely uncreate, without spot of lying or deceit, having in Himself no confusion, nor unlikeness to His Father.

Chapter 18.

The errors of the Arians are mentioned in the Nicene Definition of the Faith, to prevent their deceiving anybody. These errors are recited, together with the anathema pronounced against them, which is said to have been not only pronounced at Nicæa, but also twice renewed at Ariminum.

118. Christ, therefore, is God of God, Light of Light, very God of very God; begotten of the Father, not made; of one substance with the Father.

119. So, indeed, following the guidance of the Scriptures, our fathers declared, holding, moreover, that impious doctrines should be included in the record of their decrees, in order that the unbelief of Arius should discover itself, and not, as it were, mask itself with dye or face-paint. For they give a false color to their thoughts who dare not unfold them openly. After the manner of the censor's rolls, then, the Arian heresy is not discovered by name, but marked out by the condemnation pronounced, in order that he who is curious and eager to hear it should be preserved from falling by knowing that it is condemned already, before he hears, it set forth to the end that he should believe.

120. Those, runs the decree, who say that there was a time when the Son of God was not, and that before He was born He was not, and who say that he was made out of nothing, or is of another substance or οὐσία, or that He is capable of changing, or that with Him is any shadow of turning — them the Catholic and Apostolic Church declares accursed.

121. Your sacred Majesty has agreed that they who utter such doctrines are rightly condemned. It was of no determination by man, of no human counsel, that three hundred and eighteen bishops met, as I showed above more at length, in Council, but that in their number the Lord Jesus might prove, by the sign of His Name and Passion, that He was in the midst, where His own were gathered together. Matthew 18:20 In the number of three hundred was the sign of His Cross, in that of eighteen was the sign of the Name Jesus.

122. This also was the teaching of the First Confession in the Council of Ariminum, and of the Second Correction, after that Council. Of the Confession, the letter sent to the Emperor Constantine bears witness, and the Council that followed declares the Correction.

Chapter 19.

Arius is charged with the first of the above-mentioned errors, and refuted by the testimony of St. John. The miserable death of the Heresiarch is described, and the rest of his blasphemous errors are one by one examined and disproved.

123. Arius, then, says: There was a time when the Son of God existed not, but Scripture says: He was, not that He was not. Furthermore, St. John has written: In the beginning was the Word, and the Word was with God, and the Word was God. The same was in the beginning with God. John 1:1-3 Observe how often the verb was appears, whereas was not is nowhere found. Whom, then, are we to believe?— St. John, who lay on Christ's bosom, or Arius, wallowing amid the outgush of his very bowels?— so wallowing that we might understand how Arius in his teaching showed himself like Judas, being visited with like punishment.

124. For Arius' bowels also gushed out — decency forbids to say where — and so he burst asunder in the midst, falling headlong, and besmirching those foul lips wherewith he had denied Christ. He was rent, even as the Apostle Peter said of Judas, because he bought a field with the price of evil-doing, and falling headlong he burst asunder in the midst, and all his bowels gushed out. It was no chance manner of death, seeing that like wickedness was visited with like punishment, to the end that those who denied and betrayed the same Lord might likewise undergo the same torment.

125. Let us pass on to further points. Arius says: Before He was born, the Son of God was not, but the Scripture says that all things are maintained in existence by the Son's office. How, then, could He, Who existed not, bestow existence upon others? Again, when the blasphemer uses the words when and before, he certainly uses words which are marks of time. How, then, do the Arians deny that time was ere the Son was, and yet will have things created in time to exist before the Son, seeing that the very words, when, before, and did not exist once, announce the idea of time?

126. Arius says that the Son of God came into being out of nought. How, then, is He Son of God— how was He begotten from the womb of the Father — how do we read of Him as the Word spoken of the heart's abundance, save to the end that we should believe that He came forth, as it is written, from the Father's inmost, unapproachable sanctuary? Now a son is so called either by means of adoption or by nature, as we are called sons by means of adoption. Christ is the Son of God by virtue of His real and abiding nature. How, then, can He, Who out of nothing fashioned all things, be Himself created out of nothing?

127. He who knows not whence the Son is has not the Son. The Jews therefore had not the Son, for they knew not whence He was. Wherefore the Lord said to them: You know not whence I came; John 8:14 and again: You neither have found out Who I am, nor know My Father, for he who denies that the Son is of the Father knows not the Father, of Whom the Son is; and again, he knows not the Son, because he knows not the Father.

128. Arius says: [The Son is] of another Substance. But what other substance is exalted to equality with the Son of God, so that simply in virtue thereof He is Son of God? Or what right have the Arians for censuring us because we speak, in Greek, of the οὐσία, or in Latin, of the *Substantia* of God, when they themselves, in saying that the Son of God is of another Substance, assert a divine *Substantia*.

129. Howbeit, should they desire to dispute the use of the words divine Substance or divine Nature, they shall easily be refuted, for Holy Writ oft-times has spoken of οὐσία in Greek, or *Substantia* in Latin, and St. Peter, as we read, would have us become partakers in the divine Nature. But if they will have it that the Son is of another Substance, they with their own lips confute themselves, in that they both acknowledge the term Substance, whereof they are so afraid, and rank the Son on a level with the creatures above which they feign to exalt Him.

130. Arius calls the Son of God a creature, but not as the rest of the creatures. Yet what created being is not different from another? Man is not as angel, earth is not as heaven, the sun is not as water, nor light as darkness. Arius' preference, therefore, is empty — he has but disguised with a sorry dye his deceitful blasphemies, in order to take the foolish.

131. Arius declares that the Son of God may change and swerve. How, then, is He God if He is changeable, seeing that He Himself has said: I am, I am, and I change not?

Chapter 20.

St. Ambrose declares his desire that some angel would fly to him to purify him, as once the Seraph did to Isaiah — nay more, that Christ Himself would come to him, to the Emperor, and to his readers, and finally prays that Gratian and the rest of the faithful may be exalted by the power and spell of the Lord's Cup, which he describes in mystic language.

132. Howbeit, now must I needs confess the Prophet Isaiah's confession, which he makes before declaring the word of the Lord: Woe is me, my heart is smitten, for I, a man of unclean lips, and living in the midst of a people of unclean lips, have seen the Lord of Sabaoth. Now if Isaiah said Woe is me, who looked upon the Lord of Sabaoth, what shall I say of myself, who, being a man of unclean lips, am constrained to treat of the divine generation? How shall I break forth into speech of things whereof I am afraid, when David prays that a watch may be set over his mouth in the matter of things whereof he has knowledge? O that to me also one of the Seraphim

would bring the burning coal from the celestial altar, taking it in the tongs of the two testaments, and with the fire thereof purge my unclean lips!

133. But forasmuch as then the Seraph came down in a vision to the Prophet, while You, O Lord, in revelation of the mystery have come to us in the flesh, do Thou, not by any deputy, nor by any messenger, but You Yourself cleanse my conscience from my secret sins, that I too, erstwhile unclean, but now by Your mercy made clean through faith, may sing in the words of David: I will make music to You upon a harp, O God of Israel, my lips shall rejoice, in all my song to You, and so, too, shall my soul, whom You have redeemed.

134. And so, O Lord, leaving them that slander and hate You, come unto us, sanctify the ears of our sovereign ruler, Gratian, and all besides into whose hands this little book shall come — and purge my ears, that no stains of the infidelity they have heard remain anywhere. Cleanse thoroughly, then, our ears, not with water of well, river, or rippling and purling brook, but with words cleansing like water, clearer than any water, and purer than any snow — even the words You have spoken — Though your sins be as scarlet, I will make them white as snow. Isaiah 1:18

135. Moreover, there is a Cup, which You use to purify the hidden chambers of the soul, a Cup not of the old order, nor filled from a common Vine — a new Cup, brought down from heaven to earth, filled with wine pressed from the wondrous cluster, which hung in fleshly form upon the tree of the Cross, even as the grape hangs upon the Vine. From this Cluster, then, is the Wine that makes glad the heart of man, Judges 9:13 uplifts the sorrowful, is fragrant with, pours into us, the ecstasy of faith, true devotion, and purity.

136. With this Wine, therefore, O Lord my God, cleanse the spiritual ears of our sovereign Emperor, to the end that, just as men, being uplifted with common wine, love rest and quietness, cast out the fear of death, have no feeling of injuries, seek not that which belongs to others, and forget their own; and so he, too, intoxicated with your wine, may love peace, and, confident in the exultation of faith, may never know the death of unbelief, and may display loving patience, have no part in other men's profanities, and hold the faith of more account even than kindred and children, as it is written: Leave all that you have, and come, follow Me. Matthew 19:21

137. With this Wine, also, Lord Jesus, purify our senses, that we may adore You, and worship You, the Creator of things visible and invisible. Truly, You can not fail of being Yourself invisible and good, Who hast given invisibility and goodness to the works of Your Hands.

EXPOSITION ON THE CHRISTIAN FAITH

Book II.

Introduction.

Twelve names of the Son of God are recounted, being distributed into three classes. These names are so many proofs of the eternity not only of the Son, but of the Father also. Furthermore, they are compared with the twelve stones in the High Priest's breastplate, and their inseparability is shown by a new distribution of them. Returning to the comparison with the High Priest's breastplate, the writer sets forth the beauty of the woven-work and the precious stones of the mystic raiment, and the hidden meaning of that division into woven-work and precious stones, which being done, he expounds the comparison drawn by him, showing that faith must be woven in with works, and adds a short summary of the same faith, as concerning the Son.

1. Enough has been said, as I think, your sacred Majesty, in the book preceding to show that the Son of God is an eternal being, not diverse from the Father, begotten, not created: we have also proved, from passages of the Scriptures, that God's true Son is God, and is declared so to be by the evident tokens of His Majesty.

2. Wherefore, albeit what has already been set forth is plentiful even to overflowing for maintaining the Faith — seeing that the greatness of a river is mostly judged of from the manner in which its springs rise and flow forth — still, to the end that our belief may be the plainer to sight, the waters of our spring ought, methinks, to be parted off into three channels. There are, then, firstly, plain tokens declaring essential inherence in the Godhead; secondly, the expressions of the likeness of the Father and the Son; and lastly, those of the undoubtable unity of the Divine Majesty. Now of the first sort are the names begetting, God, Son, The Word; of the second, brightness, expression, mirror, image; and of the third, wisdom, power, truth, life.

3. These tokens so declare the nature of the Son, that by them you may know both that the Father is eternal, and that the Son is not diverse from Him; for the source of generation is He Who is, and as begotten of the Eternal, He is God; coming forth from the Father, He is the Son; from God, He is the Word; He is the radiance of the Father's glory, the expression of His substance, the counterpart of God, the image of His majesty; the Bounty of Him Who is bountiful, the Wisdom of Him Who is wise, the Power of the Mighty One, the Truth of Him Who is true, the Life of the Living One. In agreement, therefore, stand the attributes of Father and Son, that none may suppose any diversity, or doubt but that they are of one Majesty. For each and all of these names would we furnish examples of their use were we not constrained by a desire to maintain our discourse within bounds.

4. Of these twelve, as of twelve precious stones, is the pillar of our faith built up. For these are the precious stones — sardius, jasper, smaragd, chrysolite, and the rest — woven into the robe of holy Aaron, even of him who bears the likeness of Christ, that is, of the true Priest; stones set in gold, and inscribed with the names of the sons of Israel, twelve stones close joined and fitting one into another, for if any should sunder or separate them, the whole fabric of the faith falls in ruins.

5. This, then, is the foundation of our faith— to know that the Son of God is begotten; if He be not begotten, neither is He the Son. Nor yet is it sufficient to call Him Son, unless you shall also distinguish Him as the Only-begotten Son. If He is a creature, He is not God; if He is not God, He is not the Life; if He is not the Life, then is He not the Truth.

6. The first three tokens, therefore, that is to say, the names generation, Son, Only-begotten, do show that the Son is of God originally and by virtue of His own nature.

7. The three that follow — to wit, the names God, Life, Truth, reveal His Power, whereby He has laid the foundations of, and upheld, the created world. For, as Paul said, in Him we live and move and have our being; Acts 17:28 and therefore, in the first three the Son's natural right, in the other three the unity of action subsisting between Father and Son is made manifest.

8. The Son of God is also called the image and effulgence and expression [of God], for these names have disclosed the Father's incomprehensible and unsearchable Majesty dwelling in the Son, and the expression of His likeness in Him. These three names, then, as we see, refer to [the Son's] likeness [to the Father].

9. We have yet the operations of Power, Wisdom, and Justice left, wherewith, severally, to prove [the Son's] eternity.

10. This, then, is that robe, adorned with precious stones; this is the amice of the true Priest; this the bridal garment; here is the inspired weaver, who well knew how to weave that work. No common woven work is it, whereof the Lord spoke by His Prophet: Who gave to women their skill in weaving? No common stones again, are they — stones, as we find them called, of filling; for all perfection depends on this condition, that there be nought lacking. They are stones joined together and set in gold — that is, of a spiritual kind; the joining of them by our minds and their setting in convincing argument. Finally Scripture teaches us how far from common are these stones, inasmuch as, while some brought one kind, and others another, of less precious offerings, these the devout princes brought, wearing them upon their shoulders, and made of them the breastplate of judgment, that is, a piece of woven work. Now we have a woven work, when faith and action go together.

11. Let none suppose me to be misguided, in that I made at first a threefold division, each part containing four, and afterwards a fourfold division, each part containing three terms. The beauty of a good thing pleases the more, if it be shown under various aspects. For those are good things, whereof the texture of the priestly robe was the token, that is to say, either the Law, or the Church, which latter has made two garments for her spouse, as it is written — the one of action, the other of spirit, weaving together the threads of faith and works. Thus, in one place, as we read, she makes a groundwork of gold, and afterwards weaves thereon blue, and purple, with scarlet, and white. Again, [as we read] elsewhere, she first makes little flowerets of blue and other colors, and attaches gold, and there is made a single priestly robe, to the end that adornments of diverse grace and beauty, made up of the same bright colors, may gain fresh glory by diversity of arrangement.

12. Moreover (to complete our interpretation of these types), it is certain that by refined gold and silver are designated the oracles of the Lord, whereby our faith stands firm. The oracles of the Lord are pure oracles, silver tried in the fire, refined of dross, purified seven times. Now blue is like the air we breathe and draw in; purple, again, represents the appearance of water; scarlet signifies fire; and white linen, earth, for its origin is in the earth. Of these four elements, again, the human body is composed.

13. Whether, then, you join to faith already present in the soul, bodily acts agreeing thereto; or acts come first, and faith be joined as their companion, presenting them to God — here is the robe of the minister of religion, here the priestly vestment.

14. Faith is profitable, therefore, when her brow is bright with a fair crown of good works. James 2:14-26 This faith— that I may set the matter forth shortly — is contained in the following principles, which cannot be overthrown. If the Son had His origin in nothing, He is not Son; if He is a creature, He is not the Creator; if He was made, He did not make all things; if He needs to learn, He has no foreknowledge; if He is a receiver, He is not perfect; if He progress, He is not God. If He is unlike (the Father) He is not the (Father's) image; if He is Son by grace, He is not such by nature; if He have no part in the Godhead, He has it in Him to sin. There is none good, but Godhead. Mark 10:18

Chapter 1.

The Arian argument from S. Mark 10:18 , There is none good but one, that is, God, refuted by explanation of these words of Christ.

15. The objection I have now to face, your sacred Majesty, fills me with bewilderment, my soul and body faint at the thought that there should be men, or rather not men, but beings with the outward appearance of men, but inwardly full of brutish folly — who can, after receiving at the hands of the Lord benefits so many and so great, say that the Author of all good things is Himself not good.

16. It is written, say they, that There is none good but God alone. I acknowledge the Scripture— but there is no falsehood in the letter; would that there were none in the Arians' exposition thereof. The written signs are guiltless, it is the meaning in which they are taken that is to blame. I acknowledge the words as the words of our Lord and Saviour — but let us bethink ourselves when, to whom, and with what comprehension He speaks.

17. The Son of God is certainly speaking as man, and speaking to a scribe — to him, that is, who called the Son of God Good Master, but would not acknowledge Him as God. What he believes not, Christ further gives him to understand, to the end that he may believe in God's Son not as a good master, but as the good God, for if, wheresoever the One God is named, the Son of God is never sundered from the fullness of that unity, how, when God alone is said to be good, can the Only-begotten be excluded from the fullness of Divine Goodness? The Arians must therefore either deny that the Son of God is God, or confess that God is good.

18. With divinely inspired comprehension, then, our Lord said, *not* There is none good but the Father alone, but There is none good but God alone, and Father is the proper name of Him Who begets. But the unity of God by no means excludes the Godhead of the Three Persons, and therefore it is His Nature that is extolled. Goodness, therefore, is of the nature of God, and in the nature of God, again, exists the Son of God— wherefore that which the predicate expresses belongs not to one single Person, but to the [complete] unity [of the Godhead].

19. The Lord, then, does not deny His goodness — He rebukes this sort of disciple. For when the scribe said, Good Master, the Lord answered, Why do you call Me good?— which is to say, It is not enough to call Him good, Whom you believe not to be God. Not such do I seek to be My disciples— men who rather consider My manhood and reckon Me a good master, than look to My Godhead and believe Me to be the good God.

Chapter 2.

The goodness of the Son of God is proved from His works, namely, His benefits that He showed towards the people of Israel under the Old Covenant, and to Christians under the New. It is to one's own interest to believe in the goodness of Him Who is one's Lord and Judge. The Father's testimony to the Son. No small number of the Jewish people bear witness to the Son; the Arians therefore are plainly worse than the Jews. The words of the Bride, declaring the same goodness of Christ.

20. Howbeit, I would not that the Son should rely on the mere prerogative of His nature and the claims of peculiar rights of His Majesty. Let us not call Him good, if He merit not the title; and if He merit not this by works, by acts of lovingkindness, let Him waive the right He enjoys by virtue of His nature, and be submitted to our judgment. He Who is to judge us disdains not to be brought to judgment, that He may be justified in His saying, and clear when He is judged.

21. Is He then not good, Who has shown me good things? Is He not good, Who when six hundred thousand of the people of the Jews fled before their pursuers, suddenly opened the tide of the Red Sea, an unbroken mass of waters?— so that the waves flowed round the faithful, and were walls to them, but poured back and overwhelmed the unbelievers.

22. Is He not good, at Whose command the seas became firm ground for the feet of them that fled, and the rocks gave forth water for the thirsty? so that the handiwork of the true Creator might be known, when the fluid became solid, and the rock streamed with water? That we might acknowledge this as the handiwork of Christ, the Apostle said: And that rock was Christ. 1 Corinthians 10:4

23. Is He not good, Who in the wilderness fed with bread from heaven such countless thousands of the people, lest any famine should assail them, without need of toil, in the enjoyment of rest?— so that, for the space of forty years, their raiment grew not old, nor were their shoes worn, a figure to the faithful of the Resurrection

that was to come, showing that neither the glory of great deeds, nor the beauty of the power wherewith He has clothed us, nor the stream of human life is made for nought?

24. Is He not good, Who exalted earth to heaven, so that, just as the bright companies of stars reflect His glory in the sky, as in a glass, so the choirs of apostles, martyrs, and priests, shining like glorious stars, might give light throughout the world.

25. Not only, then, is He good, but He is more. He is a good Shepherd, not only for Himself, but to His sheep also, for the good shepherd lays down his life for his sheep. Aye, He laid down His life to exalt ours — but it was in the power of His Godhead that He laid it down and took it again: I have power to lay down My life, and I have power to take it. No man takes it from Me, but I lay it down of Myself.

26. You see His goodness, in that He laid it down of His own accord: you see His power, in that He took it again — do you deny His goodness, when He has said of Himself in the Gospel, If I am good, why is your eye evil? Ungrateful wretch what are you doing? Do you deny His goodness, in Whom is your hope of good things — if, indeed, you believe this? Do you deny His goodness, Who has given us what eye has not seen, nor ear heard?

27. It concerns my interest to believe Him to be good, for It is a good thing to trust in the Lord. It is to my interest to confess Him Lord, for it is written: Give thanks unto the Lord, for He is good.

28. It is to my interest to esteem my Judge to be good, for the Lord is a righteous Judge to the house of Israel. If, then, the Son of God is Judge, surely, seeing that the Judge is the righteous God and the Son of God is Judge, [it follows that] He who is Judge and Son of God is the righteous God.

29. But perchance you believe not others, nor the Son. Hear, then, the Father saying: My heart has brought forth out of its depth the good Word. The Word, then, is good— the Word, of Whom it is written: And the Word was with God, and the Word was God. John 1:1 If, therefore, the Word is good, and the Son is the Word of God, surely, though it displease the Arians, the Son of God is God. Let them now at least blush for shame.

30. The Jews used to say: He is good. Though some said: He is not, yet others said: He is good,— and you do *all* deny His goodness.

31. He is good who forgives the sin of one man; is He not good Who has taken away the sin of the world? For it was of Him that it was said: Behold the Lamb of God, behold Him Who takes away the sin of the world.

32. But why do we doubt? The Church has believed in His goodness all these ages, and has confessed its faith in the saying: Let Him kiss me with the kisses of His mouth; for your breasts are better than wine; Song of Songs 1:1 and again: And your throat is like the goodliest wine. Of His goodness, therefore, He nourishes us with the breasts of the Law and Grace, soothing men's sorrows with telling them of

heavenly things; and do we, then, deny His goodness, when He is the manifestation of goodness, expressing in His Person the likeness of the Eternal Bounty, even as we showed above that it was written, that He is the spotless reflection and counterpart of that Bounty? Song of Songs 7:9

Chapter 3.

Forasmuch as God is One, the Son of God is God, good and true.

33. Yet what think you, who deny the goodness and true Godhead of the Son of God, though it is written that there is no God but One? 1 Corinthians 8:4 For although there be gods so-called, would you reckon Christ among them which are called gods, but are not, seeing that eternity is of His Essence, and that beside Him there is none other that is good and true God, forasmuch as God is in Him; John 17:22-23 while it follows from the very nature of the Father, that after Him there is no other true God, because God is One, neither confounding [the Persons of] the Father and Son, as the Sabellians do, nor, like the Arians, severing the Father and the Son. For the Father and the Son, as Father and Son, are distinct persons, but they admit no division of their Godhead.

Chapter 4.

The omnipotence of the Son of God, demonstrated on the authority of the Old and the New Testament.

34. Seeing, then, that the Son of God is true and good, surely He is Almighty God. Can there be yet any doubt on this point? We have already cited the place where it is read that the Lord Almighty is His Name. Because, then, the Son is Lord, and the Lord is Almighty, the Son of God is Almighty.

35. But hear also such a passage as you can build no doubts upon: Behold, He comes, says the Scripture, with the clouds, and every eye shall see Him, and they which pierced Him, and all the tribes of the earth shall mourn because of Him. Yea, amen. I am Alpha and Omega, says the Lord God, Who is, and Who was, and Who is to come, the Almighty. Revelation 1:8 Whom, I ask, did they pierce? For Whose coming hope we but the Son's? Therefore, Christ is Almighty Lord, and God.

36. Hear another passage, your sacred Majesty, — hear the voice of Christ. Thus says the Lord Almighty: After His glory has He sent me against the nations which have made spoil of you, forasmuch as he that touches you is as he that touches the pupil of His eye. For lo, I lay my hand upon them which despoiled you, and I will save you, and they shall be for a spoil, which made spoil of you, and they shall know that the Lord Almighty has sent Me. Plainly, He Who speaks is the Lord Almighty, and He Who has sent is the Lord Almighty. By consequence, then, almighty power appertains both to the Father and to the Son; nevertheless, it is One Almighty God, for there is oneness of Majesty.

37. Moreover, that your most excellent Majesty may know that it is Christ which has spoken as in the Gospel, so also in the prophet, He says by the mouth of Isaiah, as

though foreordaining the Gospel: I Myself, Who spoke, have come, that is to say, I, Who spoke in the Law, am present in the Gospel.

38. Elsewhere, again, He says: All things that the Father has are Mine. John 16:25 What means He by all things? Clearly, not things created, for all these were made by the Son, but the things that the Father has — that is to say, Eternity, Sovereignty, Godhead, which are His possession, as begotten of the Father. We cannot, then, doubt that He is Almighty, Who has all things that the Father has (for it is written: All things that the Father has are Mine).

Chapter 5.

Certain passages from Scripture, urged against the Omnipotence of Christ, are resolved; the writer is also at especial pains to show that Christ not seldom spoke in accordance with the affections of human nature.

39. Although it is written concerning God, Blessed and only Potentate, 1 Timothy 5:15 yet I have no misgiving that the Son of God is thereby severed from Him, seeing that the Scripture entitled God, not the Father by Himself, the only Potentate. The Father Himself also declares by the prophet, concerning Christ, that I have set help upon one that is mighty. It is not the Father alone, then, Who is the only Potentate; God the Son also is Potentate, for in the Father's praise the Son is praised too.

40. Aye, let some one show what there is that the Son of God cannot do. Who was His helper, when He made the heavens, — Who, when He laid the foundations of the world? Had He any need of a helper to set men free, Who needed none in constituting angels and principalities? Colossians 1:15-16

41. It is written, say they: 'My Father, if it be possible, take away this cup from Me.' If, then, He is Almighty, how comes He to doubt of the possibility? Which means that, because I have proved Him to be Almighty, I have proved Him unable to doubt of possibility.

42. The words, you say, are the words of Christ. True — consider, though, the occasion of His speaking them, and in what character He speaks. He has taken upon Him the substance of man, and therewith its affections. Again, you find in the place above cited, that He went forward a little further, and fell on His face, praying, and saying: Father, if it be possible. Not as God, then, but as man, speaks He, for could God be ignorant of the possibility or impossibility of anything? Or is anything impossible for God, when the Scripture says: For You nothing is impossible? Job 22:17

43. Of Whom, howbeit, does He doubt— of Himself, or of the Father? Of Him, surely, Who says: Take away from Me,— being moved as man is moved to doubt. The prophet reckons nothing impossible with God. The prophet doubts not; think you that the Son doubts? Will you put God lower than man? What — God has doubts of His Father, and is fearful at the thought of death! Christ, then, is afraid —

afraid, while Peter fears nothing. Peter says: I will lay down my life for Your sake. John 13:37 Christ says: My soul is troubled. John 12:27

44. Both records are true, and it is equally natural that the person who is the less should not fear, as that He Who is the greater should endure this feeling, for the one has all a man's ignorance of the might of death, while the other, as being God inhabiting a body, displays the weakness of the flesh, that the wickedness of those who deny the mystery of the Incarnation might have no excuse. Thus, then, has He spoken, yet the Manichæan believed not; Valentinus denied, and Marcion judged Him to be a ghost.

45. But indeed He so far put Himself on a level with man, such as He showed Himself to be in the reality of His bodily frame, as to say, Nevertheless, not as I will, but as You will, Matthew 26:39 though truly it is Christ's special power to will what the Father wills, even as it is His to do what the Father does.

46. Here, then, let there be an end of the objection which it is your custom to oppose to us, on the ground that the Lord said, Not as I will, but as You will; and again, For this cause I came down from heaven, not to do My own will, but the will of Him that sent Me. John 6:38

Chapter 6.

The passages of Scripture above cited are taken as an occasion for a digression, wherein our Lord's freedom of action is proved from the ascription to the Spirit of such freedom, and from places where it is attributed to the Son.

47. Let us now, for the present, explain more fully why our Lord said, If it be possible, and so call a truce, as it were, while we show that He possessed freedom of will. You deny — so far are you gone in the way of iniquity — that the Son of God had a free will. Moreover, it is your wont to detract from the Holy Spirit, though you cannot deny that it is written: The Spirit does breathe, where He will. Where He will, says the Scripture, not where He is ordered. If, then, the Spirit does breathe where He will, cannot the Son do what He will? Why, it is the very same Son of God Who in His Gospel says that the Spirit has power to breathe where He will. Does the Son, therefore, confess the Spirit to be greater, in that He has power to do what is not permitted to Himself?

48. The Apostle also says that all is the work of one and the same Spirit, distributing to each according to His will. 1 Corinthians 12:11 According to His will, mark you — that is, according to the judgment of a free will, not in obedience to compulsion. Furthermore, the gifts distributed by the Spirit are no mean gifts, but such works as God is wont to do — the gift of healing and of working deeds of power. While the Spirit, then, distributes as He will, the Son of God cannot set free whom He will. But hear Him speak when He does even as He will: I have willed to do Your will, O my God; and again: I will offer You a freewill offering.

49. The holy Apostle later knew that Jesus had it in His power to do as He would, and therefore, seeing Him walk upon the sea, said: Lord, if it be You, bid me come to You over the waters. Matthew 14:28 Peter believed that if Christ commanded, the natural conditions could be changed, so that water might support human footsteps, and things discrepant be reduced to harmony and agreement. Peter asks of Christ to command, not to request: Christ requested not, but commanded, and it was done — and Arius denies it!

50. What indeed is there that the Father will have, but the Son will not, or that the Son will have, but the Father will not? The Father quickens whom He will, and the Son quickens whom He will, even as it is written. John 5:21 Tell me now whom the Son has quickened, and the Father would not quicken. Since, however, the Son quickens whom He will, and the action [of Father and Son] is one, you see that not only does the Son the Father's will, but the Father also does the Son's. For what is quickening but quickening through the passion of Christ? But the passion of Christ is the Father's will. Whom, therefore, the Son quickens, He quickens by the will of the Father; therefore their will is one.

51. Again, what was the will of the Father, but that Jesus should come into the world and cleanse us from our sins? Hear the words of the leper: If You will, You can make me clean. Matthew 8:2 Christ answered, I will, and straightway health, the effect, followed. See you not that the Son is master of His own will, and Christ's will is the same as the Father's. Indeed, seeing that He has said, All things that the Father has are Mine, John 16:15 nothing of a certainty being excepted, the Son has the same will that the Father has.

Chapter 7.

The resolution of the difficulty set forth for consideration is again taken in hand. Christ truly and really took upon Him a human will and affections, the source of whatsoever was not in agreement with His Godhead, and which must be therefore referred to the fact that He was at the same time both God and man.

52. There is, therefore, unity of will where there is unity of working; for in God His will issues straightway in actual effect. But the will of God is one, and the human will another. Further, to show that life is the object of human will, because we fear death, while the passion of Christ depended on the Divine Will, that He should suffer for us, the Lord said, when Peter would have detained Him from suffering: You savour not of the things which be of God, but the things which be of men. Matthew 16:23

53. My will, therefore, He took to Himself, my grief. In confidence I call it grief, because I preach His Cross. Mine is the will which He called His own, for as man He bore my grief, as man He spoke, and therefore said, Not as I will, but as You will. Mine was the grief, and mine the heaviness with which He bore it, for no man exults when at the point to die. With me and for me He suffers, for me He is sad, for me He is heavy. In my stead, therefore, and in me He grieved Who had no cause to grieve for Himself.

54. Not Your wounds, but mine, hurt You, Lord Jesus; not Your death, but our weakness, even as the Prophet says: For He is afflicted for our sakes Isaiah 53:4 — and we, Lord, esteemed You afflicted, when You grieved not for Yourself, but for me.

55. And what wonder if He grieved for all, Who wept for one? What wonder if, in the hour of death, He is heavy for all, Who wept when at the point to raise Lazarus from the dead? *Then*, indeed, He was moved by a loving sister's tears, for they touched His human heart — here by secret grief He brought it to pass that, even as His death made an end of death, and His stripes healed our scars, so also His sorrow took away our sorrow.

56. As being man, therefore, He doubts; as man He is amazed. Neither His power nor His Godhead is amazed, but His soul; He is amazed by consequence of having taken human infirmity upon Him. Seeing, then, that He took upon Himself a soul He also took the affections of a soul, for God could not have been distressed or have died in respect of His being God. Finally, He cried: My God, My God, why have You forsaken Me? As being man, therefore, He speaks, bearing with Him my terrors, for when we are in the midst of dangers we think ourself abandoned by God. As man, therefore, He is distressed, as man He weeps, as man He is crucified.

57. For so has the Apostle Paul likewise said: Because they have crucified the flesh of Christ. And again the Apostle Peter says: Christ having suffered according to the flesh. 1 Peter 4:1 It was the flesh, therefore, that suffered; the Godhead above secure from death; to suffering His body yielded, after the law of human nature; can the Godhead die, then, if the soul cannot? Fear not them, said our Lord, which can kill the body, but cannot kill the soul. Matthew 10:28 If the soul, then, cannot be killed, how can the Godhead?

58. When we read, then, that the Lord of glory was crucified, let us not suppose that He was crucified as in His glory. 1 Corinthians 2:8 It is because He Who is God is also man, God by virtue of His Divinity, and by taking upon Him of the flesh, the man Christ Jesus, that the Lord of glory is said to have been crucified; for, possessing both natures, that is, the human and the divine, He endured the Passion in His humanity, in order that without distinction He Who suffered should be called both Lord of glory and Son of man, even as it is written: Who descended from heaven. John 3:13

Chapter 8.

Christ's saying, The Father is greater than I, is explained in accordance with the principle just established. Other like sayings are expounded in like fashion. Our Lord cannot, as touching His Godhead, be called inferior to the Father.

59. It was due to His humanity, therefore, that our Lord doubted and was sore distressed, and rose from the dead, for that which fell does also rise again. Again, it

was by reason of His humanity that He said those words, which our adversaries use to maliciously turn against Him: Because the Father is greater than I. John 14:28

60. But when in another passage we read: I came out from the Father, and have come into the world; again, I leave the world, and go to the Father, John 16:28 how does He go, except through death, and how comes He, save by rising again? Furthermore, He added, in order to show that He spoke concerning His Ascension: Therefore have I told you before it come to pass, in order that, when it shall have come to pass, you may believe. John 14:20 For He was speaking of the sufferings and resurrection of His body, and by that resurrection they who before doubted were led to believe— for, indeed, God, Who is always present in every place, passes not from place to place. As it is a man who goes, so it is He Himself Who comes. Furthermore, He says in another place: Rise, let us go hence. John 14:31 In that, therefore, does He go and come, which is common to Him and to us.

61. How, indeed, can He be a lesser God when He is perfect and true God? Yet in respect of His humanity He is less — and still you wonder that speaking in the person of a man He called the Father greater than Himself, when in the person of a man He called Himself a worm, and not a man, saying: But I am a worm, and no man; and again: He was led as a sheep to the slaughter. Isaiah 53:7

62. If you pronounce Him less than the Father in this respect, I cannot deny it; nevertheless, to speak in the words of Scripture, He was not begotten inferior, but made lower, Hebrews 2:9 that is, *made* inferior. And how was He made lower, except that, being in the form of God, He thought it not a prey that He should be equal with God, but emptied Himself; Philippians 2:6-7 not, indeed, parting with what He was, but taking up what He was not, for He took the form of a servant. Philippians 2:6-7

63. Moreover, to the end that we might know Him to have been made lower, by taking upon Him a body, David has shown that he is prophesying of a man, saying: What is man, that You are mindful of him, or the son of man, but that You visit him? You have made him a little lower than the angels. And in interpreting this same passage the Apostle says: For we see Jesus, made a little lower than the angels, crowned with glory and honour because that He suffered death, in order that apart from God He might taste death for all. Hebrews 2:9

64. Thus, the Son of God was made lower than, not only the Father, but angels also. And if you will turn this to His dishonour; [I ask] is then the Son, in respect of His Godhead, less than His angels who serve Him and minister to Him? Thus, in your purpose to diminish His honour, you run into the blasphemy of exalting the nature of angels above the Son of God. But the servant is not above his master. Matthew 10:24 Again, angels ministered to Him even after His Incarnation, to the end that you should acknowledge Him to have suffered no loss of majesty by reason of His bodily nature, for God could not submit to any loss of Himself, while that which He has taken of the Virgin neither adds to nor takes away from His divine power.

65. He, therefore, possessing the fullness of Divinity and glory, Colossians 2:9 is not, in respect of His Divinity, inferior. Greater and less are distinctions proper to

corporeal existences; one who is greater is so in respect of rank, or qualities, or at any rate of age. These terms lose their meaning when we come to treat of the things of God. He is commonly entitled the greater who instructs and informs another, but it is not the case with God's Wisdom that it has been built up by teaching received from another, forasmuch as Itself has laid the foundation of all teaching. But how wisely wrote the Apostle: In order that apart from God He might taste death for all,— lest we should suppose the Godhead, not the flesh, to have endured that Passion!

66. If our opponents, then, have found no means to prove [the Father] greater [than the Son], let them not pervert words unto false reports, but seek out their meaning. I ask them, therefore, as touching what do they esteem the Father the greater? If it is because He is the Father, then [I answer] here we have no question of age or of time — the Father is not distinguished by white hairs, nor the Son by youthfulness — and it is on these conditions that the greater dignity of a father depends. But father and son are names, the one of the parent, the other of the child — names which seem to join rather than separate; for dutifulness inspires no loss of personal worth, inasmuch as kinship binds men together, and does not rend them asunder.

67. If, then, they cannot make the order of nature a support for any questioning, let them now believe the witness [of Scripture]. Now the Evangelist testifies that the Son is not lower [than the Father] by reason of being the Son; nay, he even declares that, in being the Son, He is equal, saying, For the Jews sought to kill Him for this cause, that not only did He break the Sabbath, but even called God His own Father, making Himself equal to God. John 5:10

68. This is not what the Jews said — it is the Evangelist who testifies that, in calling Himself God's own Son, He made Himself equal to God, for the Jews are not presented as saying, For this cause we sought to kill Him; the Evangelist, speaking for himself, says, For the Jews sought to kill Him for this cause. Moreover, he has discovered the cause, [in saying] that the Jews were stirred with desire to slay Him because, when as God He broke the Sabbath, and also claimed God as His own Father, He ascribed to Himself not only the majesty of divine authority in breaking the Sabbath, but also, in speaking of His Father, the right appertaining to eternal equality.

69. Most fitting was the answer which the Son of God made to these Jews, proving Himself the Son and equal of God. Whatsoever things, He said, the Father has done, the Son does also in like wise. John 5:19 The Son, therefore, is both entitled and proved the equal of the Father — a true equality, which both excludes difference of Godhead, and discovers, together with the Son, the Father also, to Whom the Son is equal; for there is no equality where there is difference, nor again where there is but one person, inasmuch as none is by himself equal to himself. Thus has the Evangelist shown why it is fitting that Christ should call Himself the Son of God, that is, make Himself equal with God.

70. Hence the Apostle, following this revelation, has said: He thought it not a prey that He should be equal with God. For that which a man has not he seeks to carry off as a prey. Equality with the Father, therefore, which, as God and Lord, He possessed

in His own substance, He had not as a spoil wrongfully seized. Wherefore the Apostle added [the words]: He took the form of a servant. Now surely a servant is the opposite of an equal. Equal, therefore, is the Son, in the form of God, but inferior in taking upon Him of the flesh and in His sufferings as a man. For how could *the same* nature be both lower and equal? And how, if [the Son] be inferior, can He do the same things, in like manner, as the Father does? How, indeed, can there be sameness of operation with diversity of power? Can the inferior ever work such effects as the greater, or can there be unity of operation where there is diversity of substance?

71. Admit, therefore, that Christ, as touching His Godhead, cannot be called inferior [to the Father]. Christ speaks to Abraham: By Myself have I sworn. Genesis 22:16 Now the Apostle shows that He Who swears by Himself cannot be lower than any. Thus he says, When God rewarded Abraham with His promise, He swore by Himself, forasmuch as He had none other that was greater, saying, Surely with blessing will I bless you, and with multiplying will I multiply you. Hebrews 6:13-14 Christ had, therefore, none greater, and for that cause swore He by Himself. Moreover, the Apostle has rightly added, for men swear by one greater than themselves, forasmuch as men have one who is greater than themselves, but God has none.

72. Otherwise, if our adversaries will understand this passage as referred to the Father, then the rest of the record does not agree with it. For the Father did not appear to Abraham, nor did Abraham wash the feet of God the Father, but the feet of Him in Whom is the image of the man that shall be. Moreover, the Son of God says, Abraham saw My day, and rejoiced. John 8:56 It is He, therefore, Who swore by Himself, [and] Whom Abraham saw.

73. And how, indeed, has He any greater than Himself Who is one with the Father in Godhead? John 10:30 Where there is unity, there is no dissimilarity, whereas between greater and less there is a distinction. The teaching, therefore, of the instance from Scripture before us, with regard to the Father and the Son, is that neither is the Father greater, nor has the Son any that is above Him, inasmuch as in Father and Son there is no difference of Godhead parting them, but one majesty.

Chapter 9.

The objection that the Son, being sent by the Father, is, in that regard at least, inferior, is met by the answer that He was also sent by the Spirit, Who is yet not considered greater than the Son. Furthermore, the Spirit, in His turn, is sent by the Father to the Son, in order that Their unity in action might be shown forth. It is our duty, therefore, carefully to distinguish what utterances are to be fitly ascribed to Christ as God, and what to be ascribed to Him as man.

74. I have no fears in the matter of that commonly advanced objection, that Christ is inferior because He was sent. For even if He be inferior, yet this is not so proved; on the other hand, His equal title to honour is in truth proved. Since all honour the Son

as they honour the Father, John 5:23 it is certain that the Son is not, in so far as being sent, inferior.

75. Regard not, therefore, the narrow bounds of human language, but the plain meaning of the words, and believe facts accomplished. Bethink you that our Lord Jesus Christ said in Isaiah that He had been sent by the Spirit. Is the Son, therefore, less than the Spirit because He was sent by the Spirit? Thus you have the record, that the Son declares Himself sent by the Father and His Spirit. I am the beginning, He says, Isaiah 48:12 and I live for ever, and My hand has laid the foundations of the earth, My right hand has made the heaven to stand abidingly; and further on: I have spoken, and I have called; I have brought him, and have made his way to prosper. Draw near to Me, and hear these things: not in secret have I spoken from the beginning. When they were made, I was there: and now has the Lord and His Spirit sent Me. Isaiah 48:15-16 Here, indeed, He Who made the heaven and the earth Himself says that He is sent by the Lord and His Spirit. You see, then, that the poverty of language takes not from the honour of His mission. He, then, is sent by the Father; by the Spirit also is He sent.

76. And that you may gather that there is no separating difference of majesty, the Son in turn sends the Spirit, even as He Himself has said: But when the Comforter has come, whom I will send you from My Father — the Spirit of truth, who comes forth from My Father. John 15:26 That this same Comforter is also to be sent by the Father He has already taught, saying, But the Comforter, that Holy Spirit, whom the Father will send in My name. John 14:26 Behold their unity, inasmuch as whom God the Father sends, the Son sends also, and Whom the Father sends, the Spirit sends also. Else, if the Arians will not admit that the Son was sent, because we read that the Son is the right hand of the Father, then they themselves will confess with respect to the Father, what they deny concerning the Son, unless perchance they discover for themselves either another Father or another Son.

77. A truce, then, to vain wranglings over words, for the kingdom of God, as it is written, consists not in persuasive words, but in power plainly shown forth. Let us take heed to the distinction of the Godhead from the flesh. In each there speaks one and the same Son of God, for each nature is present in Him; yet while it is the same Person Who speaks, He speaks not always in the same manner. Behold in Him, now the glory of God, now the affections of man. As God He speaks the things of God, because He is the Word; as man He speaks the things of man, because He speaks in my nature.

78. This is the living bread, which came down from heaven. John 6:51 This bread is His flesh, even as He Himself said: This bread which I will give is My flesh. John 7:52 This is He Who came down from heaven, this is He Whom the Father has sanctified and sent into this world. Even the letter itself teaches us that not the Godhead but the flesh needed sanctification, for the Lord Himself said, And I sanctify Myself for them, John 17:19 in order that you may acknowledge that He is both sanctified in the flesh for us, and sanctifies by virtue of His Divinity.

79. This is the same One Whom the Father sent, but born of a woman, born under the law, Galatians 4:4 as the Apostle has said. This is He Who says: The Spirit of the Lord is upon Me; wherefore He has anointed Me, to bring good tidings to the poor has He sent Me: This is He Who says: My doctrine is not Mine, but His, Who sent Me. If any man will do His will, he shall know of the doctrine, whether it be of God, or whether I speak of Myself. John 7:16 Doctrine that is of God, then, is one thing; doctrine that is of man, another; and so when the Jews, regarding Him as man, called in question His teaching, and said, How knows this man letters, having never learned? Jesus answered and said, My doctrine is not Mine, for, in teaching without elegance of letters, He seems to teach not as man, but rather as God, having not learned, but devised His doctrine.

80. For He has found and devised all the way of discipline, as we read above, inasmuch as of the Son of God it has been said: This is our God, and none other shall be accounted of in comparison with Him, Who has found all the way of discipline. After these things He was seen on earth, and conversed with men. How, then, could He, as divine, not have His own doctrine — He Who has found all the way of discipline before He was seen on earth? Or how is He inferior, of Whom it is said, None shall be accounted of in comparison with Him? Surely He is entitled incomparable, in comparison of Whom none other can be accounted of — yet so that He cannot be accounted of before the Father. Now if men suppose that the Father is spoken of, they shall not escape running into the blasphemy of Sabellius, of ascribing the assumption of human nature to the Father.

81. Let us proceed with what follows. He who speaks of himself, seeks his own glory. John 7:18 See the unity wherein Father and Son are plainly revealed. He who speaks cannot but be; yet that which He speaks cannot be solely from Him, for in Him all that is, is naturally derived from the Father.

82. What now is the meaning of the words seeks his own glory? That is, not a glory in which the Father has no part — for indeed the Word of God is His glory. Again, our Lord says: that they may see My glory. John 17:24 But that glory of the Word is also the glory of the Father, even as it is written: The Lord Jesus Christ is in the glory of God the Father. In regard of His Godhead, therefore, the Son of God so has His own glory, that the glory of Father and Son is one: He is not, therefore, inferior in splendour, for the glory is one, nor lower in Godhead, for the fullness of the Godhead is in Christ.

83. How, then, you ask, is it written, Father, the hour has come; glorify Your Son? John 17:1 He Who says these words needs to be glorified, say you. Thus far you have eyes to see; the remainder of the Scripture you have not read, for it proceeds: that Your Son may glorify You. Hath ever the Father need of any, in that He is to be glorified by the Son?

Chapter 10.

The objection taken on the ground of the Son's obedience is disproved, and the unity of power, Godhead, and operation in the Trinity set forth, Christ's

obedience to His mother, to whom He certainly cannot be called inferior, is noticed.

84. In like manner our adversaries commonly make a difficulty of the Son's obedience, forasmuch as it is written: And being found in appearance as a man, He humbled Himself, and became obedient even unto death. Philippians 2:7-8 The writer has not only told us that the Son was obedient even unto death, but also first shown that He was man, in order that we might understand that obedience unto death was the part not of His Godhead but of His Incarnation, whereby He took upon Himself both the functions and the names belonging to our nature.

85. Thus we have learned that the power of the Trinity is one, as we are taught both in and after the Passion itself: for the Son suffers through His body, which is the earnest of it; the Holy Spirit is poured upon the apostles: into the Father's hands the spirit is commended; furthermore, God is with a mighty voice proclaimed the Father. We have learned that there is one form, one likeness, one sanctification, of the Father and of the Son, one activity, one glory, finally, one Godhead.

86. There is, therefore, but one only God, for it is written: You shall worship the Lord your God, and Him only shall you serve. Deuteronomy 6:13 One God, not in the sense that the Father and the Son are the same Person, as the ungodly Sabellius affirms — but forasmuch as there is one Godhead of the Father and of the Son and of the Holy Ghost. But where there is one Godhead, there is one will, one purpose.

87. Again, that you may know that the Father is, and the Son is, and that the work of the Father and of the Son is one, follow the saying of the Apostle: Now may God Himself, and our Father, and our Lord Jesus Christ direct our way unto you. 1 Thessalonians 3:11 Both Father and Son are named, but there is unity of direction, because unity of power. So also in another place we read: Now may our Lord Himself, Jesus Christ, and God and our Father, Who has loved us, and given us eternal consolation, and good hope in grace, console and strengthen your hearts. 2 Thessalonians 2:15-16 How perfect a unity it is that the Apostle presents to us, insomuch that the fount of consolation is not many, but one. Let doubt be dumb, then, or, if it will not be overcome by reason, let the thought of our Lord's gracious kindliness bend it.

88. Let us call to mind how kindly our Lord has dealt with us, in that He taught us not only faith but manners also. For, having taken His place in the form of man, He was subject to Joseph and Mary. Luke 2:51 Was He less than all mankind, then, because He was subject? The part of dutifulness is one, that of sovereignty is another, but dutifulness does not exclude sovereignty. Wherein, then, was He subject to the Father's law? In His body, surely, wherein He was subject to His mother.

Chapter 11.

The purpose and healing effects of the Incarnation. The profitableness of faith, whereby we know that Christ bore all infirmities for our sakes — Christ, Whose Godhead revealed Itself in His Passion; whence we understand that the

mission of the Son of God entailed no subservience, which belief we need not fear lest it displease the Father, Who declares Himself to be well pleased in His Son.

89. Let us likewise deal kindly, let us persuade our adversaries of that which is to their profit, let us worship and lament before the Lord our Maker. For we would not overthrow, but rather heal; we lay no ambush for them, but warn them as in duty bound. Kindliness often bends those whom neither force nor argument will avail to overcome. Again, our Lord cured with oil and wine the man who, going down from Jerusalem to Jericho, fell among thieves; having forborne to treat him with the harsh remedies of the Law or the sternness of Prophecy.

90. To Him, therefore, let all come who would be made whole. Let them receive the medicine which He has brought down from His Father and made in heaven, preparing it of the juices of those celestial fruits that wither not. This is of no earthly growth, for nature nowhere possesses this compound. Of wondrous purpose took He our flesh, to the end that He might show that the law of the flesh had been subjected to the law of the mind. He was incarnate, that He, the Teacher of men, might overcome as man.

91. Of what profit would it have been to me, had He, as God, bared the arm of His power, and only displayed His Godhead inviolate? Why should He take human nature upon Him, but to suffer Himself to be tempted under the conditions of my nature and my weakness? It was right that He should be tempted, that He should suffer with me, to the end that I might know how to conquer when tempted, how to escape when hard pressed. He overcame by force of continence, of contempt of riches, of faith; He trampled upon ambition, fled from intemperance, bade wantonness be far from Him.

92. This medicine Peter beheld, and left His nets, that is to say, the instruments and security of gain, renouncing the lust of the flesh as a leaky ship, that receives the bilge, as it were, of multitudinous passions. Truly a mighty remedy, that not only removed the scar of an old wound, but even cut the root and source of passion. O Faith, richer than all treasure-houses; O excellent remedy, healing our wounds and sins!

93. Let us bethink ourselves of the profitableness of right belief. It is profitable to me to know that for my sake Christ bore my infirmities, submitted to the affections of my body, that for me, that is to say, for every man, He was made sin, and a curse, that for me and in me was He humbled and made subject, that for me He is the Lamb, the Vine, the Rock, the Servant, the Son of an handmaid, knowing not the day of judgment, for my sake ignorant of the day and the hour.

94. For how could He, Who has made days and times, be ignorant of the day? How could He not know the day, Who has declared both the season of Judgment to come, and the cause? A curse, then, He was made not in respect of His Godhead, but of His flesh; for it is written: Cursed is every one that hangs on a tree. In and after the flesh, therefore, He hung, and for this cause He, Who bore our curses, became a curse. He

wept that thou, man, might not weep long. He endured insult, that you might not grieve over the wrong done to you.

95. A glorious remedy — to have consolation of Christ! For He bore these things with surpassing patience for our sakes — and we forsooth cannot bear them with common patience for the glory of His Name! Who may not learn to forgive, when assailed, seeing that Christ, even on the Cross, prayed — yea, for them that persecuted Him? See you not that those weaknesses, as you please to call them, of Christ's are your *strength?* Why question Him in the matter of remedies for us? His tears wash us, His weeping cleanses us — and there is strength in *this* doubt, at least, that if you begin to doubt, you will despair. The greater the insult, the greater is the gratitude due.

96. Even in the very hour of mockery and insult, acknowledge His Godhead. He hung upon the Cross, and all the elements did Him homage. Matthew 27:51 The sun withdrew his rays, the daylight vanished, darkness came down and covered the land, the earth trembled; yet He Who hung there trembled not. What was it that these signs betokened, but reverence for the Creator? That He hangs upon the Cross — this, thou Arian, you regard, that He gives the kingdom of God — this, you regard not. That He tasted of death, you read, but that He also invited the robber into paradise, Luke 23:43 to this you give no heed. You gaze at the women weeping by the tomb, but not upon the angels keeping watch by it. John 20:11-12 What He *said*, you read, what He *did*, thou dost not read. You say that the Lord said to the Canaanitish woman: I am not sent, but to the lost sheep of the house of Israel, Matthew 15:24 thou dost not say that He did what He was besought by her to do.

97. You should hereby understand that His being sent means not that He was compelled, at the command of another, but that He acted, of free will, according to His own judgment, otherwise thou dost accuse Him of despising His Father. For if, according to your expounding, Christ had come into Jewry, as one executing the Father's commands, to relieve the inhabitants of Jewry, and none besides, and yet before that was accomplished, set free the Canaanitish woman's daughter from her complaint, surely He was not only the executor of another's instruction, but was free to exercise His own judgment. But where there is freedom to act as one will, there can be no transgressing the terms of one's mission.

98. Fear not that the Son's act displeased the Father, seeing that the Son Himself says: Whatsoever things are His good pleasure, I do always, and The works that I do, He Himself does. How, then, could the Father be displeased with that which He Himself did through the Son? For it is One God, Who, as it is written, has justified circumcision in consequence of faith, and uncircumcision through faith. Romans 3:30

99. Read all the Scriptures, mark all diligently, you will then find that Christ so manifested Himself that God might be discerned in man. Misunderstand not maliciously the Son's exultation in the Father, when you hear the Father declaring His pleasure in the Son.

Chapter 12.

Do the Catholics or the Arians take the better course to assure themselves of the favour of Christ as their Judge? An objection grounded on **Psalm 110:1** *is disposed of, it being shown that when the Son is invited by the Father to sit at His right hand, no subjection is intended to be signified — nor yet any preferment, in that the Son sits at the Father's right hand. The truth of the Trinity of Persons in God, and of the Unity of their Nature, is shown to be proved by the angelic Trisagion.*

100. Howbeit, if our adversaries cannot be turned by kindness, let us summon them before the Judge. To what Judge, then, shall we go? Surely to Him Who has the Judgment. To the Father, then? Nay, but the Father judges no man, for He has given all judgment to the Son. John 5:22 He has given, that is to say, not as of largess, but in the act of generation. See, then, how unwilling He was that you should dishonour His Son — even so that He gave Him to be your Judge.

101. Let us see, then, before the judgment which has the better cause, thou or I? Surely it is the care of a prudent party to a suit to gain first the favourable regard of the judge. You honour man — do you not honour God? Which of the two, I ask, wins the favour of the magistrate — respect or contempt? Suppose that I am in error— as I certainly am not: is Christ displeased with the honour shown Him? We are all sinners — who, then, will deserve forgiveness, he who renders worship, or he who displays insolence?

102. If reasoning move you not, at least let the plain aspect of the judgment move you! Raise your eyes to the Judge, see Who it is that is seated, with Whom He is seated, and where. Christ sits at the right hand of the Father. If with your eyes you can not perceive this, hear the words of the prophet: The Lord said to my Lord, Sit on My right hand. The Son, therefore, sits at the right hand of the Father. Tell me now, thou who holdest that the things of God are to be judged of from the things of this world — say whether you think Him Who sits at the right hand to be lower? Is it any dishonour to the Father that He sits at the Son's left hand? The Father honours the Son, and you make it to be insult! The Father would have this invitation to be a sign of love and esteem, and you would make it an overlord's command! Christ has risen from the dead, and sits at the right hand of God.

103. But, you object, the Father *said*. Good, hear now a passage where the Father does not speak, and the Son prophesies: Hereafter you shall see the Son of Man sitting at the right hand of power. Matthew 26:64 This He said with regard to taking back to Himself His body — to Him the Father said: Sit at My right hand. If indeed you ask of the eternal abode of the Godhead, He said — when Pilate asked Him whether He were the King of the Jews— For this I was born. And so indeed the Apostle shows that it is good for us to believe that Christ sits at the right hand of God, not by command, nor of any boon, but as God's most dearly beloved Son. For it is written for you: Seek the things that are above, where Christ is, sitting at the right hand of God; savour the things that are above. Colossians 3:2 This is to savour the things that be above — to believe that Christ, in His sitting, does not obey as one

who receives a command, but is honoured as the well-beloved Son. It is with regard, then, to Christ's Body that the Father says: Sit at My right hand, until I make Your enemies Your footstool.

104. If, again, you seek to pervert the sense of these words, I will make Your enemies Your footstool, I answer that the Father also brings to the Son such as the Son raises up and quickens. For No man, says Christ, can come to Me, except the Father, Which has sent Me, draw him, and I will raise him up at the last day. John 6:44 And you say that the Son of God is subject by reason of weakness — the Son, to Whom the Father brings men that He may raise them up in the last day. Seems this in your eyes to be subjection, I pray you, where the kingdom is prepared for the Father, and the Father brings to the Son and there is no place for perversion of words, since the Son gives the kingdom to the Father, and none is preferred before Him? For inasmuch as the Father renders to the Son, and the Son, again, to the Father, here are plain proofs of love and regard: seeing that They so render, the One to the Other, that neither He Who receives obtains as it were what was another's, nor He That renders loses.

105. Moreover, the sitting at the right hand is no preferment, nor does that at the left hand betoken dishonour, for there are no degrees in the Godhead, Which is bound by no limits of space or time, which are the weights and measures of our puny human minds. There is no difference of love, nothing that divides the Unity.

106. But wherefore roam so far afield? You have looked upon all around you, you have seen the Judge, you have remarked the angels proclaiming Him. *They* praise, and *thou* revilest Him! Dominations and powers fall down before Him — you speak evil of His Name! All His Saints adore Him, but the Son of God adores not, nor the Holy Spirit. The seraphim say: Holy, Holy, Holy! Isaiah 6:3

107. What means this threefold utterance of the same name Holy? If thrice repeated, why is it but one act of praise? If one act of praise, why a threefold repetition? Why the threefold repetition, unless that the Father and the Son and the Holy Spirit are one in holiness? The seraph spoke the name, not once, lest he should exclude the Son; not twice, lest he should pass by the Holy Spirit; not four times, lest he should conjoin created beings [in the praise of the Creator]. Furthermore, to show that the Godhead of the Trinity is One, he, after the threefold Holy, added in the singular number the Lord God of Sabaoth. Holy, therefore, is the Father, holy the Son, holy likewise the Spirit of God, and therefore is the Trinity adored, but adores not, and is praised, but praises not. As for me, I will rather believe as the seraphim, and adore after the manner of all the principalities and powers of heaven.

Chapter 13.

The wicked and dishonourable opinions held by Arians, Sabellians, and Manichæans as concerning their Judge are shortly refuted. Christ's remonstrances regarding the rest of His adversaries being set forth, St. Ambrose expresses a hope of milder judgment for himself.

108. Let us proceed, then, with your accusations, and see how you gain the favour of your Judge. Speak now, speak, I say, and tell Him: I consider You, O Christ, to be unlike Your Father; and He will answer: Mark, if you can, mark, I say, and tell Me wherein you hold Me to differ.

109. Say again: I judge You to be a created being; and Christ will reply: If the witness of two men is true, ought you not to have believed both Me and My Father, Who has called Me His Son?

110. Then you will say: I deny Your [perfect] goodness; and He will answer: Be it unto you according to your faith; so will I not be good to you.

111. That You are Almighty, I hold not; and He will answer, in turn: Then can I not forgive you your sins.

112. You are a subject being. Whereto He will reply: Why, then, do you seek freedom and pardon of Him Whom you think to be subject as a slave?

113. I see your accusation halt here. I press you not, forasmuch as I myself know my own sins. I grudge you not pardon, for I myself would obtain indulgence, but I would know the object of your prayers. Look, then, while I recite before the Judge your desires. I betray not your sins, but look to behold your prayers and wishes set forth in their order.

114. Speak, therefore, those desires, which all alike would have granted to them. Lord, make me in the image of God. Whereto He will answer: In what image? The image which you have denied?

115. Make me incorruptible. Surely His reply will be: How can I make you incorruptible, I, Whom you call a created being, and so would make out to be corruptible? The dead shall rise purified from corruption — do you call Him corruptible Whom you see to be God?

116. Be good to me. Why do you ask what you have denied [to Me]? I would have had you to be good, and I said 'Be holy, for I Myself am holy,' Leviticus 19:2 and you set yourself to deny that I am good? Do *you* then look for forgiveness of sins? Nay, none can forgive sins, but God alone. Mark 2:7 Seeing, then, that to you I am not the true and only God, I cannot by any means forgive you your sins.

117. Thus let the followers of Arius and Photinus speak. I deny Your Godhead. To whom the Lord will make answer: 'The fool has said in his heart: There is no God?' Of whom, think you, is this said?— of Jew or Gentile, or of the devil. Whosoever he be of whom it is said, O disciple of Photinus, he is more to be borne with, who held his peace; thou, nevertheless, hast dared to lift up your voice to utter it, that you might be proved more foolish than the fool. You deny My Godhead, whereas I said, 'You are gods, and you are all the children of the Most High?' And you deny Him to be God, Whose godlike works you see around you.

118. Let the Sabellian speak in his turn. I consider You, by Yourself, to be at once Father and Son and Holy Spirit. To whom the Lord: You hear neither the Father nor the Son. Is there any doubt on this matter? The Scripture itself teaches you that it is the Father Who gives over the judgment, and the Son Who judges. John 5:22 You have not given ear to My words: 'I am not alone, but I and the Father, Who sent Me.'

119. Now let the Manichæan have his word. I hold that the devil is the creator of our flesh. The Lord will answer him: What, then, are you doing in the heavenly places? Depart, go your way to your creator. 'My will is that they be with Me, whom my Father has given Me.' John 17:24 You, Manichæan, hold yourself for a creature of the devil; hasten, then, to his abode, the place of fire and brimstone, where the fire thereof is not quenched, lest ever the punishment have an end.

120. I set aside other heretical— not persons, but portents. What manner of judgment awaits them, what shall be the form of their sentence? To all these He will, indeed, reply, rather in sorrow than in anger: O My people, what have I done unto you, wherein have I vexed you? Did I not bring you up out of Egypt, and lead you out of the house of bondage into liberty?

121. But it is not enough to have brought us out of Egypt into freedom, and to have saved us from the house of bondage: a greater boon than this, You have given Yourself for us. You will say then: Have I not borne all your sufferings? Isaiah 53:4 Have I not given My Body for you? Have I not sought death, which had no part in My Godhead, but was necessary for your redemption? Are *these* the thanks I am to receive? Is it this that My Blood has gained, even as I spoke in times past by the mouth of the prophet: 'What profit is there in My Blood, for that I have gone down to corruption?' Is this the profit, that you should wickedly deny Me — you, for whom I endured those things?

122. As for me, Lord Jesu, though I am conscious within myself of great sin, yet will I say: I have not denied You; You may pardon the infirmity of my flesh. My transgression I confess; my sin I deny not. If You will You can make me clean. Matthew 8:2 For this saying, the leper obtained his request. Enter not, I pray, into judgment with Your servant. I ask, not that You may judge, but that You may forgive.

Chapter 14.

The sentence of the Judge is set forth, the counterpleas of the opposers are considered, and the finality of the sentence, from which there is no appeal, proved.

123. What verdict do we look for from Christ? That do I know. Do I say, what verdict *will* He give? Nay, He has already pronounced sentence. We have it in our hands. Let all, says He, honour the Son, even as they honour the Father. He that honours not the Son, honours not the Father, Who has sent Him. John 5:23

124. If the sentence please you not, appeal to the Father, cancel the judgment that the Father has given. Say that He has a Son Who is unlike Him. He will reply: Then have I lied, I, Who said to the Son, 'Let us make man in Our image and likeness.' Genesis 1:26

125. Tell the Father that He has created the Son, and He will answer: Why, then, have you worshipped One Whom you thought to be a created being?

126. Tell Him that He has begotten a Son Who is inferior to Himself, and He will reply: Compare Us, and let Us see.

127. Tell Him that you owed no credence to the Son, whereto He will answer: Did I not say to you, 'This is My well-beloved Son, in Whom I am well pleased: hear Him'? Matthew 17:5 What mean these words hear Him, if not Hear Him when He says: 'All things that the Father has are Mine'? This did the apostles hear, even as it is written: And they fell upon their faces, and were greatly afraid. Matthew 17:6 If they who confessed Him fell to the earth, what shall they do who have denied Him? But Jesus laid His hand upon His apostles, and raised them up — you He will suffer to lie prone, that you may see not the glory you have denied.

128. Let us look to it, then, forasmuch as whom the Son condemns, the Father condemns also, and therefore let us honour the Son, even as we honour the Father, that by the Son we may be able to come to the Father.

Chapter 15.

St. Ambrose deprecates any praise of his own merits: in any case, the Faith is sufficiently defended by the authoritative support of holy Scripture, to whose voice the Arians, stubborn as the Jews, are deaf. He prays that they may be moved to love the truth; meanwhile, they are to be avoided, as heretics and enemies of Christ.

129. These arguments, your Majesty, I have set forth, briefly and summarily, in the rough, rather than in any form of full explanation and exact order. If indeed the Arians regard them as imperfect and unfinished, I indeed confess that they are scarce even begun; if they think that there be any still to be brought forward, I allow that there be nearly all; for whereas the unbelievers are in uttermost need of arguments, the faithful have enough and to spare. Indeed, Peter's single confession was abundant to warrant faith in Christ: You are the Christ, the Son of the living God; for it is enough to know His Divine Generation, without division or diminution, being neither derivation nor creation.

130. This, indeed, is declared in the books of Holy Writ, one and all, and yet is still doubted by misbelievers: For, as it is written, the heart of this people has become gross, and with their ears they have been dull of hearing, and their eyes have they darkened, lest ever they should see with their eyes, and hear with their ears, and understand in their heart. Isaiah 6:10 For, like the Jews, the Arians' wont is to stop their ears, or make an uproar, as often as the Word of salvation is heard.

131. And what wonder, if unbelievers doubt the word of man, when they refuse to believe the Word of God? The Son of God, as you will find it written in the Gospel, said: Father, glorify Your Name, and from heaven was heard the voice of the Father, saying: I have both glorified it, and again will glorify. John 12:28 These words the unbelievers heard, but believed not. The Son spoke, the Father answered, and the Jews said: A peal of thunder answered Him; others said: An angel spoke to Him. John 12:29

132. Paul, moreover, as it is written in the Acts of the Apostles, Acts 22:9 when by the Voice of Christ he received the call of grace, several companions journeying with him at the same time, alone said that he had heard Christ's Voice. Thus, your sacred Majesty, he who believes, hears — and he hears, that he may believe, while he who believes not, hears not, nay, he will not, he cannot hear, lest he should believe!

133. As for me, indeed, would that they might have a will to hear, that they might believe— to hear with true love and meekness, as men seeking what is true, and not assailing all truth. For it is written that we pay no heed to endless fables and genealogies, which do rather raise disputes than set forward the godly edification, which is in faith. But the aim of the charge is love from a pure heart, and a good conscience, and faith unfeigned, whence some have erred and betaken themselves to empty babbling, desirous of being teachers of the law, without understanding the words they say, nor the things whereof they speak with assurance. In another place also the same Apostle says: But foolish and ignorant questionings do thou avoid. 2 Timothy 2:23

134. Such men, who sow disputes — that is to say, heretics— the Apostle bids us leave alone. Of them he says in yet another place, that certain shall depart from the faith, giving heed to deceitful spirits, and the doctrines of devils. 1 Timothy 4:1

135. John, likewise, says that heretics are Antichrists, plainly marking out the Arians. For this [Arian] heresy began to be after all other heresies, and has gathered the poisons of all. As it is written of the Antichrist, that he opened his mouth to blasphemy against God, to blaspheme His Name, and to make war with His saints, Revelation 13:6 so do they also dishonour the Son of God, and His martyrs have they not spared. Moreover, that which perchance Antichrist will not do, they have falsified the holy Scriptures. And thus he who says that Jesus is not the Christ, the same is Antichrist; he who denies the Saviour of the world, denies Jesus; he who denies the Son, denies the Father also, for it is written; Every one which denies the Son, denies the Father likewise. 1 John 2:23

Chapter 16.

St. Ambrose assures Gratian of victory, declaring that it has been foretold in the prophecies of Ezekiel. This hope is further stayed upon the emperor's piety, the former disasters being the punishment of Eastern heresy. The book closes with a prayer to God, that He will now show His mercy, and save the army, the land, and the sovereign of the faithful.

136. I must no further detain your Majesty, in this season of preparation for war, and the achievement of victory over the Barbarians. Go forth, sheltered, indeed, under the shield of faith, and girt with the sword of the Spirit; go forth to the victory, promised of old time, and foretold in oracles given by God.

137. For Ezekiel, in those far-off days, already prophesied the minishing of our people, and the Gothic wars, saying: Prophesy, therefore, Son of Man, and say: O Gog, thus says the Lord — Shall you not, in that day when My people Israel shall be established to dwell in peace, rise up and come forth from your place, from the far north, and many nations with you, all riders upon horses, a great and mighty gathering, and the valour of many hosts? Yea, go up against my people Israel, as clouds to cover the land, in the last days.

138. That Gog is the Goth, whose coming forth we have already seen, and over whom victory in days to come is promised, according to the word of the Lord: And they shall spoil them, who had been their despoilers, and plunder them, who had carried off their goods for a prey, says the Lord. And it shall be in that day, that I will give to Gog — that is, to the Goths — a place that is famous, for Israel an high-heaped tomb of many men, of men who have made their way to the sea, and it shall reach round about, and close the mouth of the valley, and there [the house of Israel shall] overthrow Gog and all his multitude, and it shall be called the valley of the multitude of Gog: and the house of Israel shall overwhelm them, that the land may be cleansed.

139. Nor, furthermore, may we doubt, your sacred Majesty, that we, who have undertaken the contest with alien unbelief, shall enjoy the aid of the Catholic Faith that is strong in you. Plainly indeed the reason of God's wrath has been already made manifest, so that belief in the Roman Empire was first overthrown, where faith in God gave way.

140. No desire have I to recount the deaths, tortures, and banishments of confessors, the offices of the faithful made into presents for traitors. Have we not heard, from all along the border — from Thrace, and through Dacia by the river, Mœsia, and all Valeria of the Pannonians — a mingled tumult of blasphemers preaching and barbarians invading? What profit could neighbours so bloodthirsty bring us, or how could the Roman State be safe with such defenders?

141. Enough, yea, more than enough, Almighty God, have we now atoned for the deaths of confessors, the banishment of priests, and the guilt of wickedness so overweening, by our own blood, our own banishment — sufficiently plain is it that they, who have broken faith, cannot be safe. Turn again, O Lord, and set up the banners of Your faith.

142. No military eagles, no flight of birds, here lead the van of our army, but Your Name, Lord Jesus, and Your worship. This is no land of unbelievers, but the land whose custom it is to send forth confessors — Italy; Italy, ofttimes tempted, but never drawn away; Italy, which your Majesty has long defended, and now again rescued from the barbarian. No wavering mind in our emperor, but faith firm fixed.

143. Show forth now a plain sign of Your Majesty, that he who believes You to be the true Lord of Hosts, and Captain of the armies of heaven; he who believes that You are the true Power and Wisdom of God, no being of time nor of creation, but even as it is written, the eternal Power and Divinity of God, 1 Corinthians 1:24 may, upheld by the aid of your Might Supreme, win the prize of victory for his Faith.

EXPOSITION ON THE CHRISTIAN FAITH

Book III.

Chapter 1.

Statement of the reasons wherefore the matters, treated of shortly in the two former, are dealt with more at length in the three later books. Defence of the employment of fables, which is supported by the example of Holy Writ, wherein are found various figures of poetic fable, in particular the Sirens, which are figures of sensual pleasures, and which Christians ought to be taught to avoid, by the words of Paul and the deeds of Christ.

1. Forasmuch as your most gracious Majesty had laid command upon me to write for your own instruction some treatise concerning the Faith, and had yourself called me to your presence and encouraged my timidity, I, being as one on the eve of battle, composed but two books only, for the pointing out of certain ways and paths by which our faith progresses.

2. Seeing, however, that certain malicious minds, bent on sowing disputes, have not yet exhausted the force of their assaults, while your gracious Majesty's pious anxiety calls me to further labours, inasmuch as you desire to try in more things him whom you have proved in a few, I am resolved to deal somewhat more particularly with the matters whereof I have already treated in a few words, lest it should be thought, not that I have advanced those propositions in quietness and confidence, but that I, having asserted them, doubted and so abandoned their defense.

3. Again, seeing that we spoke of the Hydra and Scylla (I. vi. 46), and brought them in by way of comparison, to show how we must beware, whether of the ever-renewed outgrowths of infidelity, or the ill-omened shipwrecks made upon its shallows, if any one holds that such embellishments of an argument, borrowed from the romances of poets, are unlawful, and, from lack of opportunity to speak evil of my faith, assails something in my language, then let him know that not only phrases but complete verses of poetry have been woven into the text of Holy Writ.

4. Whence, for instance, came that verse, His offspring truly are we, Acts 17:28 whereof Paul, by prophetic experience, taught, makes use? The course of prophetic speech avoids neither the Giants nor the Valley of the Titans, and Isaiah spoke of sirens and the daughters of ostriches. Jeremiah also has prophesied concerning Babylon, that the daughters of sirens shall dwell therein, in order to show that the snares of Babylon, that is, of the tumult of this world, are to be likened to stories of old-time lust, that seemed upon this life's rocky shores to sing some tuneful song, but deadly withal, to catch the souls of youth — which the Greek poet himself tells us that the wise man escaped through being bound, as it were, in the chains of his own prudence. So hard a thing, before Christ's coming, was it esteemed, even for the stronger, to save themselves from the deceitful shows and allurements of pleasure.

5. But if the poet judged the enticement of worldly pleasure and licence destructive of men's minds and a sure cause of shipwreck, what ought we to think, for whom it has been written: Train not the flesh in concupiscence? And again: I chastise my body

and bring it into servitude, lest while I preach to others, I myself become a castaway. 1 Corinthians 9:27

6. Truly, Christ won salvation for us, not by luxury but by fasting. Moreover, it was not to obtain favour for Himself, but to instruct us, that He fasted. Nor yet did He hunger because He was overcome by the weakness of the body, but by His hunger He proved that He had verily taken upon Himself a body; that so He might teach us that He had taken not only our body, but also the weaknesses of that body, even as it is written: Surely He has taken our infirmities and borne our sicknesses.

Chapter 2.

The incidents properly affecting the body which Christ for our sake took upon Him are not to be accounted to His Godhead, in respect whereof He is the Most Highest. To deny which is to say that the Father was incarnate. When we read that God is one, and that there is none other beside Him, or that He alone has immortality, this must be understood as true of Christ also, not only to avoid the sinful heresy above-mentioned (Patripassianism), but also because the activity of the Father and the Son is declared to be one and the same.

7. It was a bodily weakness, then, that is to say, a weakness of ours, that He hungered; when He wept, and was sorrowful even unto death, it was of our nature. Why ascribe the properties and incidents of our nature to the Godhead? That He was even, as we are told, made, is a property of a body. Thus, indeed, we read: Sion our mother shall say: 'He is a man,' and in her He was made man, and the Most High Himself laid her foundations. He was made man, mark you, not He was made God.

8. But what is He Who is at once the Most High and man, what but the Mediator between God and man, the man Christ Jesus Who gave Himself as a ransom for us? 1 Timothy 2:5 This place indeed refers properly to His Incarnation, for our redemption was made by His Blood, our pardon comes through His Power, our life is secured through His Grace. He gives as the Most High, He prays as man. The one is the office of the Creator, the other of a Redeemer. Be the gifts as distinct as they may, yet the Giver is one, for it was fitting that our Maker should be our Redeemer.

9. Who indeed can deny that we have plain evidence that Christ is the Most High? He who knows otherwise makes the sacrament of Incarnation to be the work of God the Father. But that Christ is the Most High is removed beyond doubt by what Scripture has said in another place, concerning the mystery of the Passion: The Most High sent forth His Voice, and the earth was shaken. And in the Gospel you may read: And thou, child, shall be called the Prophet of the Highest; for you shall go before the face of the Lord, to prepare His ways. Luke 1:76 Who is the Highest? The Son of God. He, then, Who is the Most High God is Christ.

10. Again, while God is everywhere said to be One God, the Son of God is not separated from this Unity. For He Who is the Most High is alone, as it is written:

And let them know that Your Name is the Lord: You alone are Most High over all the earth.

11. And so the adversaries' injurious conclusion is rejected with contempt and disgrace, which they drew from the Scripture speaking of God: Who alone has immortality and dwells in light unapproachable; 1 Timothy 6:16 for these words are written of God, which Name belongs equally to Father and to Son.

12. If, indeed, wheresoever they read the Name of God, they deny that there is any thought of the Son [as well as the Father], they blaspheme, inasmuch as they deny the Son's Divine Sovereignty, and they shall appear as though they shared the sinful error of the Sabellians in teaching the Incarnation of the Father. Let them, indeed explain how they can fail to interpret in a sense blasphemous to the Father the words of the Apostle: In Whom you also rose again, by faith in the working of God, Who raised Him from the dead. Colossians 2:12 Let them also take warning from what follows of what they are running upon — for this is what comes after: And though you were dead in your sins and the uncircumcision of your flesh, He quickened us with Him, pardoning us all our offenses, blotting out the handwriting of the Ordinance, which was opposed to us, and removed it from our midst, nailing it to His Cross, divesting Himself of the flesh. Colossians 2:13-14

13. We are not, then, to suppose that the Father Who raised the flesh is alone [God]; nor, again, are we to suppose the like of the Son, Whose Body was raised again. He Who raised, did surely also quicken; and He who quickened, also pardoned sins; He who pardoned sins, also blotted out the handwriting; He Who blotted out the handwriting, also nailed it to the Cross: He who nailed it to the Cross, divested Himself of the flesh. But it was not the Father Who divested Himself of the flesh; for *not* the Father, but, as we read, the Word was made flesh. John 1:14 You see, then, that the Arians, in dividing the Father from the Son, run into danger of saying that the Father endured the Passion.

14. We, however, can easily show that the words treat of the Son's action, for the Son Himself indeed raised His own Body again, as He Himself said: Destroy this Temple, and in three days I will raise it again. John 2:19 And He Himself quickens us together with His Body: For as the Father raises the dead and quickens them, so also the Son quickens Whom He will. John 5:21 And He Himself has granted forgiveness for sins, saying, Your sins be forgiven you. Luke 5:20 He too has nailed the handwriting of the record to His Cross, in that He was crucified, and suffered in the body. Nor did any divest Himself of the flesh, save the Son of God, Who invested Himself therewith. He, therefore, Who has achieved the work of our resurrection is plainly pointed out to be very God.

Chapter 3.

That the Father and the Son must not be divided is proved by the words of the Apostle, seeing that it is befitting to the Son that He should be blessed, only Potentate, and immortal, by nature, that is, and not by grace, as even the angels themselves are immortal, and that He should dwell in the unapproachable light. How it is that the Father and the Son are alike and equally said to be alone.

15. When, therefore, you read the Name God, separate neither Father nor Son, for the Godhead of the Father and the Son is one and the same, and therefore separate them not, when you read the words blessed and only Potentate, 1 Timothy 6:15 for the words are spoken of God, even as you may read: I charge you before God, Who quickens all things. 1 Timothy 6:13 Christ also indeed does quicken, and therefore the Name of God is meetly given both to the Father and to the Son, inasmuch as the effect of their activity is in agreement. Let us go on to the words following: I charge you, he says, before God, Who quickens all things, and Jesus Christ.

16. The Word is in God, even as it is written: In God will I praise His Word. In God is His Eternal Power, even Jesus; in [speaking of] God, therefore, the Apostle has witnessed to the unity of the Godhead, while by the Name of Christ he has witnessed to the sacrament of the Incarnation.

17. Furthermore, to show that he has spoken of the Incarnation of Christ, he added: Who bore witness under Pontius Pilate with the good confession, [I charge you] keep undefiled the commandment, until the coming of our Lord Jesus Christ, Which in His own good time the blessed and only Potentate shall manifest, the King of kings and Lord of lords, Who alone has immortality, and dwells in light unapproachable, Whom no man has seen, nor can see. 1 Timothy 6:13-16 Those words, then, are written with regard to God, of which Name the dignity and truth are common to [both the Father and] the Son.

18. Why, then, should there be no thought of the Son in this place, seeing that all these things hold good of the Son also? If they do not so, then deny His Godhead, and so may thou deny what is proper to be said of God. His Blessedness cannot be denied, Who bestows blessings, for Blessed are they whose iniquities are forgiven. He cannot but be called Blessed, Who has given us wholesome teaching, even as it is written: Which is according to the Gospel of the beauty of the Blessed God. 1 Timothy 1:11 His Power cannot be denied, of Whom the Father says: I have laid help upon One that is mighty. And who dare refuse to acknowledge Him to be immortal, when He Himself has made others also immortal, as it is written of the Wisdom of God: By her shall I possess immortality. Wisdom 8:13

19. But the immortality of His Nature is one thing, that of ours is another. Things perishable are not to be compared to things divine. The Godhead is the one only Substance that death cannot touch, and therefore it is that the Apostle, though knowing both the [human] soul and angels to be immortal, declared that God only had immortality. In truth, even the soul may die: The soul that sins, it shall die, Ezekiel 18:20 and an angel is not absolutely immortal, his immortality depending on the will of the Creator.

20. Do not hastily reject this, because Gabriel dies not, nor Raphaël, nor Uriel. Even in their nature there is a capacity of sin, though not one of improvement by discipline, for every reasonable creature is exposed to influences from without itself,

and liable to judgment. It is on the influences which work upon us that the award of judgment, and corruption, or advance to perfection, do depend, and therefore Ecclesiastes says: For God shall bring all His work to judgment. Every creature, then, has within it the possibility of corruption and death, even though it do not [at present] die or commit sin; nor, if in anything it deliver not itself over to sin, has it this boon of its immortal nature, but of discipline or of grace. Immortality, then, that is of a gift is one thing: immortality without the possibility of change is another.

21. Do we deny the immortality of Christ's Godhead, because He tasted death for all in the flesh? Then is Gabriel better than Christ, for Gabriel never died, but Christ gave up the ghost. But the servant is not above his lord, Matthew 10:24 and we must discern the weakness of flesh from the eternity of Godhead. Christ's Death had its source in the flesh, immortality is of the nature of Christ's sovereignty. But if the Godhead brought it to pass that the flesh saw not corruption, the flesh being surely by nature liable to corruption, how could the Godhead itself have died?

22. And how is it that the Son dwells not in light unapproachable, if He is in the bosom of the Father, if the Father is Light, and the Son also is Light, because God is Light? 1 John 1:5 Or, if we suppose some other light, beside the Light of the Godhead, to be the unapproachable Light, is, then, this Light better than the Father, so that He is not in that Light, Who, as it is written, is both with the Father and in the Father? Let men, therefore, not exclude the thought of the Son, when they read only of *God*— and let them not exclude that of the Father, when they read of the *Son* only. John 16:32

23. On earth, the Son is not without *l.c.*John 10:30 the Father, and you think that the Father is without the Son in heaven? The Son is in the flesh — (when I say He is in the flesh or He is on earth, I speak as though we lived in the days whose story is in the Gospel, for now we no longer know Christ after the flesh 2 Corinthians 5:16)— He is in the flesh, and He is not alone, as it is written: And I am not alone, because the Father is with Me, John 8:16 and think you that the Father dwells alone in the Light?

24. Lest you should regard this argument as mere speculation take this sentence of authority. No man, says the Scripture, John 1:18 has seen God at any time, save the Only-begotten Son, Who is in the bosom of the Father; He has revealed Him. How can the Father be in solitude, if the Son be in the bosom of the Father? How does the Son reveal Him, Whom He sees not? The Father, then, exists not alone.

25. Observe now what the solitude of the Father and of the Son is. The Father is alone, because there is no other Father; the Son is alone, because there is no other Son; God is alone, because the Godhead of the Trinity is One.

Chapter 4.

We are told that Christ was only made so far as regards the flesh. For the redemption of mankind He needed no means of aid, even as He needed none in order to His Resurrection, whereas others, in order to raise the dead, had need of recourse to prayer. Even when Christ prayed, the prayer was offered by Him in His capacity as human; while He must be accounted divine from the fact that He commanded (that such and such things should be done). On this point the devil's testimony is truer than the Arians' arguments. The discussion concludes with an explanation of the reason why the title of mighty is given to the Son of Man.

26. It is now sufficiently made plain that the Father is not God in solitude, without the Son, and that the Son cannot be thought of as God alone, without the Father, for it is in respect of His flesh that we read that the Son of God was made, not in respect of His generation from God the Father.

27. Indeed, in what sense He was made He has declared by the mouth of the holy patriarch, saying: For My soul is filled with sorrow to overflowing, and My life has drawn near unto hell. I have been counted with them that go down into the pit; I have been made as a man free, without help, among the dead. Here, then, we read: I have been made as a man, not I have been made as God; and again: My soul overflows with sorrows. My soul, mark you, not My Godhead. He was made in so far as that was concerned wherein He was due to hell, wherein He was reckoned with others, for the Godhead admits of no likeness which may be ground for classing it with others. Yet mark how the majesty of Godhead shows itself in Christ, even in that flesh which was appointed to death. Although He was made as a man, and made as flesh, yet He was made free among the dead, free, without help.

28. But how can the Son say here that He was without help, when it has already been said: I have laid help upon One that is mighty? Distinguish here also the two natures present. The flesh has need of help, the Godhead has no need. He is free, then, because the chains of death had no hold upon Him. He was not made prisoner by the powers of darkness, it is He Who exerted power among them. He is without help, because He Himself, the Lord, has by no office of messenger or ambassador, but by His own might, saved His people. How could He, Who raised others to life, require any help in order to raise His own body?

29. And though men also have raised the dead, still they did this not of their own power, but in the Name of Christ. To ask is one thing, to command is another; to obtain is different from bestowing.

30. Elijah, then, raised the dead, but he prayed— he did not command. Elisha raised one to life after laying himself upon the dead body, in accordance with its posture; 2 Kings 4:34 and, again, the very contact of Elisha's corpse gave life to the dead, that the prophet might foreshow the coming of Him, Who, being sent in the likeness of sinful flesh, should, even after His burial, raise the dead to life.

31. Peter, again, when he healed Aeneas, said: In the Name of Jesus of Nazareth, rise and walk. Not in his own name, but in the Name of Christ. But rise is a command; on the other hand, it is an instance of confidence in one's right, SeeMark 16:17-18 not an arrogant claim to power, and the authority of the command stood in the effective influence of the Name, not in its own might. What answer, then, make the Arians?

Peter commands in the Name of Christ — this on the one hand: on the other, they will have it that the Son of God did not command, but requested.

32. We read, they objected, of His uttering a prayer. John 11:41 But take note of the difference. He prays as Son of *Man*, He commands as Son of *God*. Will you not ascribe unto the Son of God what even the devil has ascribed? Will you accuse yourselves of greater wickedness than Satan's? The devil says: If You be the Son of God, command this stone that it become bread. Luke 4:3 Satan says command, you say entreat. The devil believes that, at the word of God's Son, the nature of an elementary substance may be exchanged for that of a composite one; you think that, unless the Son of God prefers a request, even His Will cannot be done. Again, the devil thinks that the Son of God is to be esteemed from His power, Romans 1:4 you that He is to be esteemed from His infirmity. The devil's temptations are more tolerable than the Arians' disputings.

33. Let us not, then, be troubled if we find the Son of Man entitled mighty in one place, and yet in another, that the Lord of glory was crucified. 1 Corinthians 2:8 What might is greater than sovereignty over the powers of heaven? But this was in the hands of Him Who ruled over thrones, principalities, angels; for, although He was among the wild beasts, as it is written, yet angels ministered to Him, that you may perceive the difference between what is proper to the Incarnation, and what is proper to Sovereignty. So far as His flesh is concerned, then, He endures the assault of wild beasts; in regard of His Godhead, He is adored by angels.

34. We have learned, then, that He was made man, and that His being made must be referred to His manhood. Furthermore, in another passage of Scripture, you may read: Who was made for Him of the seed of David, Romans 1:3 that is to say, in respect of the flesh He was made of the seed of David, but He was God begotten of God before the worlds.

Chapter 5.

Passages brought forward from Scripture to show that made does not always mean the same as created; whence it is concluded that the letter of Holy Writ should not be made the ground of captious arguments, after the manner of the Jews, who, however, are shown to be not so bad as the heretics, and thus the principle already set forth is confirmed anew.

35. At the same time, becoming does not always imply *creation;* for we read: Lord, You have become our refuge, and You have become my salvation. Plainly, here is no statement of the fact or purpose of a *creation*, but God is said to have become my refuge and have turned to my salvation, even as the Apostle has said: Who became for us 1 Corinthians 1:30 Wisdom from God, and Righteousness, and Sanctification, and Redemption, that is, that Christ was made for us, of the Father, not *created*. Again, the writer has explained in the sequel in what sense he says that Christ was made Wisdom for us: But we preach the Wisdom of God in doctrine of mystery, which Wisdom is hidden, foreordained by God before the existence of the world for our glory, and which none of the princes of this world knew, for had they known they

would never have crucified the Lord of glory. When the mystery of the Passion is set forth, surely there is no speaking of an eternal process of generation.

36. The Lord's Cross, then, is my wisdom; the Lord's Death my redemption; for we are redeemed with His precious blood, as the Apostle Peter has said. 1 Peter 1:19 With His blood, then, as man, the Lord redeemed us, Who also, as God, has forgiven sins. Mark 2:8-12

37. Let us not, therefore, lay snares as it were in words, and eagerly seek out entanglements therein; let us not, because misbelievers make out the written word to mean that it means not, set forth only what this letter bears on the face of it, instead of the underlying sense. This way went the Jews to destruction, despising the deep-hidden meaning, and following only after the bare form of the word, for the letter kills, but the Spirit makes alive. 2 Corinthians 3:6

38. And yet, of these two grievous impieties, to ascribe to the Godhead what is true only of manhood is perchance more detestable than to attribute to spirit what belongs only to letter. The Jews feared to believe in manhood taken up into God, and therefore have lost the grace of redemption, because they reject that on which salvation depends; the Arians degrade the majesty of Godhead to the weakness of humanity. Detestable as are the Jews, who crucified the Lord's flesh, more detestable still do I hold them who have believed that the Godhead of Christ was nailed to the Cross. So one who ofttimes had dealings with Jews said: Avoid a heretic, after once reproving him Titus 3:10

39. Nor, again, are these men careful to avoid doing dishonour to the Father, in their impious application of the fact, that Christ was made Wisdom for us, to His incomprehensible generation, that transcends all limits and divisions of time; for, leaving it out of account that dishonour done to the Son is an insult to the Father, they do even carry their blasphemy in assault upon the Father, of Whom it is written: Let God be made truthful, but every man a liar. Romans 3:4 If indeed they think that the Son is spoken of, they do not foreclose against His generation, but in that they rest on the authority of this text they do confess that which they reject, namely, that Christ is God, and true God.

40. It would be a lengthy matter were I to pass in review each several place where we read of His being made, not indeed by nature, but by way of gracious dispensation. Moses, for example, says: You are made my Helper and Protector, to save me; Exodus 15:2 and David: Be unto me for a God of salvation, and a house of refuge, that You may save me; and Isaiah: He has become an Helper for every city that is lowly. Isaiah 25:4 Of a surety the holy men say not to God: You have been created, but By Your grace You are made a Protector and Helper unto us.

Chapter 6.

In order to dispose of an objection grounded on a text in St. John, St. Ambrose first shows that the Arian interpretation lends countenance to the Manichæans; then, after setting forth the different ways of dividing the words

in this same passage, he shows plainly that it cannot, without dishonour to the Father, be understood with such reference to the Godhead as the Arians give it, and expounds the true meaning thereon.

41. We have no reason, therefore, to fear the argument which the Arians, in their reckless manner of expounding, use to construct, showing that the Word of God was made, for, say they, it is written: That which has been made in Him is life.

42. First of all, let them understand that if they make the words That which has been made to refer to the Godhead, they entangle themselves in the difficulties raised by the Manichæans, for these people argue: If that which has been made in Him is life, then there is something which has not been made in Him, and is death, so that they may impiously bring in two principles. But this teaching the Church condemns.

43. Again, how can the Arians prove that the Evangelist actually said this? The most part of those who are learned in the Faith read the passage as follows: All things were made by Him, and without Him was not anything made that has been made. Others read thus: All things were made by Him, and without Him was nothing made. Then they proceed: What has been made, and to this they join the words in Him; that is to say, But whatsover is has been made in Him. But what mean the words in Him? The Apostle tells us, when he says: In Him we have our being, and live, and move. Acts 17:28

44. Howbeit, let them read the passage as they will, they cannot diminish the majesty of God the Word, in referring to His Person, as subject, the words That which was made, without also doing dishonour to God the Father, of Whom it is written: But he who does the truth comes to the light, that his works may be made manifest that they are wrought in God. John 3:21 See then — here we read of man's works being wrought in God, and yet for all that we cannot understand the Godhead as the subject of them. We must either recognize the works as wrought through Him, as the Apostle's affirmation shows that all things are through Him, and were created in Him, and He is before all, and all things *exist together* in Him, or, as the witness of the text here cited teaches us, we ought to regard the virtues whereby the fruit of life eternal is gained, as wrought in God — chastity, piety, devoutness, faith, and others of this kind, whereby the will of God is expressed.

45. Just as the works, then, are the expression of the will and power of God the Father, so are they of Christ's, even as we read: Created in Christ in good works; Ephesians 2:10 and in the psalm: Peace be made in Your power; and again: In wisdom have You made them all. In wisdom have You made, mark you — not You have made wisdom; for since all things have been made in wisdom, and Christ is the Wisdom of God, then this Wisdom is plainly not an accident, but a substance, and an everlasting one, but if the Wisdom has been made, then is it made in a worse condition than all things, forasmuch as it could not, by itself, be made Wisdom. If, then, being made is oftentimes referred to something accidental, not to the essence of a thing, so may creation also be referred to some end had in view.

Chapter 7.

Solomon's words, The Lord created Me, etc., mean that Christ's Incarnation was done for the redemption of the Father's creation, as is shown by the Son's own words. That He is the beginning may be understood from the visible proofs of His virtuousness, and it is shown how the Lord opened the ways of all virtues, and was their true beginning.

46. Hereby we are brought to understand that the prophecy of the Incarnation, The Lord created me the beginning of His ways for His works, Proverbs 8:22 means that the Lord Jesus was created of the Virgin for the redeeming of the Father's works. Truly, we cannot doubt that this is spoken of the mystery of the Incarnation, forasmuch as the Lord took upon Him our flesh, in order to save the works of His hands from the slavery of corruption, so that He might, by the sufferings of His own body, overthrow him who had the power of death. For Christ's flesh is for the sake of things created, but His Godhead existed before them, seeing that He is before all things, while all things exist together in Him. Colossians 1:16

47. His Godhead, then, is not by reason of creation, but creation exists because of the Godhead; even as the Apostle showed, saying that all things exist because of the Son of God, for we read as follows: But it was fitting that He, through Whom and because of Whom are all things, after bringing many sons to glory, should, as Captain of their salvation, be made perfect through suffering. Hebrews 2:10 Has he not plainly declared that the Son of God, Who, by reason of His Godhead, was the Creator of all, did in after time, for the salvation of His people, submit to the taking on of the flesh and the suffering of death?

48. Now for the sake of what works the Lord was created of a virgin, He Himself, while healing the blind man, has shown, saying: In Him must I work the works of Him that sent Me. Furthermore He said in the same Scripture, that we might believe Him to speak of the Incarnation: As long as I am in this world, I am the Light of this world, John 9:5 for, so far as He is man, He is in this world for a season, but as God He exists at all times. In another place, too, He says: Lo, I am with you even unto the end of the world. Matthew 28:20

49. Nor is there any room for questioning with respect to the beginning, seeing that when, during His earthly life, He was asked, Who are You? He answered: The beginning, even as I tell you. This refers not only to the essential nature of the eternal Godhead, but also to the visible proofs of virtues, for hereby has He proved Himself the eternal God, in that He is the beginning of all things, and the Author of each several virtue, in that He is the Head of the Church, as it is written: Because He is the Head of the Body, of the Church; Colossians 1:18 Who is the beginning, first-begotten from the dead. Ephesians 4:15-16

50. It is clear, then, that the words beginning of His ways, which, as it seems, we must refer to the mystery of the putting on of His body, are a prophecy of the Incarnation. For Christ's purpose in the Incarnation was to pave for us the road to heaven. Mark how He says: I go up to My Father and your Father, to My God and your God. John 20:17 Then, to give you to know that the Almighty Father appointed His ways to the Son, after the Incarnation, you have in Zechariah the words of the angel

speaking to Joshua clothed in filthy garments: Thus says the Lord Almighty: If you will walk in My ways and observe My precepts. Zechariah 3:7 What is the meaning of that filthy garb save the putting on of the flesh?

51. Now the ways of the Lord are, we may say, certain courses taken in a good life, guided by Christ, Who says, I am the Way, and the Truth, and the Life. John 14:6 The way, then, is the surpassing power of God, for Christ, is our way, and a good way, too, is He, a way which has opened the kingdom of heaven to believers. Moreover, the ways of the Lord are straight, as it is written: Make Your ways known unto me, O Lord. Chastity is a way, faith is a way, abstinence is a way. There is, indeed, a way of virtue, and there is a way of wickedness; for it is written: And see if there be any way of wickedness in me.

52. Christ, then, is the beginning of our virtue. He is the beginning of purity, Who taught maidens not to look for the embraces of men, but to yield the purity of their bodies and minds to the service of the Holy Spirit rather than to a husband. Christ is the beginning of frugality, for He became poor, though He was rich.
1 Corinthians 8:9 Christ is the beginning of patience, for when He was reviled, He reviled not again, when He was struck, He did not strike back. Christ is the beginning of humility, for He took the form of a servant, though in the majesty of His power He was equal with God the Father. From Him each several virtue has taken its origin.

53. For this cause, then, that we might learn these various virtues, a Son was given us, Whose beginning was upon His shoulder. That beginning is the Lord's Cross — the beginning of strong courage, wherewith a way has been opened for the holy martyrs to enter the sufferings of the Holy War.

Chapter 8.

The prophecy of Christ's Godhead and Manhood, contained in the verse of Isaiah just now cited, is unfolded, and its force in refuting various heresies demonstrated.

54. This beginning did Isaiah see, and therefore he says: A Child is born, a Son is given to us, as also did the Magi, and therefore worshipped they, when they saw the little One in the stable, and said: A Child is born, and, when they saw the star, declared, A Son is given to us. On the one hand, a gift from earth — on the other, a gift from heaven — and both are One Person, perfect in respect of each, without any changeableness in the Godhead, as without any taking away from the fullness of the Manhood. One Person did the Magi adore, to one and the same they offered their gifts, to show that He Who was seen in the stall was the very Lord of heaven.

55. Mark how the two verbs differ in their import: A Child is born, a Son is given. Though born of the Father, yet is He not born, but given to us, forasmuch as the Son is not for our sakes, but we for the Son's. For indeed He was not born to us, being born before us, and the maker of all things created. nor is He now brought to life for the first time, Who was always, and was in the beginning; John 1:1 on the other hand, that which before-time was not is born to us. Again we find it thus recorded, how

that the angel, when he spoke to the shepherds, said that He had been born: Who is this day born to us a Saviour, Who is Christ the Lord, in the city of David. Luke 2:11 To us, then, was born that which was not before — that is, a child of the Virgin, a body from Mary — for this was made after man had been created, whereas [the Godhead] was before us.

56. Some manuscripts read as follows: A Child is born to us a Son is given to us; that is to say, He, Who is Son of God, is born as Mary's child for us, and given to us. As for the fact that He is given, listen to the prophet's words: And grant us Your salvation. But that which is above us is given: what is from heaven is given: even as indeed we read concerning the Spirit, that the love of God is shed abroad in our hearts by the Holy Spirit, Who is given unto us. Romans 5:5

57. But note how this passage is as water upon fire to a crowd of heresies. A Child is born to *us*, not to the Jews; to *us*, not to the Manichæans; to *us*, not to the Marcionites. The prophet says to *us*, that is, to those who believe, not to unbelievers. And He indeed, in His pitifulness, was born for all, but it is the disloyalty of heretics that has brought it to pass that the birth of Him Who was born for all should not profit all. For the sun is bidden to rise upon the good and the bad, but to them that see not there is no appearance of sunrise.

58. Even as the Child, then, is born not unto all, but unto the faithful: so the Son is given to the faithful and not to the unbelieving. He is given to us, not to the Photinians; for they affirm that the Son of God was not given unto us, but was born and first began to exist among us. To us is He given, not to the Sabellians, who will not hear of a Son being given, maintaining that Father and Son are one and the same. Unto us is He given, not unto the Arians, in whose judgment the Son was not given for salvation, but sent over subject and inferior, to whom, moreover, He is no Counsellor, inasmuch as they hold that He knows nought of the future, no Son, since they believe not in His eternity, though of the Word of God it is written: That which was in the beginning; and again: In the beginning was the Word. John 1:1-2 To return to the passage we set before us to discuss. In the beginning, says the Scripture, before He made the earth, before He made the deeps, before He brought forth the springs of water, before all the hills He begot Me.

Chapter 9.

The preceding quotation from Solomon's Proverbs receives further explanation.

59. Perchance you will ask how I came to cite, as referring to the Incarnation of Christ, the place, The Lord created Me, seeing that the creation of the universe took place before the Incarnation of Christ? But consider that the use of holy Scripture is to speak of things to come as though already past, and to make intimation of the union of two natures, Godhead and Manhood, in Christ, lest any should deny either His Godhead or His Manhood.

60. In Isaiah, for example, you may read: A Child is born unto us, and a Son is given unto us; so here also [in the Proverbs] the prophet sets forth first the creation of the flesh, and joined thereto the declaration of the Godhead, that you might know that Christ is not two, but One, being both begotten of the Father before the worlds, and in the last times created of the Virgin. And thus the meaning is: I, Who am begotten before the worlds, am He Who was created of mortal woman, created for a set purpose.

61. Again, immediately before the declaration, The Lord created Me, He says, I will tell of the things which are from eternity, and before saying, He begot, He premised, In the beginning, before He made the earth, before all hills. In its extent, the preposition before reaches back into the past without end or limit, and so Before Abraham was, I am, John 8:58 clearly need not mean after Adam, just as before the Morning Star need not mean after the angels. But when He said before, He intended, not that He was included in any one's existence, but that all things are included in His, for thus it is the custom of Holy Writ to show the eternity of God. Finally, in another passage you may read: Before the mountains were brought forth, or ever the earth and the world were made, You are from everlasting to everlasting.

62. Before all created things, then, is the Son begotten; within all and for the good of all is He made; begotten of the Father, above the Law, Mark 2:28 brought forth of Mary, under the Law. Galatians 4:4

Chapter 10.

Observations on the words of John the Baptist (John 1:30), which may be referred to divine fore-ordinance, but at any rate, as explained by the foregoing considerations, must be understood of the Incarnation. The precedence of Christ is mystically expounded, with reference to the history of Ruth.

63. But [say they] it is written: After me comes a Man, Who is made before me, because He was before me; John 1:30 and so they argue: See, He Who was aforetime is 'made.' Let us take the words by themselves. After me comes a Man. He, then, Who came is a Man, and this is the Man Who was made. But the word man connotes sex, and sex is attributed to human nature, but never to the Godhead.

64. I might argue: The Man [Christ Jesus] was in pre-existence so far as His body was foreknown, though His power is from everlasting — for both the Church and the Saints were foreordained before the worlds began. But here I lay aside this argument, and urge that the being made concerns not the Godhead, but the nature of the Incarnation, even as John himself said: This is He of Whom I said: After me comes a Man, Who was made before me.

65. The Scripture, then, having, as I showed above, discovered the twofold nature in Christ, that you might understand the presence of both Godhead and Manhood, here begins with the flesh; for it is the custom of Holy Writ to begin without fixed rule sometimes with the Godhead of Christ, and descend to the visible tokens of Incarnation; sometimes, on the other hand, to start from its humility, and rise to the

glory of the Godhead, as oftentimes in the Prophets and Evangelists, and in St. Paul. Here, then, after this use, the writer begins with the Incarnation of our Lord, and then proclaims His Divinity, not to confound, but to distinguish, the human and the divine. But Arians, like Jew vintners, mix water with the wine, confounding the divine generation with the human, and ascribing to the majesty of God what is properly said only of the lowliness of the flesh.

66. I have no fears of a certain objection they are likely to put forward, namely, that in the words cited we have a *man*— for some have, Who comes after me. But here, too, let them observe what precedes. The Word, it is said, was made flesh. John 1:14 Having said that the Word was made *flesh*, the Evangelist added no mention of *man*. We understand man there in the mention of flesh, and flesh by the mention of man. After the statement made, then, that the Word was made *flesh*, there was no need here to particularly mention man, whom he already intended by using the name flesh.

67. Later on, St. John uses the lamb, that takes away the sins of the world, as an example; and to teach you plainly the Incarnation of Him, of Whom he had spoken before, he says: This is He of Whom I said before: After me comes a Man, Who is made before me, to wit, of Whom I said that He was made as being man, not as being God. However, to show that it was He Who was before the worlds, and none other, that became flesh, lest we should suppose two Sons of God, he adds: because He was before me. If the words was made had referred to the divine generation, what need was there that the writer should add this, and repeat himself? But, having first said, with regard to the Incarnation only, After me comes a Man, Who is made before me, he added: because He was before me, because it was needful to teach the eternity of [Christ's] Godhead; and this is the reason why St. John acknowledged Christ's priority, that He, Who is His own Father's eternal Power, may be presented as on that account duly preferred.

68. But the abounding activity of the spiritual understanding makes it a pleasing exercise to sally forth and drive into a corner the Arians, who will understand the term made in this passage, not of the manhood, but of the Godhead [of Christ]. What ground, indeed, is left for them to take their stand upon, when the Baptist has declared that after me comes One Who is made before me, that is, Who, though in the course of earthly life He comes after me, yet is placed above the degree of my worth and grace, and Who has title to be worshipped as God. For the words comes after me belong to an event in time, but was before me signify Christ's eternity; and is made before me refer to His pre-eminence, forasmuch as, indeed, the mystery of the Incarnation is above human deserving.

69. Again, St. John Baptist also taught in less weighty language what ideas they were he had combined, saying: After me comes a Man, Whose shoes I am not worthy to bear, setting forth at least the more excellent dignity [of Christ], though not the eternity of His Divine Generation. Now these words are so fully intended of the Incarnation, that Scripture has given us, in an earlier book, a human counterpart of the mystic sandal. For, by the Law, when a man died, the marriage bond with his wife was passed on to his brother, or other man next of kin, in order that the seed of the brother or next of kin might renew the life of the house, and thus it was that Ruth,

though she was foreign-born, but yet had possessed a husband of the Jewish people, who had left a kinsman of near relation, being seen and loved of Boaz while gleaning and maintaining herself and her mother-in-law with that she gleaned, was yet not taken of Boaz to wife, until she had first loosed the shoe from [the foot of] him whose wife she ought, by the Law, to have become.

70. The story is a simple one, but deep are its hidden meanings, for that which was done was the outward betokening of somewhat further. If indeed we should rack the sense so as to fit the letter exactly, we should almost find the words an occasion of a certain shame and horror, that we should regard them as intending and conveying the thought of common bodily intercourse; but it was the foreshadowing of One Who was to arise from Jewry — whence Christ was, after the flesh — Who should, with the seed of heavenly teaching, revive the seed of his dead kinsman, that is to say, the people, and to Whom the precepts of the Law, in their spiritual significance, assigned the sandal of marriage, for the espousals of the Church.

71. Moses was not the Bridegroom, for to him comes the word, Loose your shoe from off your foot, Exodus 3:5 that he might give place to his Lord. Nor was Joshua, the son of Nun, the Bridegroom, for to him also it was told, saying, Loose your shoe from off your foot, Joshua 5:16 lest, by reason of the likeness of his name, he should be thought the spouse of the Church. None other is the Bridegroom but Christ alone, of Whom St. John said: He Who has the bride is the Bridegroom. John 3:29 They, therefore, loose their shoes, but His shoe cannot be loosed, even as St. John said: I am not worthy to loose the latchet of His shoe. John 1:27

72. Christ alone, then, is the Bridegroom to Whom the Church, His bride, comes from the nations, and gives herself in wedlock; aforetime poor and starving, but now rich with Christ's harvest; gathering in the hidden bosom of her mind handfuls of the rich crop and gleanings of the Word, that so she may nourish with fresh food her who is worn out, bereaved by the death of her son, and starving, even the mother of the dead people — leaving not the widow and destitute, while she seeks new children.

73. Christ, then, alone is the Bridegroom, grudging not even to the synagogue the sheaves of His harvest. Would that the synagogue had not of her own will shut herself out! She had sheaves that she might herself have gathered, but, her people being dead, she, like one bereaved by the death of her son, began to gather sheaves, whereby she might live, by the hand of the Church— the which sheaves they who come in joyfulness shall carry, even as it is written: Yet surely shall they come with joy, bringing their sheaves with them.

74. Who, indeed, but Christ could dare to claim the Church as His bride, whom He alone, and none other, has called from Libanus, saying: Come hither from Libanus, my bride; come hither from Libanus? Song of Songs 4:8 Or of Whom else could the Church have said: His throat is sweetness, and He is altogether desirable? Song of Songs 5:26 And seeing that we entered upon this discussion from speaking of the shoes of His feet — to Whom else but the Word of God incarnate can those words apply? His legs are pillars of marble, set upon bases of gold. Song of Songs 5:15 For Christ alone walks in the souls and makes His path in the

minds of His saints, in which, as upon bases of gold and foundations of precious stone the heavenly Word has left His footprints ineffaceably impressed.

75. Clearly we see, then, that both the man and the type point to the mystery of the Incarnation.

Chapter 11.

St. Ambrose returns to the main question, and shows that whenever Christ is said to have been made (or become), this must be understood with reference to His Incarnation, or to certain limitations. In this sense several passages of Scripture — especially of St. Paul — are expounded. The eternal Priesthood of Christ, prefigured in Melchizedek. Christ possesses not only likeness, but oneness with the Father.

76. When, therefore, Christ is said to have been made, to have become, the phrase relates, not to the substance of the Godhead, but often to the Incarnation — sometimes indeed to a particular office; for if you understand it of His Godhead, then God was made into an object of insult and derision inasmuch as it is written: But you have rejected your Christ, and brought Him to nought; you have driven Him to wander; and again: And He was made the derision of His neighbours. Of His neighbours, mark you — not of them of His household, not of them who clave to Him, for he who cleaves to the Lord is one Spirit; 1 Corinthians 6:17 he who is neighbour does not cleave to Him. Again, He was made a derision, because the Lord's Cross is to Jews a stumbling-block, and to Greeks is foolishness: 1 Corinthians 1:23 for to them that are wise He is, by that same Cross, *made* higher than the heavens, higher than angels, and is made the Mediator of the better covenant, even as He was Mediator of the former.

77. Mark how I repeat the phrase; so far am I from seeking to avoid it. Yet take notice in what sense He is made.

78. In the first place, having made purification, He sits on the right hand of Majesty on high, being made so much better than the angels. Hebrews 1:3-4 Now where purification is, there is a victim; where there is a victim, there is also a body; where a body is, there is oblation; where there is the office of oblation, there also is sacrifice made with suffering.

79. In the next place, He is the Mediator of a better covenant. But where there is testamentary disposition, the death of the testator must first come to pass, as it is written a little further on. Howbeit, the death is not the death of His eternal Godhead, but of His weak human frame.

80. Furthermore, we are taught how He is made higher than the heavens. Unspotted, says the Scripture, Hebrews 7:26-27 separate from sinners, and made higher than the heavens; not having daily need, as the priests have need, to offer a victim first for his own sins, and then for those of the people. For this He did by sacrificing Himself once and for all. None is said to be made higher, save he who has in some respect

been lower; Christ, then, is, by His sitting at the right hand of the Father, made higher in regard of that wherein, being made lower than the angels, He offered Himself to suffer.

81. Finally, the Apostle himself says to the Philippians, that being made in the likeness of man, and found in outward appearance as a man, He humbled Himself, being made obedient even unto death. Philippians 2:7-8 Mark that, in regard whereof He is made, He is made, the Apostle says, in the likeness of man, not in respect of Divine Sovereignty, and He was made obedient unto death, so that He displayed the obedience proper to man, and obtained the kingdom appertaining of right to Godhead.

82. How many passages need we cite further in evidence that His being made must be understood with reference to His Incarnation, or to some particular dispensation? Now whatsoever is made, the same is also created, for He spoke and they were made; He gave also the word, and they were created. The Lord created me. These words are spoken with regard to His Manhood; and we have also shown, in our First Book, that the word created appears to have reference to the Incarnation.

83. Again, the Apostle himself, by declaring that no worship is to be rendered to a created existence, has shown that the Son has not been created, but begotten, of God. Romans 1:25 At the same time he shows in other places what there was in Christ that was created, in order to make plain in what sense he has read in Solomon's book: The Lord created Me.

84. Let us now review a whole passage in order. Seeing, then, that the sons have parts of flesh and blood, He too likewise was made to have part in the same, to the end that by death He might overthrow him who had the power of death. Hebrews 2:14 Who, then, is He Who would have us to be partakers in His own flesh and blood? Surely the Son of God. How, save by means of the flesh, was He made partaker with us, or by what, save by bodily death, broke He the chains of death? For Christ's endurance of death was made the death of Death. 1 Corinthians 15:54-55 This text, then, speaks of the Incarnation.

85. Let us see what follows: For He did not indeed [straightway] put on Him the nature of angels, but that of Abraham's seed. And thus was He able to be made like to His brethren in all things throughout, that He might become a compassionate and faithful Prince, a Priest unto God, to make propitiation for the sins of the people; for in that He Himself suffered He is able also to help them that are tempted. Wherefore, brethren most holy, you who have each his share in a heavenly calling, look upon the Apostle and High Priest of our confession, Jesus, regard His faithfulness to His Creator, even as Moses was in his house. These, then, are the Apostle's words.

86. You see what it is in respect whereof the writer calls Him created: In so far as He took upon Him the seed of Abraham; plainly asserting the begetting of a body. How, indeed, but in His body did He expiate the sins of the people? In what did He suffer, save in His body — even as we said above: Christ having suffered in the flesh? In what is He a priest, save in that which He took to Himself from the priestly nation?

87. It is a priest's duty to offer something, and, according to the Law, to enter into the holy places by means of blood; seeing, then, that God had rejected the blood of bulls and goats, this High Priest was indeed bound to make passage and entry into the holy of holies in heaven through His own blood, in order that He might be the everlasting propitiation for our sins. Priest and victim, then, are one; the priesthood and sacrifice are, however, exercised under the conditions of humanity, for He was led as a lamb to the slaughter, and He is a priest after the order of Melchizedek.

88. Let no man, therefore, when he beholds an order of human establishment, contend that in it resides the claim of Divinity; for even that Melchizedek, by whose office Abraham offered sacrifice, the Church does certainly not hold to be an angel (as some Jewish triflers do), but a holy man and priest of God, who, *prefiguring* our Lord, is described as without father or mother, without history of his descent, without beginning and without end, in order to show beforehand the coming into this world of the eternal Son of God, Who likewise was incarnate and then brought forth without any father, begotten as God without mother, and was without history of descent, for it is written: His generation who shall declare? Isaiah 53:8

89. This Melchizedek, then, have we received as a priest of God made upon the model of Christ, but the one we regard as the type, the other as the original. Now a type is a shadow of the truth, and we have accepted the royalty of the one in the name of a single city, but that of the other as shown in the reconciliation of the whole world; for it is written: God was in Christ, reconciling the world to Himself; 2 Corinthians 5:19 that is to say, [in Christ was] eternal Godhead: or, if the Father is in the Son, even as the Son is in the Father, then Their unity in both nature and operation is plainly not denied.

90. But how, indeed, could our adversaries justly deny this, even if they would, when the Scripture says: But the Father, Who abides in Me, even He does the works; and The works that I do, He Himself works? John 14:10 Not He *also* does the works, but one should regard it as similarity rather than unity of work; in saying, The things that I do, He Himself does, the Apostle has left it clear that we ought to believe that the work of the Father and the work of the Son is one.

91. On the other hand, when He would have similarity, not unity, of works, to be understood, He said: He that believes in Me, the works which I do, shall he do also. John 14:12 Skilfully inserting here the word also, He has allowed us similarity, and yet has not ascribed natural unity. One, therefore, is the work of the Father and the work of the Son, whether the Arians please so to think or not.

Chapter 12.

The kingdom of the Father and of the Son is one and undivided, so likewise is the Godhead of each.

92. I would now ask how they suppose the kingdom of the Father and the Son to be divided, when the Lord has said, as we showed above: Every kingdom divided against itself shall be speedily overthrown. Matthew 12:25

93. Indeed, it was to debar the impious teaching of Arian enmity that Saint Peter himself asserted the dominion of the Father and the Son to be one, saying: Wherefore, my brethren, labour to make your calling and election sure, for so doing you shall not go astray, for thus your entrance into the eternal realm of God and our Lord and Saviour Jesus Christ shall be granted with the greater abundance of grace. 1 Peter 2:10-11

94. Now, if it be thought that Christ's dominion alone is spoken of, and the place be therefore understood in such sense that the Father and the Son are regarded as divided in authority — yet it will be still acknowledged that it is the dominion of the Son, and that an eternal one, and thus not only will two kingdoms, separate, and so liable to fail, be brought in, but, furthermore, inasmuch as no kingdom is to be compared with God's kingdom, which they cannot, however greatly they may desire to, deny to be the kingdom of the Son, they must either turn back upon their opinion, and acknowledge the kingdom of the Father and the Son to be one and the same; or they must ascribe to the Father the government of a lesser kingdom — which is blasphemy; or they must acknowledge Him, Whom they wickedly declare to be inferior in respect of Godhead, to possess an equal kingdom, which is inconsistent.

95. But this [their teaching] squares not, agrees not, holds not [with its premisses]. Let them confess, then, that the kingdom is one, even as we confess and prove, not indeed on our own evidence, but upon testimony vouchsafed from heaven.

96. To begin with, learn, from further testimonies [of Scripture], how that the kingdom of heaven is also the kingdom of the Son: Verily, verily, I say unto you, that there are some among those which stand here with us, who shall not taste death, until they see the Son of Man coming into His kingdom. Matthew 16:28 There is therefore no room for doubt that the kingdom appertains to the Son of God.

97. Now learn that the kingdom of the Son is the very same as the kingdom of the Father: Verily, I say unto you that there be some of those which stand around us, who shall not taste death until they see the kingdom of God coming in power. Mark 8:39 So far, indeed, is it one kingdom, that the reward is one, the inheritor is one and the same, and so also the merit, and He Who promises [the reward].

98. How can it but be one kingdom, above all when the Son Himself has said of Himself: Then shall the righteous shine like the sun in the kingdom of My Father? Matthew 13:43 For that which is the Father's, by fitness to His majesty, is also the Son's, by unity in the same glory. John 17:5 The Scripture, therefore, has declared the kingdom to be the kingdom both of the Father and of the Son.

99. Now learn that where the kingdom of God is named, there is no putting aside of the authority either of the Father or of the Son, because both the kingdom of the Father and the kingdom of the Son is included under the single name of God, saying: When you shall see Abraham, Isaac, and Jacob, and all the prophets, in the kingdom of God. Luke 13:28 Do we deny that the prophets are in the kingdom of the Son, when even to a dying robber who said, Remember me, when You come into Your kingdom, the Lord made answer: Verily, I say unto you, today shall you be with Me in

paradise. Luke 23:42-43 What, indeed, do we understand by being in the kingdom of God, if not the having escaped eternal death? But they who have escaped eternal death see the Son of Man coming into His kingdom.

100. How, then, can He not have in His power that which He gives, saying: To you will I give the keys of the kingdom of heaven? Matthew 16:19 See the gulf between [the one and the other]. The servant opens, the Lord bestows; the One through Himself, the other through Christ; the minister receives the keys, the Lord appoints powers: the one is the right of a giver, the other the duty of a steward.

101. See now yet another proof that the kingdom, the government, of the Father and the Son is one. It is written in the Epistle to Timothy: Paul, an apostle of Jesus Christ, according to the government of God, our Saviour, and Christ Jesus, our Hope. 1 Timothy 1:1 One, therefore, the kingdom of the Father and the Son is plainly declared to be, even as Paul the Apostle also asserted, saying: For know this, that no shameless person, none that is impure, or covetous (which means idolatry), has inheritance in the kingdom of Christ and of God. Ephesians 5:5 It is, therefore, one kingdom, one Godhead.

102. Oneness in Godhead the Law has proved, which speaks of one God, Deuteronomy 6:4 as also the Apostle, by saying of Christ; In Whom dwells all the fullness of the Godhead bodily. For if, as the Apostle says, all the fullness of the Godhead, bodily, is in Christ, then must the Father and the Son be confessed to be of one Godhead; or if it is desired to sunder the Godhead of the Son from the Godhead of the Father, while the Son possesses all the fullness of the Godhead bodily, what is supposed to be further reserved, seeing that nothing remains over and above the fullness of perfection? Therefore the Godhead is one.

Chapter 13.

The majesty of the Son is His own, and equal to that of the Father, and the angels are not partakers, but beholders thereof.

103. Now, we having already laid down that the Father and the Son are of one image and likeness, it remains for us to show that They are also of one majesty. And we need not go far afield for proof, inasmuch as the Son Himself has said of Himself: When the Son of Man shall come in His majesty, and all the angels with Him, then shall He sit upon the throne of His majesty. Matthew 25:31 Behold, then, the majesty of the Son declared! What lacks He yet, Whose uncreated majesty cannot be denied? Majesty, then, belongs to the Son.

104. Let our adversaries now hold it proved beyond doubt that the majesty of the Father and of the Son is one, forasmuch as the Lord Himself has said: For he who shall be ashamed of Me and of My words, of Him shall the Son of Man be ashamed, when He comes in His majesty and His Father's, and the majesty of the holy angels. Luke 9:26 What is the force of the words and the majesty of the holy angels, but that the servants derive honour from the worship of their Lord?

105. The Son, therefore, ascribed His majesty to His Father as well as to Himself, not, indeed, in such sort that the angels should share in that majesty on equal terms with the Father and the Son, but that they should behold the surpassing glory of God; for truly not even angels possess a majesty of their own, after the manner in which Scripture speaks of the Son: When He shall sit upon the throne of His majesty, but they stand in the presence, that they may see the glory of the Father and the Son, in such degrees of vision as they are either worthy of or able to bear.

106. Furthermore, the God-given words themselves declare their own meaning, that you may understand that glory of the Father and the Son not to be held in common with them by angels, for thus they run: But when the Son of Man shall come in His majesty, and all the angels with Him. Again, to show that His Father's majesty and glory and His own majesty and glory are one and the same, our Lord Himself says in another book: And the Son of Man shall confound him, when He shall come in the glory of His Father, with the holy angels. Mark 8:38 The angels come in obedience, He comes in glory: they are His retainers, He sits upon His throne: they stand, He is seated — to borrow terms of the daily dealings of human life, He is the Judge: they are the officers of the court. Note that He did not place first His Father's divine majesty, and then, in the second place, His own and the angels', lest He should seem to have made out a sort of descending order, from the highest to lower natures. He placed His own majesty first, and then spoke of His Father's, and the majesty of the angels (because the Father could not appear lower than they), in order that He might not, by placing mention of Himself between that of His Father and that of the angels, seem to have made out some ascending scale, leading from angels to the Father through increase of His own dignity; nor, again, be believed to have, contrariwise, shown a descent from the Father to angels, entailing diminution of that dignity. Now we who confess one Godhead of the Father and the Son suppose no such order of distinction as the Arians do.

Chapter 14.

The Son is of one substance with the Father.

108. And now, your Majesty, with regard to the question of the substance, why need I tell you that the Son is of one substance with the Father, when we have read that the Son is the image of the Father's substance, that you may understand that there is nothing wherein, so far as Godhead is regarded, the Son differs from the Father.

109. In virtue of this likeness Christ said: All things that the Father has are Mine. John 16:15 We cannot, then, deny substance to God, for indeed He is not unsubstantial, Who has given to others the ground of their being, though this be different in God from what it is in the creature. The Son of God, by Whose agency all things endure, could not be unsubstantial.

110. And therefore, the Psalmist says: My bones are not hidden, which You made in secret, and my substance in the underworld. For to His power and Godhead, the things that before the foundation of the world were done, though their magnificence was [as yet] invisible, could not be hidden. Here, then, we find mention of substance.

111. But it may be objected that the mention of His substance is the consequence of His Incarnation. I have shown that the word substance is used more than once, and that not in the sense of inherited possessions, as you would construe it. Now, if it please you, let us grant that, in accordance with the mystic prophecy, the substance of Christ was present in the underworld — for truly He did exert His power in the lower world to set free, in the soul which animated His own body, the souls of the dead, to loose the bands of death, to remit sins. 1 Peter 3:19

112. And, indeed, what hinders you from understanding, by that substance, His divine substance, seeing that God is everywhere, so that it has been said to Him: If I go up into heaven, You are there; if I go down into hell, You are present.

113. Furthermore, the Psalmist has in the words following made it plain that we must understand the divine substance to be mentioned when he says: Your eyes did see My being, [as] not the effect of working; inasmuch as the Son is not made, nor one of God's works, but the begotten Word of eternal power. He called Him ἀχατέργαστον, meaning that the Word neither made nor created, is begotten of the Father without the witnessing presence of any created being. Howbeit, we have abundance of testimony besides this. Let us grant that the substance here spoken of is the bodily substance, provided you also yourself say not that the Son of God is something effected by working, but confess His uncreated Godhead.

114. Now I know that some assert that the mystic incarnate form was uncreated, forasmuch as nothing was done therein through intercourse with a man, because our Lord was the offspring of a virgin. If, then, many have, on the strength of this passage, asserted that neither that which was brought forth of Mary was produced by creative operation, dare you, disciple of Arius, think that the Word of God is something so produced?

115. But is this the only place where we read of substance? Hath it not also been said in another passage: The gates of the cities are broken down, the mountains are fallen, and His substance is revealed? What, does the word mean something created here also? Some, I know, are accustomed to say that the substance is substance in money. Then, if you give this meaning to the word, the mountains fell, in order that some one's possessions of money might be seen.

116. But let us remember *what* mountains fell, those, namely, of which it has been said: If you shall have faith as a grain of mustard seed you shall say to this mountain: Be removed, and be cast into the sea! Matthew 17:19 By mountains, then, are meant high things that exalt themselves. 2 Corinthians 10:5

117. Moreover, in the Greek, the rendering is this: The palaces are fallen. What palaces, save the palace of Satan, of whom the Lord said: How shall His kingdom stand? We are reading, therefore, of the things which are the devil's palaces as being very mountains, and therefore in the fall of those palaces from the hearts of the faithful, the truth stands revealed, that Christ, the Son of God, is of the Father's eternal substance. What, again, are those mountains of bronze, from the midst of which four chariots come forth? Zechariah 6:1

118. We behold that height, lifting up itself against the knowledge of God, cast down by the word of the Lord, when the Son of God said: Hold your peace, and come forth, you foul spirit. Mark 1:25 Concerning whom the prophet also said: Behold, I have come to you, you mount of corruption!

119. *Those* mountains, then, are fallen, and it is revealed that in Christ was the substance of God, in the words of those who had seen Him: Truly You are the Son of God, Luke 4:41 for it was in virtue of divine, not human power, that He commanded devils. Jeremiah also says: Make mourning upon the mountains, and beat your breasts upon the desert tracks, for they have failed; forasmuch as there are no men, they have not heard the word of substance: from flying fowl to beasts of burden, they trembled, they have failed.

120. Nor has it escaped us, that in another place also, setting forth the frailties of man's estate, in order to show that He had taken upon Himself the infirmity of the flesh, and the affections of our minds, the Lord said, by the mouth of His prophet: Remember, O Lord, what My substance is, because it was the Son of God speaking in the nature of human frailty.

121. Of Him the Scripture says, in the passage cited, in order to discover the mysteries of the Incarnation: But You have rejected, O Lord, and counted for nought — You have cast out Your Christ. You have overthrown the covenant made with Your Servant, and trampled His holiness in the earth. What was it, in regard whereof the Scripture called Him Servant, but His flesh?— seeing that He did not hold equality with God as a prey, but emptied Himself, taking the form of a servant, being made into the likeness of men, and found in fashion as a man. Philippians 2:6-7 So, then, in that He took upon Himself My nature, He was a servant, but by virtue of His own power He is the Lord.

122. Furthermore, what means it that you read, Who has stood in the *truth* (*substantia*) of the Lord? and again: Now if they had stood in My *truth*, and had given ear to My words, and had taught My people, I would have turned them from their follies and transgressions?

Chapter 15.

The Arians, inasmuch as they assert the Son to be of another substance, plainly acknowledge substance in God. The only reason why they avoid the use of this term is that they will not, as Eusebius of Nicomedia has made it evident, confess Christ to be the true Son of God.

123. How can the Arians deny the substance of God? How can they suppose that the word substance which is found in many places of Scripture ought to be debarred from use, when they themselves do yet, by saying that the Son is ἑτεροούσιος, that is, of another substance, admit substance in God?

124. It is not the term itself, then, but its force and consequences, that they shun, because they will not confess the Son of God to be true [God]. For though the

process of the divine generation cannot be comprehended in human language, still the Fathers judged that their faith might be fitly distinguished by the use of such a term, as against that of ἑτεροούσιος, following the authority of the prophet, who says: Who has stood in the truth (*substantia*) of the Lord, and seen His Word? Jeremiah 23:18 Arians, therefore, admit the term substance when it is used so as to square with their blasphemy; contrariwise, when it is adopted in accordance with the pious devotion of the faithful, they reject and dispute against it.

125. What other reason can there be for their unwillingness to have the Son spoken of as ὁ μοούσιος, of the same substance, with the Father, but that they are unwilling to confess Him the true Son of God? This is betrayed in the letter of Eusebius of Nicomedia. If, writes he, we say that the Son is true God and uncreate, then we are in the way to confess Him to be of one substance (ὁμοούσιος) with the Father. When this letter had been read before the Council assembled at Nicæa, the Fathers put this word in their exposition of the Faith, because they saw that it daunted their adversaries; in order that they might take the sword, which their opponents had drawn, to smite off the head of those opponents' own blasphemous heresy. 1 Samuel 17:51

126. Vain, however, is their plea, that they avoid the use of the term, because of the Sabellians; whereby they betray their own ignorance, for a being is of the same substance (ὁ μοούσιον) with another, not with itself. Rightly, then, do we call the Son ὁ μοούσιος (of the same substance), with the Father, forasmuch as that term expresses both the distinction of Persons and the unity of nature.

127. Can they deny that the term οὐσία is met with in Scripture, when the Lord has spoken of bread, that is, ἑ πιούσιος, and Moses has written ὑμεῖς ἔσεσθέ μοι λαὸς περιούσιος ? Exodus 19:6 What does οὐσία mean, whence comes the name, but from οὖσα ἀεί, that which endures for ever? For He Who *is*, and *is* for ever, is God; and therefore the Divine Substance, abiding everlastingly, is called οὐσία . Bread is ἐπιούσιος, because, taking the substance of abiding power from the substance of the Word, it supplies this to heart and soul, for it is written: And bread strengthens man's heart.

128. Let us, then, keep the precepts of our forefathers, nor with rude and reckless daring profane the symbols bequeathed to us. That sealed book of prophecy, whereof we have heard, neither elders, nor powers, nor angels, nor archangels, ventured to open; for Christ alone is reserved the peculiar right of opening it. Revelation 5:5 Who among us dare unseal the book of the priesthood, sealed by confessors, and long hallowed by the testimony of many? They who have been constrained to unseal, nevertheless have since, respecting the deceit put upon them, sealed again; they who dared not lay sacrilegious hands upon it, have stood forth as martyrs and confessors. How can we deny the Faith held by those whose victory we proclaim?

Chapter 16.

In order to forearm the orthodox against the stratagems of the Arians, St. Ambrose discloses some of the deceitful confessions used by the latter, and

shows by various arguments, that though they sometimes call the Son God, it is not enough, unless they also admit His equality with the Father.

129. Let none fear, let none tremble; he who threatens gives the advantage to the faithful. The soothing balms of deceitful men are poisoned — then must we be on our guard against them, when they pretend to preach that they do deny. Thus were those aforetime, who lightly trusted to them, deceived, so that they fell into the snares of treachery, when they thought all was good faith.

130. Let him be accursed, say they, who says that Christ is a creature, after the manner of the rest of created beings. Plain folks have heard this, and put faith in it, for, as it is written, the simple man believes every word. Proverbs 14:15 Thus have they heard and believed, being taken in by the first sound thereof, and, like birds, eager for the bait of faith, have not noted the net spread for them, and so, pursuing after faith, have caught the hook of ungodly deceit. Wherefore be wise as serpents, says the Lord, and harmless as doves. Matthew 10:16 Wisdom is put foremost, in order that harmlessness may be unharmed.

131. For those are serpents, such as the Gospel intends, who put off old habits, in order to put on new manners: Putting off the old man, together with his acts, and putting on the new man, made in the image of Him Who created him. Colossians 3:9-10 Let us learn then, the ways of those whom the Gospel calls the serpents, throwing off the slough of the old man, that so, like serpents, we may know how to preserve our life and beware of fraud.

132. It would have been sufficient to say, Accursed be he who says that Christ is a created being. Why, then, Arian, do you mingle poison with the good that is in your confession, and so defile the whole body of it? For by addition of after the manner of the rest of created beings, you deny not that Christ is a being created, but that He is a created being like [all] others — for created being you do entitle Him, albeit you assign to Him dignity transcending the rest of creation. Furthermore, Arius, the first teacher of this ungodly doctrine, said that the Son of God was a perfect created being, and not as the rest of created beings. See you, then, how that you have adopted language bequeathed you from your father. To deny that Christ is a being created is enough: why add but not as the rest of beings created? Cut away the gangrened part, lest the contagion spread — it is poisonous, deadly.

133. Again, you say sometimes that Christ is God. Nay, but so call Him true God, as meaning, that you acknowledge Him to possess the fullness of the Father's Godhead — for there are gods, so called, alike in heaven or upon earth. The name God, then, is not to be used as a mere manner of address and mention, but with the understanding that you affirm, of the Son, that same Godhead which the Father has, as it is written: For as the Father has life in Himself, so has He given to the Son also to have life in Himself; John 5:26 that is to say, He has given it to Him, as to His Son, through begetting Him — not by grace, as to one indigent.

134. And He has given Him power to execute judgment, because He is the Son of Man. John 5:27 Note well this addition, that you may not take occasion, upon a word,

to preach falsehood. You read that He is the Son of Man; do you therefore deny that He accepts [the power given]? Deny God, then, if all things proper to God are not given to the Son, for whereas He has said, All things that the Father has are Mine, John 16:15 why not acknowledge that all the properties and attributes of Divinity are in the Son [as they are in the Father]? For He who says, All things that the Father has are Mine, what does He except as having not?

135. Why is it that you recount with insistence and in such sincere language, Christ's raising the dead to life, walking upon the waters, healing the sicknesses of men? These powers, indeed, He has given to His bondmen to display as well as Himself. They do the more arouse my wonder when seen present in men, forasmuch as God has given them power so great. I would hear somewhat concerning Christ that is His distinctly and peculiarly, and cannot be held in common with Him by created beings, now that He is begotten, the only Son of God, very God of very God, sitting at the Father's right hand.

136. Wheresoever I read of the Father and Son sitting side by side, I find the Son always upon the right hand. Is that because the Son is above the Father? Nay, we say not so; but He Whom God's love honours is dishonoured by man's ungodliness. The Father knew that doubts as concerning the Son must needs be sown, and He has given us an example of reverence for us to follow after, lest we dishonour the Son.

Chapter 17.

An objection based on St. Stephen's vision of the Lord standing *is disposed of, and from the prayers of the same saint, addressed to the Son of God, the equality of the Son with the Father is shown.*

137. There is just one place, in which Stephen has said that he saw the Lord Jesus *standing* at the right hand of God. Acts 7:55 Learn now the import of these words, that you may not use them to raise a question upon. Why (you would ask) do we read every where else of the Son as sitting at the right hand of God, but in one place of His standing? He sits as Judge of quick and dead; He stands as His people's Advocate. He stood, then, as a Priest, while He was offering to His Father the sacrifice of a good martyr; He stood, as the Umpire, to bestow, as it were, upon a good wrestler the prize of so mighty a contest.

138. Receive also the Spirit of God, that you may discern those things, even as Stephen received the Spirit; and you may say, as the martyr said: Behold, I see the heavens opened, and the Son of Man standing at the right hand of God. Acts 7:55 He who has the heavens opened to him, sees Jesus at the right hand of God: he whose soul's eye is closed, sees not Jesus at the right hand of God. Let us, then, confess Jesus at God's right hand, that to us also the heavens may be opened. They who confess otherwise close the gates of heaven against themselves.

139. But if any urge in objection that the *Son* was standing, let them show upon this passage that the Father was seated, for though Stephen said that the Son of Man was standing, still he did not further say here that the Father was sitting.

140. Howbeit, to make it more abundantly clear and known that the standing implied no dishonour, but rather sovereignty, Stephen prayed to the Son, being desirous to commend himself the more to the Father, saying: Lord Jesu, receive my spirit. Acts 7:58 Again, to show that the sovereignty of the Father and of the Son is one and the same, he prayed again, saying, Lord, lay not this sin to their charge. Acts 7:51 These are the words that the Lord, in His own Passion, speaks to the Father, as the Son of Man— these the words of Stephen's prayer, in his own martyrdom to the Son of God. When the same grace is sought of both the Father and the Son, the same power is affirmed of each.

141. Otherwise, if our opponents will have it that Stephen addressed himself to the Father, let them consider what, on their own showing, they affirm. We indeed are unmoved by their arguments; howbeit, let them, to whom the letter and sequence is all important, take notice that the *first* petition is addressed to the Son. Now we, even on their understanding of the passage, prove from it the unity of the Father's and the Son's majesty; for when the Son is addressed in prayer as well as the Father, the equality which the prayer assigns points to unity in action. But if they will not allow that the Son was addressed with the title Lord, we see that they do indeed seek to deny that He is Lord.

142. Seeing, however, that so great a martyr's crown has been brought forth, let us abate the eagerness of disputation, and bring today's discourse to a close. Let us sing the praises of the holy martyr, as is fitting always after a mighty conflict — the martyr bleeding indeed from the enemy's blows, but rewarded with the crown bestowed by Christ.

EXPOSITION ON THE CHRISTIAN FAITH

Book IV.

Chapter 1.

The marvel is, not that men have failed to know Christ, but that they have not listened to the words of the Scriptures. Christ, indeed, was not known, even of angels, save by revelation, nor again, by His forerunner. Follows a description of Christ's triumphal ascent into heaven, and the excellence of its glory over the assumption of certain prophets. Lastly, from exposition of the conversation with angels upon this occasion, the omnipotence of the Son is proved, as against the Arians.

1. On consideration, your Majesty, of the reason wherefore men have so far gone astray, or that many — alas!— should follow diverse ways of belief concerning the Son of God, the marvel seems to be, not at all that human knowledge has been baffled in dealing with superhuman things, but that it has not submitted to the authority of the Scriptures.

2. What reason, indeed, is there to wonder, if by their worldly wisdom men failed to comprehend the mystery of God the Father and the Lord Jesus Christ, in Whom all the treasures of wisdom and knowledge are hidden, Colossians 2:3 that mystery of which not even angels have been able to take knowledge, save by revelation?

3. For who could by force of imagination, and not by faith, follow the Lord Jesus, now descending from the highest heaven to the shades below, now rising again from Hades to the heavenly places; in a moment self-emptied, that He might dwell among us, and yet never made less than He was, the Son being ever in the Father and the Father in the Son?

4. Even Christ's forerunner, though only in so far as representing the synagogue, doubted concerning Him, even he who was appointed to go before the face of the Lord, and at last sending messengers, enquired: Are You He that should come, or do we look for another? Matthew 11:3

5. Angels, too, stood spellbound in wonder at the heavenly mystery. And so, when the Lord rose again, and the heights of heaven could not bear the glory of His rising from the dead, Who of late, so far as regarded His flesh, had been confined in the narrow bounds of a sepulchre, even the heavenly hosts doubted and were amazed.

6. For a Conqueror came, adorned with wondrous spoils, the Lord was in His holy Temple, before Him went angels and archangels, marvelling at the prey wrested from death, and though they knew that nothing can be added to God from the flesh, because all things are lower than God, nevertheless, beholding the trophy of the Cross, whereof the government was upon His shoulder, and the spoils borne by the everlasting Conqueror, they, as if the gates could not afford passage for Him Who had gone forth from them, though indeed they can never o'erspan His greatness — they sought some broader and more lofty passage for Him on His return — so entirely had He remained undiminished by His self-emptying.

---

7. However, it was meet that a new way should be prepared before the face of the new Conqueror — for a Conqueror is always, as it were, taller and greater in person than others; but, forasmuch as the Gates of Righteousness, which are the Gates of the Old and the New Testament, wherewith heaven is opened, are eternal, they are not indeed changed, but raised, for it was not merely one man but the whole world that entered, in the person of the All-Redeemer.

8. Enoch had been translated, Elias caught up, but the servant is not above his Master. For No man has ascended into heaven, but He Who came down from heaven; John 3:13 and even of Moses, though his corpse was never seen on earth, we do nowhere read as of one abiding in celestial glory, unless it was after that the Lord, by the earnest of His own Resurrection, burst the bonds of hell and exalted the souls of the godly. Enoch, then, was translated, and Elias caught up; both as servants, both in the body, but not after resurrection from the dead, nor with the spoils of death and the triumphal train of the Cross, had they been seen of angels.

9. And therefore [the angels] descrying the approach of the Lord of all, first and only Vanquisher of Death, bade their princes that the gates should be lifted up, saying in adoration, Lift up the gates, such as are princes among you, and be lifted up, O everlasting doors, and the King of glory shall come in.

10. Yet there were still, even among the hosts of heaven, some that were amazed, overcome with astonishment at such pomp and glory as they had never yet beheld, and therefore they asked: Who is the King of glory? Howbeit, seeing that the angels (as well as ourselves) acquire their knowledge step by step, and are capable of advancement, they certainly must display differences of power and understanding, for God alone is above and beyond the limits imposed by gradual advance, possessing, as He does, every perfection from everlasting.

11. Others, again — those, to wit, who had been present at His rising again, those who had seen or who already recognized Him — made reply: It is the Lord, strong and mighty, the Lord mighty in battle.

12. Then, again, sang the multitude of angels, in triumphal chorus: Lift up the gates, O you that are their princes, and be lifted up, you everlasting doors, and the King of glory shall come in.

13. And back again came the challenge of them that stood astonished: Who is that King of glory? For we saw Him having neither form nor comeliness; Isaiah 53:2 if then it be not He, *who* is that King of glory?

14. Whereto answer they which know: The Lord of Hosts, He is the King of glory. Therefore, the Lord of Hosts, He is the Son. How then do the Arians call Him fallible, Whom we believe to be Lord of Hosts, even as we believe of the Father? How can they draw distinctions between the sovereign powers of Each, when we have found the Son, even as also the Father, entitled Lord of Sabaoth? For, in this very passage, the reading in many copies is: The Lord of Sabaoth, He is the King of glory. Now the translators have, for the Lord of Sabaoth, rendered in some places the

Lord of Hosts, in others the Lord the King, and in others the Lord Omnipotent. Therefore, since He Who ascended is the Son, and, again, He Who ascended is the Lord of Sabaoth, it surely follows that the Son of God is omnipotent!

Chapter 2.

None can ascend to heaven without faith; in any case, he who has so ascended there will be cast out wherefore, faith must be zealously preserved. We ourselves each have a heaven within, the gates whereof must be opened and be raised by confession of the Godhead of Christ, which gates are not raised by Arians, nor by those who seek the Son amongst earthly things, and who must therefore, like the Magdalene, be sent back to the apostles, against whom the gates of hell shall not prevail. Scriptures are cited to show that the servant of the Lord must not diminish any of his Master's honour.

15. What shall we do, then? How shall we ascend unto heaven? There, powers are stationed, principalities drawn up in order, who keep the doors of heaven, and challenge him who ascends. Who shall give me passage, unless I proclaim that Christ is Almighty? The gates are shut — they are not opened to any and every one; not every one who will shall enter, unless he also believes according to the true Faith. The Sovereign's court is kept under guard.

16. Suppose, however, that one who is unworthy has crept up, has stolen past the principalities who keep the gates of heaven, has sat down at the supper of the Lord; when the Lord of the banquet enters, and sees one not clad in the wedding garment of the Faith, He will cast him into outer darkness, where is weeping and gnashing of teeth, Matthew 22:11 if he keep not the Faith and peace.

17. Let us, therefore, keep the wedding garment which we have received, and not deny Christ that which is His own, Whose omnipotence angels announce, prophets foretel, apostles witness to, even as we have already shown above.

18. Perchance, indeed, the prophet has spoken of His entering in not only with regard to the gates of the universal heaven; for there be other heavens also whereinto the Word of God passes, whereof it is said: We have a great Priest, a High Priest, Who has passed through the heavens, Jesus, the Son of God. Hebrews 4:14 What are those heavens, but even the heavens whereof the prophet says that the heavens declare the glory of God?

19. For Christ stands at the door of your soul. Hear Him speaking. Behold, I stand at the door, and knock: if any man open to Me, I will come in to him, and I will sup with him, and he with Me. Revelation 3:20 And the Church says, speaking of Him: The voice of my brother sounds at the door. Song of Songs 5:2

20. He stands, then — but not alone, for before Him go angels, saying: Lift up the gates, O you the princes. What gates? Even those of the which the Psalmist sings in another place also: Open to me the gates of righteousness. Open, then, your gates to

Christ, that He may come into you — open the gates of righteousness, the gates of chastity, the gates of courage and wisdom.

21. Believe the message of the angels: Be lift up, you everlasting doors, and the King of glory shall come in, the Lord of Sabaoth. Your gate is the loud confession made with faithful voice; it is the door of the Lord, which the Apostle desires to have opened for him, as he says: That a door of the word may be opened for me, to proclaim the mystery of Christ. Colossians 4:3

22. Let your gate, then, be opened to Christ, and let it be not only opened, but lifted up, if, indeed, it be eternal and not condemned to ruin; for it is written: And be lifted up, you *everlasting* doors. The lintel was lift up for Isaiah, when the seraph touched his lips and he saw the Lord of Sabaoth.

23. Your gates shall be lifted up, then, if you believe the Son of God to be eternal, omnipotent, above and beyond all praise and understanding, knowing all things, both past and to come, while if you judge Him to be of limited power and knowledge, and subordinate, you lift not up the everlasting doors.

24. Be your gates lifted up, then, that Christ may come in unto you, not such a Christ as the Arians take Him to be — petty, and weak, and menial — but Christ in the form of God, Christ with the Father; that He may enter such as He is, exalted above the heaven and all things; and that He may send forth upon you His Holy Spirit. It is expedient for you that you should believe that He has ascended and is sitting at the right hand of the Father, for if in impious thought you detain Him among things created and earthly, if He depart not for you, ascend not for you, then to you the Comforter shall not come, even as Christ Himself has told us: For if I go not away, the Comforter will not come unto you, but if I depart, I will send Him unto you. John 16:7

25. But if you should seek Him among earthly beings, even as Mary of Magdala sought Him, take heed lest He say to you, as unto her: Touch Me not, for I am not yet ascended unto My Father. John 20:17 For your gates are narrow — they give me no passage — they cannot be lifted up, and therefore I cannot come in.

26. Go your way, therefore, to my brethren — that is, to those everlasting doors, which, as soon as they see Jesus, are lifted up. Peter is an everlasting door, against whom the gates of hell shall not prevail. Matthew 16:18 John and James, the sons of thunder, to wit, Mark 3:17 are everlasting doom. Everlasting are the doors of the Church, where the prophet, desirous to proclaim the praises of Christ, says: That I may tell all your praises in the gates of the daughter of Sion.

27. Great, therefore, is the mystery of Christ, before which even angels stood amazed and bewildered. For this cause, then, it is your duty to worship Him, and, being a servant, you ought not to detract from your Lord. Ignorance you may not plead, for to this end He came down, that you may believe; if you believe not, He has not come down for you, has not suffered for you. If I had not come, says the Scripture, and spoken with them, they would have no sin: but now have they no excuse for their sin.

He that hates Me, hates My Father also. John 15:22-23 Who, then, hates Christ, if not he who speaks to His dishonour?— for as it is love's part to render, so it is hate's to withdraw honour. He who hates, calls in question; he who loves, pays reverence.

Chapter 3.

The words, The head of every man is Christ...and the head of Christ is God misused by the Arians, are now turned back against them, to their confutation. Next, another passage of Scripture, commonly taken by the same heretics as a ground of objection, is called in to show that God is the Head of Christ, in so far as Christ is human, in regard of His Manhood, and the unwisdom of their opposition upon the text, He who plants and He who waters are one, is displayed. After which explanations, the meaning of the doctrine that the Father is in the Son, and the Son in the Father, and that the faithful are in Both, is expounded.

28. Now let us examine some other objections raised by the Arians. It is written, say they, that the head of every man is Christ, and the head of woman is man, and the head of Christ is God. 1 Corinthians 11:3 Let them, if they please, tell me what they mean by this objection — whether to join together, or to dissociate, these four terms. Suppose they mean to join them, and say that God is the Head of Christ in the same sense and manner as man is the head of woman. Mark what a conclusion they fall into. For if this comparison proceeds on the supposed equality of the terms of it, and these four — woman, man, Christ, and God — are viewed together as in virtue of a likeness resulting from their being of one and the same nature, then woman and God will begin to come under one definition.

29. But if this conclusion be not satisfactory, by reason of its impiety, let them divide, on what principle they will. Thus, if they will have it that Christ stands to God the Father in the same relation as woman to man, then surely they pronounce Christ and God to be of one substance, inasmuch as woman and man are of one nature in respect of the flesh, for their difference is in respect of sex. But, seeing that there is no difference of sex between Christ and His Father, they will acknowledge then that which is one, and common to the Son and the Father, in respect of nature, whereas they will deny the difference lying in sex.

30. Does this conclusion content them? Or will they have woman, man, and Christ to be of one substance, and distinguish the Father from them? Will this, then, serve their turn? Suppose that it will, then observe what they are brought to. They must either confess themselves not merely Arians, but very Photinians, because they acknowledge only the Manhood of Christ, Whom they judge fit only to be placed on the same scale with human beings. Or else they must, however contrary to their leanings, subscribe to our belief, by which we dutifully and in godly fashion maintain that which they have come at by an impious course of thought, that Christ is indeed, after His divine generation, the power of God, while after His putting on of the flesh, He is of one substance with all men in regard of His flesh, excepting indeed the proper glory of His Incarnation, because He took upon Himself the reality, not a phantom likeness, of flesh.

31. Let God, then, be the Head of Christ, with regard to the conditions of Manhood. Observe that the Scripture says not that the *Father* is the Head of Christ; but that *God* is the Head of Christ, because the Godhead, as the creating power, is the Head of the being created. And well said [the Apostle] the Head of Christ is God; to bring before our thoughts both the Godhead of Christ and His flesh, implying, that is to say, the Incarnation in the mention of the name of Christ, and, in that of the name of God, oneness of Godhead and grandeur of sovereignty.

32. But the saying, that in respect of the Incarnation God is the Head of Christ, leads on to the principle that Christ, as Incarnate, is the Head of man, as the Apostle has clearly expressed in another passage, where he says: Since man is the head of woman, even as Christ is the Head of the Church; Ephesians 5:23 while in the words following he has added: Who gave Himself for her. Ephesians 5:25 After His Incarnation, then, is Christ the head of man, for His self-surrender issued from His Incarnation.

33. The Head of Christ, then, is God, in so far as His form of a servant, that is, of man, not of God, is considered. But it is nothing against the Son of God, if, in accordance with the reality of His flesh, He is like men, while in regard of His Godhead He is one with the Father, for by this account of Him we do not take anything from His sovereignty, but attribute compassion to Him.

34. But who can with a good conscience deny the one Godhead of the Father and the Son, when our Lord, to complete His teaching for His disciples, said: That they may be one, even as we also are one. John 17:11 The record stands for witness to the Faith, though Arians turn it aside to suit their heresy; for, inasmuch as they cannot deny the Unity so often spoken of, they endeavour to diminish it, in order that the Unity of Godhead subsisting between the Father and the Son may seem to be such as is unity of devotion and faith among men, though even among men themselves community of nature makes unity thereof.

35. Thus with abundant clearness we disprove the objection commonly raised by Arians, in order to loosen the Divine Unity, on the ground that it is written: But he who plants and he who waters are one. This passage the Arians, if they were wise, would not quote against us; for how can they deny that the Father and the Son are One, if Paul and Apollos are one, both in nature and in faith? At the same time, we do grant that these cannot be one throughout, in all relations, because things human cannot bear comparison with things divine.

36. No separation, then, is to be made of the Word from God the Father, no separation in power, no separation in wisdom, by reason of the Unity of the Divine Substance. Again, God the Father is in the Son, as we ofttimes find it written, yet [He dwells in the Son] not as sanctifying one who lacks sanctification, nor as filling a void, for the power of God knows no void. Nor, again, is the power of the one increased by the power of the other, for there are not two powers, but one Power; nor does Godhead entertain Godhead, for there are not two Godheads, but one Godhead. We, contrariwise, shall be One in Christ through Power received [from another] and dwelling in us.

37. The letter [of the unity] is common, but the Substance of God and the substance of man are different. We shall be, the Father and the Son [already] are, one; we shall be one by grace, the Son is so by substance. Again, unity by conjunction is one thing, unity by nature another. Finally, observe what it is that Scripture has already recorded: That they may all be one, as You, Father, are in Me, and I in You. John 17:21

38. Mark now that He said not You in us, and we in You, but You in Me, and I in You, to place Himself apart from His creatures. Further He added: that they also may be in Us, in order to separate here His dignity and His Father's from us, that our union in the Father and the Son may appear the issue, not of nature, but of grace, while with regard to the unity of the Father and the Son it may be believed that the Son has not received this by grace, but possesses by natural right of His Sonship.

Chapter 4.

The passage quoted adversely by heretics, namely, The Son can do nothing of Himself, is first explained from the words which follow; then, the text being examined, word by word, their acceptation in the Arian sense is shown to be impossible without incurring the charge of impiety or absurdity, the proof resting chiefly on the creation of the world and certain miracles of Christ.

39. Again, another objection that the Arians bring up, denying that the Power of the Father and the Son can be one and the same, is rested on His saying: Verily, verily, I say unto you; the Son can do nothing of Himself, but what He has seen the Father doing. John 5:19 And therefore they affirm that the Son has done nothing of Himself, and can do nothing, save what He has seen the Father doing.

40. O wise foreknowledge of the arguments of unbelievers, which made further provision of means whereby to answer questions, by adding the words that follow: For whatsoever the Father does, the same does the Son also, in like fashion, John 5:19 for this indeed is the sequel. Why, then, is it written: The Son does the same things, and not such like things, but that you might judge that in the Son there is unity in the Father's works, not imitation of them?

41. But to put their proofs in turn upon trial: I would have them answer the question, whether the Son sees the works of the Father. Does He see, I ask, or not? If He sees them, then He also does them; if He does them, let heretics cease to deny the omnipotence of Him Whom they confess able to do all things that He has seen the Father doing.

42. But what are we to understand by has seen? Has the Son any need of bodily eyes? Nay, if they will affirm this of the Son, they will make out in the Father also a need of bodily activity, in order that the Son may see that which He Himself is to do.

43. Furthermore, what mean the words: The Son can do nothing of Himself? Let us put this question, and debate it. Now is there anything impossible to God's Power and Wisdom? These, observe, are names of the Son of God, Whose Might is certainly not a gift received from another, but just as He is the Life, John 14:6 not depending

upon another's quickening action, but Himself quickening others, because He is the Life; so also He is Wisdom, 1 Corinthians 1:24 not as one that is ignorant acquiring wisdom, but making others wise from His own store; so, too, He is Power, 1 Corinthians 1:24 not as having through weakness obtained increase of strength, but being Himself Power, and bestowing power upon the strong.

44. How, then, does Power assert, as it were, under oath: Verily, verily I say unto you, which means: Of a truth, of a truth, I tell you? John 5:19 Truly, then, You speak, Lord Jesus, and affirm, repeating indeed your solemn declaration, that You can do nothing, save what You have seen the Father doing. You made the universe. Did Your Father then make another universe, for You to take as a model? So must Your blasphemers confess that there are two, or a multitude of universes, as philosophers affirm, and thus also entangle themselves in this heathen error, or, if they will follow the truth, let them say that what You have made, You made, without any pattern.

45. Tell me, Lord, when You saw Your Father incarnate, and walking upon the sea, for I know not, I hold it impious to believe this thing of the Father, knowing that You only have taken our flesh upon You. When did You see the Father at a marriage-feast, turning water into wine? Nay, but I have read that You alone are the only Son, begotten of the Father. I have been taught that You alone, in the mystery of the Incarnation, were born of the Holy Ghost and the Virgin. The things, then, which we have cited as Your doings, the Father did not, but You alone, without guidance of any work done by Your Father, for the purchase of the world's salvation with Your Blood, came forth spotless from the Virgin's womb.

46. When they say, The Son can do nothing of Himself, they indeed except nothing, so that one blasphemer has even said: He cannot make even a gnat, mocking with so headstrong profanity and with insolence so overweening the majesty of Supreme Power; yet perhaps they may think the mystery of Your Incarnate Life a needful exception. But say, Lord Jesu, what earth the Father made without You. For without You He made no heaven, seeing that it is written: By the Word of the Lord were the heavens established.

47. But neither did the Father make the earth without You, for it is written: All things were made by Him, and without Him was not anything made. For if the Father made anything without You, God the Word, then not all things were made by the Word, and the Evangelist lies. Whereas if all things were made by the Word, and if by You all things begin to be, which before were not, then surely You Yourself, of Yourself, hast made what You did not see made by the Father; though perchance our adversaries may have recourse to that theory of Plato, and place before You the ideas supposed by philosophers, which, indeed, we know have been exploded by philosophers themselves. On the other hand, if You Yourself hast of Yourself made all things, vain are the assertions of the unbelieving, which ascribe progress in learning to the Maker of all, Who of Himself supplies the teaching of His craft.

48. But if heretics deny that either the heavens or the earth were made by You, let them take heed into what a gulf they are by their own madness hurling themselves, seeing that it is written: Perish the gods, which have not made heaven and earth.

Jeremiah 10:11 Shall He then perish, O Arian, Who has found and saved that which had perished? But to purpose.

Chapter 5.

Continuing the exposition of the disputed passage, which he had begun, Ambrose brings forward four reasons why we affirm that something cannot be, and shows that the first three fail to apply to Christ, and infers that the only reason why the Son can do nothing of Himself is His Unity in Power with the Father.

49. In what sense can the Son do nothing of Himself? Let us ask what it is that He cannot do. There are many different sorts of impossibilities. One thing is naturally impossible, another is naturally possible, but impossible by reason of some weakness. Again, there are things which are rendered possible by strength, impossible by unskilfulness or weakness, of body and mind. Further, there are things which it is impossible to change, by reason of the law of an unchangeable purpose, the endurance of a firm will, and, again, faithfulness in friendship.

50. To make this clearer, let us consider the matter in the light of examples. It is impossible for a bird to pursue a course of learning in any science or become trained to any art: it is impossible for a stone to move in any direction, inasmuch as it can only be moved by the motion of another body. Of itself, then, a stone is incapable of moving, and passing from its place. Again, an eagle cannot be taught in the ways of human learning.

51. It is, to take another example, impossible for a sick man to do a strong man's work; but in this case the reason of the impossibility is of a different kind, for the man is rendered unable, by sickness, to do what he is naturally capable of doing. In this case, then, the cause of the impossibility is sickness, and this kind of impossibility is different from the first, since the man is hindered by bodily weakness from the possibility of doing.

52. Again, there is a third cause of impossibility. A man may be naturally capable, and his bodily health may allow of his doing some work, which he is yet unable to do by reason of want of skill, or because his rank in life disqualifies him; because, that is, he lacks the required learning or is a slave.

53. Which of these three different causes of impossibility, think you, which we have enumerated (setting aside the fourth) can we meetly assign to the case of the Son of God? Is He naturally insensible and immovable, like a stone? He is indeed a stone of stumbling to the wicked, a cornerstone for the faithful; but He is not insensible, upon Whom the faithful affection of sentient peoples are stayed. He is not an immovable rock, for they drank of a Rock that followed them, and that Rock was Christ.
1 Corinthians 10:4 The work of the Father, then, is not rendered impossible to Christ by diversity of nature.

54. Perchance we may suppose some things were made impossible for Him by reason of weakness. But He was not weakly Who could heal the weaknesses of others by His word of authority. Seemed He weak when bidding the paralytic take up his bed and walk? Mark 2:11 He charged the man to perform an action of which health was the necessary condition, even while the patient was yet praying a remedy for his disease. Not weak was the Lord of hosts when He gave sight to the blind, made the crooked to stand upright, raised the dead to life, Matthew 11:5 anticipated the effects of medicine at our prayers, and cured them that besought Him, and when to touch the fringe of His robe was to be purified. Mark 6:56

55. Unless, perhaps, you thought it was weakness, you wretches, when you saw His wounds. Truly, they were wounds piercing His Body, but there was no weakness betokened by that wound, whence flowed the Life of all, and therefore was it that the prophet said: By His stripes we are healed. Isaiah 53:5 Was He, then, Who was not weak in the hour when He was wounded, weak in regard of His Sovereignty? How, then, I ask? When He commanded the devils, and forgave the offenses of sinners? Luke 5:20 Or when He made entreaty to the Father?

56. Here, indeed, our adversaries may perchance enquire: How can the Father and the Son be One, if the Son at one time commands, at another entreats? True, They are One; true also, He both commands and prays: yet while in the hour when He commands He is not alone, so also in the hour of prayer He is not weak. He is not alone, for whatsoever things the Father does, the same things does the Son also, in like manner. He is not weak, for though in the flesh He suffered weakness for our sins yet that was the chastisement of our peace upon Him, Isaiah 53:5 not lack of sovereign Power in Himself.

57. Moreover, that you may know that it is after His Manhood that He entreats, and in virtue of His Godhead that He commands, it is written for you in the Gospel that He said to Peter: I have prayed for you, that your faith fail not. Luke 22:32 To the same Apostle, again, when on a former occasion he said, You are the Christ, the Son of the living God, He made answer: You are Peter, and upon this Rock will I build My Church, and I will give you the keys of the kingdom of heaven. Matthew 16:18 Could He not, then, strengthen the faith of the man to whom, acting on His own authority, He gave the kingdom, whom He called the Rock, thereby declaring him to be the foundation of the Church? Consider, then, the manner of His entreaty, the occasions of His commanding. He entreats, when He is shown to us as on the eve of suffering: He commands, when He is believed to be the Son of God.

58. We see, then, that two sorts of impossibility furnish no explanation, inasmuch as the Power of God can be neither insensible nor weakly. Will you then proffer the third kind [as an account of the matter], namely, that He can do nothing, just as an unskilled apprentice can do nothing without his master's instructions, or a slave can do nothing without his lord. Then did You speak falsely, Lord Jesus, in calling Yourself Master and Lord, and You deceived Your disciples by Your words: You call Me Master and Lord, and you say well, for so I am. John 13:13 Nay, but You, O Truth, would never have deceived men, least of all them whom You called friends. John 15:14-15

59. Yet if our enemies sunder You from the Creator, as being unskilled, let them see how they affirm that skill was lacking to You, that is to say, to the Divine Wisdom; for all that, however, they cannot divide the unity of substance that You have with the Father. It is not, indeed, by nature, but by reason of ignorance, that the difference exists between the craftsman and the unskilled; but neither is handicraft attributable to the Father, nor ignorance to You, for there is no such thing as ignorant wisdom.

60. Therefore, if insensibility is no attribute of the Son, and if neither weakness, nor ignorance, nor servility, let unbelievers put it to their minds for meditation that both by nature and sovereignty the Son is One with the Father, and by its working His power is not at cross-purpose with the Father, inasmuch as all things that the Father has done, the Son does likewise, for no one can do in like fashion the same work that another has done, unless he shares in the unity of the same nature, while he is also not inferior in method of working.

61. Yet I would still enquire *what* it is that the Son cannot do, unless He see the Father doing it. I will take the fool's line, and propound some examples drawn from things of a lower world. I have become a fool; you have compelled me.
2 Corinthians 12:11 What indeed is more foolish than to debate over the majesty of God, which rather occasions questionings, than godly instruction which is in faith. But to arguments let arguments reply; let words make answer to them, but love to us, the love which is in God, issuing of a pure heart and good conscience and faith unfeigned. And so I stickle not to introduce even the ludicrous for the confutation of so vain a thesis.

62. How, then, does the Son see the Father? A horse sees a painting, which naturally it is unable to imitate. Not thus does the Son behold the Father. A child sees the work of a grown man, but he cannot reproduce it; certainly not thus, again, does the Son see the Father.

63. If, then, the Son can, by virtue of a common hidden power of the same nature which He has with the Father, both see and act in an invisible manner, and by the fullness of His Godhead execute every decree of His Will, what remains for us but to believe that the Son, by reason of indivisible unity of power, does nothing, save what He has seen the Father doing, forasmuch as because of His incomparable love the Son does nothing of Himself, since He wills nothing that is against His Father's Will? Which truly is the proof not of weakness but of unity.

Chapter 6.

The fourth kind of impossibility (§49) is now taken into consideration, and it is shown that the Son does nothing that the Father approves not, there being between Them perfect unity of will and power.

64. The Son, moreover — to consider now our fourth premiss — is not self-assertive, for He, the Divine Assessor, has done nought that is not in agreement with His Father's Will. Further, the Father has seen the things that the Son made, and

pronounced them very good; for so it is written in Genesis: And God said, Let there be light; and there was light. And God saw the light that it was good. Genesis 1:3-4

65. Now, did the Father say on that occasion, Let there be such light as I Myself have made, or Let there be light — light having as yet not existed; or did the Son ask what sort of light the Father made? Nay, the Son made light, according to His own Will, and so far in accordance with the Father's good pleasure, that He approved. It is of new, original work by the Son that the place speaks.

66. Again, if, as Arian, expositions of the Scriptures make out, it is a discredit to the Son to have made what He saw, whereas the Scriptures present Him as having made what He [before] saw not, and to have given being to things which as yet were not, what should they say of the Father, Who praised that He had seen, as though He could not have foreseen the things that were to be made?

67. The Son, therefore, sees the Father's work in like manner as the Father sees the Son's, and the Father praises not the work as one would praise work of another's doing, but recognizes it as His own, for whatsoever things the Father has done, the same does the Son, in like manner. [So was it written, that] you might understand one and the same work to be the work both of the Father and of the Son. And thus the Son does nothing save what is approved of by the Father, praised by the Father, willed by the Father, because His whole Being is of the Father; and He is not as the created being, which commits many faults, ofttimes offending the Will of its Creator, in lusting after and falling into sin. Nought, then, is of the Son's doing, save what is pleasing to the Father, forasmuch as one Will, one Purpose, is Theirs, one true Love, one effect of action.

68. Furthermore, to prove to you that it comes of Love, that the Son can do nothing of Himself save what He has seen the Father doing, the Apostle has added to the words, Whatsoever the Father has done, the same things does the Son also, in like manner, this reason: For the Father loves the Son, and thus Scripture refers the Son's inability to do, whereof it testifies, to unity in Love that suffers no separation or disagreement.

69. But if the inseparableness of the Persons in Love rest, as it truly does, upon [identity of] nature, then surely they are also inseparable, for the same reason, in action, and it is impossible that the work of the Son should not be in agreement with the Father's Will, when what the Son works, the Father works also, and what the Father works, the Son works also, and what the Son speaks, the Father speaks also, as it is written: My Father, Who dwells in Me, He it is that speaks, and the works that I do He Himself does. John 14:10 For the Father appointed nought save by the exercise of His Power and Wisdom, forasmuch as He made all things wisely, as it is written: In wisdom have You made them all; and likewise, God the Word made nought without the Father's participation.

70. Not without the Father does He work; not without His Father's Will did He offer Himself for that most holy Passion, the Victim slain for the salvation of the whole world; not without His Father's Will concurring did He raise the dead to life. For

example, when He was at the point to raise Lazarus to life, He lifted up His eyes and said, Father, I thank You, for that You have heard Me. And I know that You always hear Me, but for the sake of the multitude that stands round I spoke, that they may believe that You have sent Me, John 11:40 in order that, though speaking agreeably to His assumed character of man, in the flesh, He might still express His oneness with the Father in will and operation, in that the Father hears all and sees all that the Son wills, and therefore also the Father sees the Son's doings, hears the utterances of His Will, for the Son made no request, and yet said that He had been heard.

71. Again, we cannot suppose that the Father hears not all, whatsoever the Son's will resolves; and to show that He is always heard by the Father, not as a servant, not as a prophet, but as Son, He said: And I know that Thou dost always hear Me, but for the sake of the multitude which stands round I spoke, that they may believe that You have sent Me.

72. It is for our sakes, therefore, that He renders thanks, lest we should suppose that the Father and the Son are one and the same Person, when we hear of one and the same work being wrought by the Father and the Son. Further, to show us that His rendering of thanks had not been the tribute due from one wanting in power, that, on the contrary, He, as Son of God, ever claimed for Himself the possession of divine authority, He cried, Lazarus, come forth. Here, surely, is the voice of command, not of prayer.

Chapter 7.

The doctrine had in view for enforcement is corroborated by the truth that the Son is the Word of the Father — the Word, not in the sense in which we understand the term, but a living and active Word. This being so, we cannot deny Him to be of the same Will, Power, and Substance with the Father.

73. To return, however, to what we had in hand before, and finish the task set before us. The Son, as the Word, carries out His Father's Will. Now, a word, as we understand and use it, is an *utterance*. There are syllables and sounds, which, however, are not at variance with the thought of our mind, and what we apprehend and are affected by inwardly we give token of by the testimony of the spoken word, which, as it were, works [for us]. But the words we speak have no direct efficacy in themselves, it is the Word of God alone, which is neither an utterance, nor an inward concept, as they call it, but works efficaciously, is living, and has healing power.

74. Would you know what is the nature of the Word — hear the Scriptures. For the Word of God is living and mighty, yea, working effectually, sharp and keener than any the sharpest sword, piercing even to the sundering of soul and spirit, of limbs and marrow. Hebrews 4:12

75. Do you hear, then, the Word of God, and will you separate Him from the Father's Will and Power? You hear Him called the living Word, the healing Word — seek not then to compare Him with the word of our mouth; for if the word we utter, though it have not eyes to see, nor ears to hear, yet speaks, and still the knowledge of

what it speaks is wrought by virtue of hidden mysteries of man's nature, how can he escape the charge of blasphemy, who requires that some sort of bodily vision and hearing shall go along with the Godhead in the Word of God, and thinks that the Son can do nothing of Himself, save what He shall have seen the Father doing, though (as we have said) there is in the Father, Son, and Holy Spirit the same Will, both to do and not to do, and the same Power, by reason of unity in the same substance.

76. But if, though men are, as a rule, different in respect of their thoughts and feelings, they yet agree as to the meaning of a single proposition, what ought we to think as concerning the Father and the Son of God, seeing that in the Substance of the Godhead there is that is imitated by human love?

77. Let us, however, suppose — as our adversaries would have it — that the Son does, as it were, copy the pattern of that which He has seen His Father doing. But even this, we must confess, means that He is of the same substance, for none can completely imitate the working of another, unless he be one with him in the same nature.

Chapter 8.

The heretical objection, that the Son cannot be equal to the Father, because He cannot beget a Son, is turned back upon the authors of it. From the case of human nature it is shown that whether a person begets offspring or not, has nothing to do with his power. Most of all must this be true since, otherwise, the Father Himself would have to be pronounced wanting in power. Whence it follows that we have no right to judge of divine things by human, and must take our stand upon the authority of Holy Writ, otherwise we must deny all power either to the Father or to the Son.

78. There is a fool's demurrer, your Majesty, which certain persons are given to raising, in order to show the Father and the Son to be not equal together, saying that the Father is Almighty, because He has begotten the Son, but that the Son is not Almighty, because He has not been able to beget.

79. But see how wild is their blasphemy, how their philosophers' logic confutes itself. For the raising of this question must lead either to their confessing with their own mouths that the Son is co-eternal with the Father, or, if they impose a beginning upon the Son's existence, to their assigning of necessity a beginning to the Father's power. When, therefore, they deny that the Son is Almighty, they are on the road to assert — which is impious — that the Father began to be Almighty by help of the Son.

80. For if the Father is Almighty by reason of begetting the Son, then, certainly, either the Son is co-eternal with the Father, because if the Father is eternally Almighty, then the Son also is eternal, or, if there was a time when there was not an eternal Son, there was by consequence a time when there was not an Almighty Father. For when they would make out that there was a time when the Son began to be, they are sliding back into [the error of] saying that the Father's Power also has not been from

everlasting, but began to be in consequence of the generation of the Son. So, in their desire to do dishonour to the Son of God, they do so increase His honour as to seem to make Him, contrary to all right belief, the source of His Father's Power, though the Son says, All things that the Father has are Mine John 16:15 — that is to say, not the things which He has bestowed upon the Father, but which He has received from the Father, by right as the Son Whom the Father has begotten.

81. And therefore we do declare the Son to be Eternal Power; Romans 1:20 if, then, His Power and Godhead be eternal, surely His Sovereignty is eternal also. He, then, who dishonours the Son dishonours the Father, and is an enemy and offender against duty and love. Let us honour the Son, in Whom the Father is well pleased, for it is the Father's pleasure that praise be given to the Son, in Whom He Himself is well pleased.

82. Let us, however, make answer to the conclusion they strive to establish; but we seem to have sought, in pursuit of a personal appeal, to escape from the difficulty of treating the question before us. The Father, they say, has begotten a Son; the Son has not. What proof is this that they are not equal? To beget is the Father's natural function, as a Father, and no necessary outcome of His Sovereign Power. Furthermore, dutiful regard places persons on an equality with each other, and does not sunder them. Again, our own experience of what holds good among us frail mortals teaches us that it may frequently happen that weak men have sons, while stronger men have not; that slaves have children, while their masters are childless; and that the poor beget offspring, while rich men are unblessed with any.

83. But if our adversaries say that this too may be the result of infirmity, inasmuch as men may desire to beget children, but be unable to do so; then, though things divine are not to be judged of and determined by things human, yet let them understand that with men also, as with God, whether one has children or no, is not dependent upon or derived of his authoritative power, but upon the personal attributes of a father, and that begetting lies not in the power of our will, but is contingent upon our qualities of body; for if it were a matter of sovereign authority, then the mightier king would have the greater number of sons. To have sons, then, or to be childless, therefore, is not in necessary connection or relation to sovereign authority. Is it, then, so with nature?

84. If you [my Arian adversaries] regard what you object as natural weakness, and rely upon examples taken from the nature of mankind, remember that the Father's nature is the same as the Son's, and therefore you do either confess the Son to be a true Son, and dishonour the Father in the Person of the Son, by reason of Their unity in one and the same Nature (for as the Father is by Nature God, so also is the Son; whereas the Apostle says that the gods many are not so by nature, but are only so called); or, if you deny Him to be a true Son, that is to say, possessing the same Nature, then He is not begotten, and if the Son is not begotten, the Father did not beget Him.

85. The conclusion we come at, therefore, on the line of your persuasion, is that God the Father is not Almighty, because He could not beget, if He did not beget the Son, but created Him. But forasmuch as the Father is Almighty, He being, as you hold, the

Almighty in so far as He is the only Author of Being, then surely He has begotten His Son, and not created Him. Howbeit, we ought to believe His word before yours. He says: I have begotten, and that more than once, witnessing to Himself as begetting.

86. It is no sign, then, of infirmity, whether of nature or authority, in Christ, that He has not begotten, for to beget, as we have already said ofttimes, bears no relation to supremacy of authority, but to a personal property in a nature. For if the Omnipotence of the Father is thereby constituted, that He has a Son, then He might have been more Almighty had He begotten more Sons.

87. Then is His power exhausted in the begetting of One? Nay, but I will show that Christ also has sons, whom He begets every day, but with that generation, or rather regeneration, which is related to personal authority rather than nature, for adoption is the exercise and bestowal of authority, and generation the manifestation of a property, as Scripture itself has taught us: for John says that He was in this world, and the world was made by Him, and the world knew Him not. He came to His own, and His own received Him not. But as many as received Him, to them gave He power to become sons of God, to them which believe in His Name.

88. We say, therefore, that it is the function and exercise of His Authority that He has made us sons of God, whereas the oracles of God discover that His generation is in relation to personal attribute, for the Wisdom of God says: I came forth out of the mouth of the Most High, Sirach 24:5 that is to say not of compulsion, but free, not under bond of authority, but born in a hidden birth, according to personal powers of Supreme Sovereignty and rightfulness of authority. Again, concerning the same Wisdom, Which is the Lord Jesus, the Father says in another place: Out of the womb I begot You, before the morning star.

89. Now this He said, not to make us think of a bodily womb, but to show that true generation is His proper activity, for if we understand the words as speaking of generation from a body, then [we imply] the Father Almighty conceived and brought forth in travail. But far be it from us that we should make this weak bodily frame the measure of God's greatness. The word womb represents the hidden mystery, the inner sanctuary of the Father's being, into which neither angels nor archangels nor powers nor dominations, nor any created nature, has been able to enter. For the Son is always with the Father, and in the Father — with the Father, by virtue of the distinction, without division, proper to the Eternal Trinity; in the Father, by reason of the essential unity of the Divine Nature.

90. What room here, then, for one to sit in judgment upon the Godhead, to call in question the Father and the Son — the One for begetting, the Other for not begetting. No man condemns his servant or handmaid for begetting (or bearing) offspring; but those Arians condemn Christ for not begetting — they do condemn Him, for they privately pass sentence of condemnation upon Him, when they take from His glory and dignity. The question, why they have not begotten offspring, does not lead those who are joined in marriage into loss of their love, or denial of each other's merits, but the Arians, because Christ has not begotten a Son, make light of His sovereignty.

91. Why, ask they, is the Son not a Father? Because, on the other side, the Father is not a Son. Why has not Christ begotten? Even because the Father is not begotten. Yet the Son stands none the lower, because He is not a Father; nor the Father, because He is not a Son, for the Son said: All things that the Father has are Mine John 16:15 — so truly is generation involved in the Father's personal attributes, and comes not by mere right of sovereignty.

92. The Substance of the Trinity is, so to say, a common Essence in that which is distinct, an incomprehensible, ineffable Substance. We hold the distinction, not the confusion of Father, Son, and Holy Spirit; a distinction without separation; a distinction without plurality; and thus we believe in Father, Son, and Holy Spirit as each existing from and to eternity in this divine and wonderful Mystery: not in two Fathers, nor in two Sons, nor in two Spirits. For there is one God, the Father, of Whom are all things, and we in Him; and one Lord, Jesus Christ, by Whom are all things, and we by Him. 1 Corinthians 8:6 There is One born of the Father, the Lord Jesus, and therefore He is the Only-begotten. There is also One Holy Spirit, 1 Corinthians 12:11 as the same Apostle has said. So we believe, so we read, so we hold. We know the fact of distinction, we know nothing of the hidden mysteries; we pry not into the causes, but keep the outward signs vouchsafed unto us.

93. O monstrous wickedness, that they who have no power over their own procreation should claim and usurp power to enquire into the Divine Generation! Let them deny, them, that the Son is equal to the Father, forasmuch as He has not begotten; let them deny that the Son is equal to the Father, because He has a Father! But if they talked after this fashion about men, who sometimes desire to beget sons, yet cannot, we should call it an insult, just as we should so call it, if of two men, one having sons and the other childless, the latter were said to be inferior to the former on that ground. So monstrous also, I say, does it seem, in regard simply to men, that one should therefore be esteemed the more lightly because he has a father. Peradventure, indeed, the Arians suppose that Christ is in the position of one in a family, and frets because He is not set free and independent of His Father's authority, and is not empowered to administer the estate. But Christ is not under tutelage; nay, rather has He abolished all tutelage.

94. How then, let them tell us, would they have these things to be?— a true generation, the true Son begotten of God the Father, that is, of the Substance of the Father, or of another substance? If they say begotten of the Father, that is, of the Substance of God, well and good, for then they acknowledge the Son as begotten of the Substance of the Father. If, then, they are of one Substance, surely they are also of one sovereign Power. Whereas, if the Son is begotten of another substance, how can the Father be Almighty, and the Son not Almighty? For what advantage has God, if He have made His Son of another substance, when confessedly the Son, on His part, has of another substance made us sons of God? The Son, therefore, is either of one Substance with the Father, or of one sovereign Power.

95. Our adversaries' question, then, falls flat, because they cannot judge Christ — or rather, because He is clear, when He is judged. They are worthy, however, to be condemned upon their own sentence, who raise this question against us, for if the

Son be therefore not equal to the Father, because He has not begotten a Son, then by all means let them who sow discussions of this kind confess, if they have not children, that their very servants are to be preferred before themselves, inasmuch as they cannot be the equals of those who have children — whereas, if they have children, let them regard the merit thereof as due not to themselves, but of right to their sons.

96. The objection, then, holds not together, that the Son cannot be equal to the Father, by reason of the Father having begotten the Son, while the Son has begotten no Son of Himself, for the spring begets the stream, though the stream begets no spring out of itself, and light begets radiance, and not radiance light, yet the nature of radiance and light is one.

Chapter 9.

Various quibbling arguments, advanced by the Arians to show that the Son had a beginning of existence, are considered and refuted, on the ground that while the Arians plainly prove nothing, or if they prove anything, prove it against themselves, (inasmuch as He Who is the beginning of all cannot Himself have a beginning), their reasonings do not even hold true with regard to facts of human existence. Time could not be before He was, Who is the Author of time — if indeed at some time He was not in existence, then the Father was without His Power and Wisdom. Again, our own human experience shows that a person is said to exist before he is born.

97. Now that our opponents have failed to maintain their objection against the truth of His Son's equality with the Father, on the ground of His Generation, let them see that their well known device of controversy, their stock misrepresentation, is frustrated. Their common use is to propound this riddle: How can the Son be equal with the Father? If He is a Son, then before He was begotten He was not in existence. If He was in existence, why was He begotten? And men who advance difficulties raised by Arius yet sturdily deny that they are Arians.

98. Accordingly, they demand our answer, intending, if we say, The Son existed before He was begotten, to meet us with a subtle retort, that If so, then, before He was begotten, He was created, and there is no difference between Him and the rest of created beings, for He began to be a creature before He began to be the Son. To which they add: Why was He begotten, when He was already in existence? Because He was imperfect, and in order that He might afterwards be made more perfect? Whilst if we reply that the Son did not exist before He was begotten, they will immediately reply: Then by being begotten He was brought into existence, not having existed before He was begotten, so as to lead on from this to the conclusion that the Son existed, when He did not exist.

99. But let those who propound this difficulty and endeavour to enwrap the truth in a cloud tell us themselves whether the Father exerts His power of begetting within or without limits of time. If they say within limits of time, then they will attribute to the Father what they object against the Son, so as to make the Father seem to have begun

to be what He was not before. If their answer is without such limits, then what is left them but to resolve for themselves the problem they have propounded, and acknowledge that the Son is not begotten under limits and conditions of time, since they deny that the Father so begets?

100. If the Son, then, is not begotten within limits of time, we are free to judge that nothing can have existed before the Son, Whose being is not confined by time. If, indeed, there was anything in being before the Son, then it instantly follows that in Him were not created all things in heaven or in earth, and the Apostle is shown to have erred in so setting it down in his Epistle, Colossians 1:16 whereas, if before He was begotten there was nothing, I see not wherefore He, before Whom none was, should be said to have been after any.

101. With the consideration whereof we must join another most blasphemous objection of theirs, which covers a subtle purpose to confuse the sense and understanding of simple folk. They ask whether everything that comes to an end had also at any time a beginning. If they are told that what has an end also had a beginning, then they return to the charge with the question whether the Father has ceased to beget His Son. This by our consent being granted them, they conclude that the generation of the Son had a beginning. The which if you allow, it seems to follow that if the Generation had a beginning, it appears to have begun in Him Who was begotten; so that one, who had not existed before, may be called begotten— their intent being to close the inquiry by laying down as conclusive that there was a time when the Son existed not.

102. Besides this, there are other vain objections, such as persons of their glibness of tongue would readily urge. If, say they, the Son is the Word of the Father, then He is called begotten, inasmuch as He is the Word. But then since He is the Word, He is not a work. Now the Father has spoken in various manners, Hebrews 1:1 whence it follows that He has begotten many Sons, if He has spoken His Word, not created it as a work of His hands. O fools, talking as though they knew not the difference between the word uttered and the Divine Word, abiding eternally, born of the Father — born, I say, not uttered only — in Whom is no combination of syllables, but the fullness of the eternal Godhead and life without end!

103. Follows another blasphemy, whereby they enquire whether it was of His own free will, or on compulsion, that the Father begot [His Son], intending, if we say, Of His own free will, that we should appear as though we acknowledged that the Father's Will preceded the [Divine] Generation, and to answer that there being something that preceded the existence of the Son, the Son is not co-eternal with the Father, or that He, like the rest of the world, is a being created, forasmuch as it is written, He has made all things, as many as He would, though this is spoken, not of the Father and the Son, but of those creatures which the Son made. Whereas if we answered that the Father begot [His Son] on compulsion, we should seem to have attributed infirmity to the Father.

104. But in the eternal Generation there is no foregoing condition, neither of will, nor of unwillingness, and therefore I can neither say that the Father begot of His free

Will, nor yet that He begot on compulsion, for to beget depends not upon possibility as determined by will, but rather appears to stand in a certain right and property of the hidden being of the Father. For just as the Father is not good because He wills to be so, or is compelled to be so, but is above these conditions — is good, that is, by nature, — even so the putting forth of His generative power is neither of will nor of necessity.

105. Yet let us grant their proposal. Granted that the Generation depends on the Will of Him Who generates; when do they say that this act of will took place? If it was in the beginning, then, plainly, the Son was in the beginning. If the Will is eternal, then the Son also is eternal. If the Will began to exist, then God the Father, as He was, was so displeased with Himself, that He made a change in His condition, that is to say, without His Son He was displeasing to Himself; in His Son He began to be well pleased.

106. To follow out the consequences thereof. If the Father conceived, after the manner of human nature, a desire to beget, then did He also pass through all the experiences which befal men before the birth takes place — but we find that generation is not determined merely by will, but is an object of wish.

107. Thus do they betray their own ungodliness, who would have it that Christ's generation had a beginning, in order that it may seem, not that true begetting of the Word abiding, but the utterance of words that pass and are forgotten, and that by intrusion of [the premiss of] a multitude of sons, they may [be warranted to] deny Christ's personal possession of the divine attributes, to the end that He may be regarded as neither the only-begotten nor the first-begotten Son; and lastly, that given the belief that His existence had a beginning, it may also be deemed as appointed to have an end.

108. But neither had the Son of God any beginning, seeing that He already was at the beginning, nor shall He come to an end, Who is the Beginning and the End of the Universe; for being the Beginning, how could He take and receive that which He already had, or how shall He come to an end, being Himself the End of all things, so that in that End we have an abiding-place without end? The Divine Generation is not an event occurring in the course of time, and within its limits, and therefore before it time is not, and in it time has no place.

109. Again, their aimless and futile question finds no loophole for entry, even when directed upon the creation itself; nay, indeed, temporal existences appear, in certain cases, to admit of no division of time. For instance, light generates radiance, but we can neither conceive that the radiance begins to exist after the light, nor that the light is in existence before the radiance, for where there is a light, there is radiance, and where there is radiance there is also a light; and thus we can neither have a light without radiance, nor radiance without light, because both the light is in the radiance, and the radiance in the light. Thus the Apostle was taught to call the Son the Radiance of the Father's Glory, Hebrews 1:3 for the Son is the Radiance of His Father's light, co-eternal, because of eternity of Power; inseparable, by unity of brightness.

110. If then we can neither understand the mystery of, nor dissociate, these created objects in the sky above us, which we see, can we comprehend Him Whom we see not, Who is above every created existence, God, as He is in the very Holy of Holies of His own Generation? Can we make time a barrier between Him and the Son, when all time is the creation of the Son?

111. Let them cease therefore, and say no more that before He was begotten the Son was not. For the word before is a mark of time, whereas the Generation is before all times, and therefore that which comes after anything comes not before it, and the work cannot be before the maker, seeing that necessarily objects made take their commencement from the craftsman who makes them. How can the customary action of any created object be regarded as existing prior to the maker of it, while all time is a creation, and every creation has taken its being from its creator?

112. I would, therefore, further examine our opponents, who esteem themselves so cunning, and have them make good the application of their theory to human existence, seeing that they use it to disparage the glory of God's Existence, and keep far away from any confession of an inscrutable mystery in the Divine Generation. I would have them find ground for their objection in the facts of human generation. Of God's Son they assert that before He was begotten He was not — that is to say, they say this of the Wisdom, the Power, the Word of God, Whose Generation knows nothing prior to itself. But if, as they would have us believe, there was a time when the Son existed not (the which it is blasphemy to affirm), then there was a time when God lacked the fullness of Divine Perfection, if afterwards He passed through a process of begetting a Son.

113. To show them, however, the weakness and transparency of their objection, though it has no real relation to any truth, divine or human, I will prove to them that men have existed before they were born. Else, let them show that Jacob, who while yet hidden in the secret chamber of his mother's womb supplanted his brother, had not been appointed and ordained, ere ever he was born; Genesis 25:23 let them show that Jeremiah had not likewise been so, before his birth — Jeremiah, to whom the message comes: Before I formed you in your mother's womb, I knew you; and before you came forth from the belly, I sanctified you, and appointed you for a prophet among the nations. Jeremiah 1:5 What testimony can we have stronger than the case of this great prophet, who was sanctified before he was born, and known before he was shaped?

114. What, again, shall I say of John, of whom his holy mother testifies that, while he yet lay in her womb, he perceived in spirit the presence of his Lord, and leaped for joy, as we remember it to be written, his mother saying: For lo, as soon as the voice of the salutation entered mine ears, the babe leaped in my womb for joy. Luke 1:44 Was he, then, who prophesied, in existence or not? Nay, surely he was — surely he was in being who worshipped his Maker; he was in being who spoke in his mother's womb. And so Elisabeth was filled with the spirit of her son, and Mary sanctified by the Spirit of hers, for thus you may find it recorded, that the babe leaped in her womb, and Elisabeth was filled with the Holy Ghost. Luke 1:41

115. Consider the proper force of each word. Elisabeth was indeed the first to hear the voice of Mary, but John was first to feel His Lord's gracious Presence. Sweet is the harmony of prophecy with prophecy, of woman with woman, of babe with babe. The women speak words of grace, the babes move hiddenly, and as their mothers approach one another, so do they engage in mysterious converse of love; and in a twofold miracle, though in diverse degrees of honour, the mothers prophesy in the spirit of their little ones. Who, I ask, was it that performed this miracle? Was it not the Son of God, Who made the unborn to be?

116. Thus your objection fails of reconcilement with the truths of human existence—can it attain thereto with divine mysteries? What mean you by your principle that before He was begotten He was not? Was the Father engaged for some time in conception, so that certain epochs passed away before the Son was begotten? Was He, like women, in travail of birth, so that just this travail? What would you? Why seek we to pry into divine mysteries? The Scriptures tell me the necessary effects of the Divine Generation, not how it is done.

Chapter 10.

The objection that Christ, on the showing of St. John, lives because of the Father, and therefore is not to be regarded as equal with the Father, is met by the reply that for the Life of the Son, in respect of His Godhead, there has never been a time when it began; and that it is dependent upon none, while the passage in question must be understood as referring to His human life, as is shown by His speaking there of His body and blood. Two expositions of the passage are given, the one of which is shown to refer to Christ's Manhood, while the second teaches His equality with the Father, as also His likeness with men. Rebuke is administered to the Arians for the insult which they are seeking to inflict upon the Son, and the sense in which the Son can be said to live because of the Father is explained, as also the union of life with the divine Life. A further objection, based upon the Son's prayer that He may be glorified by the Father, is briefly refuted.

118. There are not a few who raise this further objection, that it is written: As the living Father has sent Me, and I live by the Father; so he that eats Me, lives also by Me. John 6:58 How, ask they, is the Son equal with the Father, when He has said that He lives by the Father?

119. Let those who oppose us on this ground tell us first what the Life of the Son is. Is it a life bestowed by the Father upon one lacking life? But how could the Son ever fail to possess life, He Himself being the Life, as He says, I am the Way, the Truth, and the Life. Isaiah 14:6 Truly, His life is eternal, even as His power is eternal. Was there a time, then, when (so to speak) Life possessed not itself?

120. Bethink you what is read this day concerning the Lord Jesus, that He died for our sakes, to the end that whether we wake or whether we sleep, we may live with Him. 1 Thessalonians 5:10 He Whose Death is Life, is not His Godhead Life, seeing that the Godhead is Life eternal?

121. But is His Life truly in the Father's power? Why, He showed that even His bodily life was not in the power of any other, as we have it on record: I lay down My life, that I may take it again. No man takes it from Me, but I lay it down of Myself. I have power to lay it down, and again I have power to take it. This commandment have I received of My Father.

122. Is His divine Life then to be regarded as depending upon the power of another, when His bodily life was subject to no other power but His own? For it would have been the power of another, but for the Unity of power. But just as He gives us to understand that His laying down His life was done of His own power, and of His free Will, so also He teaches us, in laying it down in obedience to His Father's command, the unity of His own with the Father's Will.

123. If, then, there has neither been a time when the Life of the Son took a commencement, nor any power to which it has been subjected, let us consider what His meaning was when He said: Even as the living Father has sent Me, and I live by the Father? Let us expound His meaning as best we can; nay, rather let Him expound it Himself.

124. Take notice, then, what He said in an earlier part of His discourse. Verily, verily, I say unto you. He first teaches you how you ought to listen. Verily, verily, I say unto you, unless you eat the flesh of the Son of Man, and drink His blood, you shall have no life in you. John 6:54 He first premised that He was speaking as Son of Man; do you then think that what He has said, as Son of Man, concerning His Flesh and His Blood, is to be applied to His Godhead?

125. Then He added: For My Flesh is meat indeed, and My Blood is drink [indeed]. John 6:56 You hear Him speak of His Flesh and of His Blood, you perceive the sacred pledges, [conveying to us the merits and power] of the Lord's death, John 6:52 and you dishonour His Godhead. Hear His own words: A spirit has not flesh and bones. Luke 24:39 Now we, as often as we receive the Sacramental Elements, which by the mysterious efficacy of holy prayer are transformed into the Flesh and the Blood, do show the Lord's Death.

126. Then, after calling on us to take notice that He speaks as Son of Man, and frequent repeated mention of His Flesh and His Blood, He adds: Even as the living Father has sent Me, and I live by the Father, so he that eats Me, he also lives by Me. How then do they suppose that we are to understand these words?— for the comparison can be shown as a double one. The first comparison being after the following manner: Even as the living Father has sent Me, I live by the Father; the second: Even as the living Father has sent Me, and I live by the Father, so also he that eats Me, he too lives by Me.

127. If our adversaries choose the former, the meaning is this, that, as I am sent by the Father and have come down from the Father, so (in accordance therewith) I live by the Father. But in what character was He sent, and came down, save as Son of Man, even as He Himself said before: No man has ascended into heaven, save He that has come down from heaven as Son of Man. John 3:13 Then, just as He was sent

and came down as Son of Man, so as Son of Man He lives by the Father. Furthermore, he that eats Him, as eating the Son of Man, does himself also live by the Son of Man. Thus, He has compared the effect of His Incarnation to His coming.

128. But if they choose the second method, do we not infer both the equality of the Son with the Father, and His likeness to men, together, though in clear mutual distinction? For what is the meaning of the words, Even as He Himself lives by the Father, so we also live by Him, but that the Son so quickens a man, as the Father has in the Son quickened human nature? For as the Father raises the dead and quickens them, so also the Son quickens whom He will, John 5:21 as the Lord Himself has already said.

129. Thus the equality of the Son to the Father is established simply upon unity in the action of quickening, since the Son so quickens as the Father does. Acknowledge therefore the eternity of His Life and Sovereignty. Again, our likeness with the Son is discovered, and a certain unity with Him in the flesh, because that, like as the Son of God was quickened in the flesh by the Father, so also is man quickened; for thus it is written, that as God raised Jesus Christ from the dead, so we also, as men, are quickened by the Son of God. Romans 4:24

130. According to this interpretation, then, immortality is not only applied to our condition by grace of bounty, but is also proclaimed as the property of Godhead — the latter, because it is the Godhead which quickens; the former, because manhood is quickened in Christ.

131. But if any would apply the force of either comparison to Christ's *Godhead*, then the Son of God is put on one footing with men, so that the Son of God lives by the Father just as we live by the Son of God. But the Son of God bestows eternal life by free gift, we cannot so do. If then He be placed on a level with us, He too does not bestow this gift. Let Arius' disciples then have the due reward of their faith— which is, not to obtain eternal life of the Son.

132. I would now go further. If our opponents are pleased to apply the teaching of this passage to the principle of the eternity of the Divine Substance, let them hear a third exposition: Does not our Lord plainly appear to say that as the Father is a living Father, so too the Son also lives? — and who can but observe that here we must understand a reference to unity of Life, forasmuch as the same Life is the Life of the Father and the Life of the Son? For as the Father has Life in Himself, so has He given to the Son also to have Life in Himself. John 5:26 He has given — by reason of unity with Him. He has given, not to take away, but that He may be glorified in the Son. He has given, not that He, the Father, might keep guard over it, but that the Son might have it in possession.

133. But the Arians think that they must oppose hereto the fact that He had said, I live by the Father. Of a certainty (suppose that they conceive the words as referring to His Godhead) the Son lives by the Father, because He is the Son begotten of the Father — by the Father, because He is of one Substance with the Father — by the Father, because He is the Word given forth from the heart of the Father, because He

came forth from the Father, because He is begotten of the bowels of the Father, because the Father is the Fountain and Root of the Son's being.

134. But perhaps they may urge: If you hold that the Son, in saying, 'And I live by the Father,' spoke of the unity of life subsisting between the Father and the Son, does it not follow that He discovered the unity of life between the Son and mankind in saying that 'he that eats Me, the same lives by Me'?

135. Even so. Just as I confess the unity of celestial Life subsisting in Father and Son by reason of the unity of the substance of the Godhead, so too, save as concerns the prerogatives of the Divine Nature or those which are the effect of the Incarnation of our Lord, I affirm of the Son a participation of spiritual life with us by virtue of the unity of His Manhood with ours, for as is the heavenly, such are they also that are heavenly. Further, even as in Him we sit at the right hand of the Father, not in the sense that we share His throne, but that we rest in the Body of Christ — even as, I say, we have part in Christ's session by reason of corporal unity, so too we live in Christ by reason of unity of our bodies with His Body.

136. Not only, then, have I no fears of the text, I live by the Father, but I should have none, even though Christ had said, I live by help of the Father.

137. Now another objection commonly urged by them starts from the text: This sickness is not unto death, but for the glory of God, to the end that His Son may be glorified by Him. John 11:4 But not only is the Son glorified through the Father and by the Father, as it is written: Glorify Me, Father; John 17:5 and again: Now has the Son of Man been glorified, and God has been glorified in Him, and God glorifies Him, John 13:31-32 but the Father also is glorified through the Son and by the Son, for Truth has said: I have glorified You upon earth. John 17:4

138. Even as the Son, therefore, is glorified through the Father, so too He lives by the Father. There are some who have been led by consideration of these words to the supposition that [the Greek] δόξα means opinion, belief, rather than glory, and therefore have interpreted as follows: I have given you a δόξα upon earth, I have finished the work which You gave Me to do, and now, O Father, give me a δόξα; that is to say: I have taught men so to believe concerning You, as to know that You are the true God; do Thou also establish in them, concerning Me, the belief that I am Your Son, and very God.

Chapter 11.

The particular distinction which the Arians endeavoured to prove upon the Apostle's teaching that all things are of the Father and through the Son, is overthrown, it being shown that in the passage cited the same Omnipotence is ascribed both to Father and to Son, as is proved from various texts, especially from the words of St. Paul himself, in which heretics foolishly find a reference to the Father only, though indeed there is no diminution or inferiority of the Son's sovereignty proved, even by such a reference. Finally, the three phrases,

of Whom, through Whom, in Whom, are shown to suppose or imply no difference (of power), and each and all to hold true of the Three Persons.

139. Now we come to that laughable method, attempted by some, of showing a difference of Power to subsist between Father and Son, on the strength of apostolic testimony, it being written: But for us there is One God, the Father, of Whom are all things, and we in Him, and One Lord, Jesus Christ, through Whom are all things, and we through Him. 1 Corinthians 8:6 It is urged that no small difference in degree of Divine Majesty is signified in the affirmation that all things are of the Father, and through the Son. Whereas nothing is clearer than that here a plain reason is given of the Omnipotence of the Son, inasmuch as while all things are of the Father, none the less are they all through the Son.

140. The Father is not among all things, for to Him it is confessed that all things serve You. Nor is the Son reckoned among all things, for all things were made by Him, John 1:3 and all things exist together in Him, and He is above all the heavens. Colossians 1:17 The Son, therefore, exists not among but *above* all things, being, indeed, after the flesh, of the people, of the Jews, but yet at the same time God over all, blessed for ever, having a Name which is above every name, Philippians 2:9 it being said of Him, You have put all things in subjection under His feet. But in making *all things* subject to Him, He left nothing that is not subject, even as the Apostle has said. Hebrews 2:8 But suppose that the Apostle's words were intended with reference to the Incarnate Lord; how then can we doubt the incomparable majesty of His Divine Generation?

141. Certain it is, then, that between Father and Son there can be no difference of Power. Nay, so far is such difference from being present, that the same Apostle has said that all things are of Him, by Whom are all things, as follows: For of Him and through Him and in Him are all things. Romans 11:36

142. Now if, as they suppose, it is the Father alone Who is spoken of, it cannot be that He is at once Omnipotent because all things are of Him, and not Omnipotent because all things are through Him. On their own showing, then, they will declare the Father lacking in Power, and not Omnipotent, or at the least they will be confessing with their own mouth, all against their will though it be, the Omnipotence of the Son as well as of the Father.

143. Howbeit, let them decide whether they will understand this affirmation as made concerning the Father. If they do so decide then all things are through Him also. If they decide that it is the Son Who is spoken of, then all things are of Him as well as of the Father. But if all things are through the Father also, then surely there is no argument for diminishing from the honour due to the Son; and if all things are of the Son, the Son must be honoured in like manner as the Father is.

144. In case our opponents should suspect that we are taking advantage of some intrusion of a single spurious verse into the text, let us review the whole passage. O depth of the riches of God's wisdom and knowledge! exclaims the Apostle, how unsearchable are His judgments, and His ways past finding out! For Who has known

EXPOSITION ON THE CHRISTIAN FAITH

the mind of the Lord, or who has been His counsellor? Or who has been first to give unto Him, and shall be recompensed? For of Him and through Him and in Him are all things. To Him be glory for ever!

145. Who, then, think they, is here spoken of — the Father or the Son? If it be the Father — then we answer that the Father is not the Wisdom of God, for the Son is. But what is there that is impossible to Wisdom, of Whom it is written: Seeing that she is almighty and abiding, she makes all things new in herself? Wisdom 7:27 We read of Wisdom, then, not as approaching, but as abiding. Thus have you the authority of Solomon to teach you of the Omnipotence and Eternity of Wisdom, and of her Goodness as well, for it is written: But malice overcomes not Wisdom. Wisdom 7:30

146. But to purpose. How unsearchable, says the Apostle, are His judgments! Now if the Father has given all judgment to the Son, John 5:22 it seems that the Father points to the Son as Judge.

147. But now, to show us that He is speaking of the Son, not of the Father, St. Paul proceeds: Who was first in giving to Him? For the Father has given to the Son, but it was as acknowledging the rights of Him Whom He has begotten, not by way of largess. Therefore, it being undeniable that the Son has received at the hands of the Father, as it is written, All things have been given unto Me of My Father, Matthew 11:27 yet, in saying, Who was first in giving to Him? the Apostle has not denied that the Son has received gifts of the Father, by virtue of His Nature, but he has indeed shown that, of Father and Son, Neither can be said to be before the Other, forasmuch as, albeit the Father has given gifts unto the Son, yet He has not so bestowed them as upon one that began to be after Him; because the uncreate and incomprehensible Trinity, Which is of One Eternity and Glory, admits neither difference of time nor degree of precedence.

148. If, however, we hold ourselves more bound to observe those Greek manuscripts which show τίς προσέδωχεν αὐτῷ; it is clear that He to Whom nothing can be added is not unequal to Him Who is perfect and complete. Therefore, if this passage from the Apostle, in its entirety, is better understood with reference to the Son, we see that we must also believe concerning the Son, that all things are of Him, even as it is written: For of Him and through Him and in Him are all things.

149. Be it so, nevertheless, that they suppose the passage to be intended of the Father, then let us call to mind that even as we read of all things being *of* Him, so too we read of all things being *through* Him, that is to say, the authority of the Father and of the Son is extended over the whole created universe. And, though we have already proved the Omnipotence of the Son by the Omnipotence of the Father, still — forasmuch as they are ever bent upon disparagement — let them consider that they disparage the Father as well as the Son. For if the Son be limited in might, because all things are *through* Him, do we say further, that the Father likewise is limited, because all things are through Him also?

150. But to bring them to understand that these phrases involve no difference, I will once again show that it is the same person, of whom anything is, and through whom

anything is, and that we read of things being related in both these ways to the Father. For we find: Faithful is God, through Whom you were called into the fellowship of His Son. Let our adversaries weigh the meaning of the Apostle's words. We are called through the Father — they raise no controversy: we are created through the Son — and this they have set down as a mark of inferiority. The Father has called us into fellowship with His Son, and this truth we, as in duty bound, devoutly receive. The Son has created all things, and Arius' followers imagine that here they have not the decree of a free Will, but a forced service, slavishly performed!

151. Again, to obtain fuller understanding that, forasmuch as we are called through the Father into fellowship with His Son, there is no difference of Power in the Father and the Son, [note that] the fellowship itself has its beginning of the Son, as it is written: For from His fullness have we all received, though, if we follow the Greek text of the Gospel, we ought to render *of* His fullness. John 1:16

152. See, then, how there is fellowship both *through* the Father and *of* the Son, and yet not a different fellowship, but one and the same. And that our fellowship be with the Father and with His Son Jesus Christ. 1 John 1:3

153. Observe, further, that Scripture speaks of our having one fellowship not only of the Father and the Son, but also of the Holy Spirit. The grace of Our Lord Jesus Christ, says the Apostle, and the love of God, and the fellowship of the Holy Spirit be with you all.

154. Now, I ask, wherein does He, through Whom are all things, appear less than He, of Whom are all things? Is it because He is declared to be the Worker? But the Father also works, for He is true who said, My Father works hitherto, and I work. John 5:17 Therefore, even as the Father works, so works the Son also; and so He Who works is not limitary in power nor abject, for the Father also works; which being so, that which is common to the Son with the Father, or even which the Son has by the Father, ought not to be the less esteemed, lest heretics further dishonour the Father in the Person of the Son.

155. Not to be passed over for silencing the disputings of Arian misbelief are those words of the same Saint John, which he set down in another Scripture: If you know that He is just, know that he which does righteousness is born of Him. 1 John 2:29 But who is righteous, save the Lord, Who loves righteousness? Or whom — as the foregoing texts warn us — have we to assure us of everlasting life, if we have not the Son? If, therefore, the Son of God has promised us everlasting life, and He is righteous, surely we are born of Him. Else, if our adversaries deny that we are born of the Son by grace, they likewise deny His righteousness.

156. You must therefore believe that all things are of the Son of God [even as of God the Father, for even as God is the Father of all, so likewise is the Son the Author and Creator of all. We see, then, the vanity of this their questioning, forasmuch as it holds good of the Son [as of the Father], that of Him and through Him and in Him are all things.

157. We have shown how all things are of Him, and likewise how all things are also through Him. Who then doubts that all things are in Him, when another Scripture says: For in Him are all things founded, that are in the heavens, and in Him they were created, and He is before all things, and all things consist in Him? Colossians 1:16. Of Him, then, you have grace; Himself you have for your Creator; in Him you find the foundation of all things.

Chapter 12.

The comparison, found in the Gospel of St. John, of the Son to a Vine and the Father to a husbandman, must be understood with reference to the Incarnation. To understand it with reference to the Divine Generation is to doubly insult the Son, making Him inferior to St. Paul, and bringing Him down to the level of the rest of mankind, as well as in like manner the Father also, by making Him not merely to be on one footing with the same Apostle, but even of no account at all. The Son, indeed, in so far as being God, is also the husbandman, and, as regards His Manhood, a grape-cluster. True statement of the Father's pre-eminence.

158. There is yet another Scripture, which our opponents commonly object against us, in order to prove their division of the Godhead of the Father from the Godhead of the Son, namely, our Lord's words in the Gospel: I am the true Vine and My Father is the Husbandman. The vine and the husbandman, say they, are of different natures, and the vine is in the power of the husbandman.

159. Thus, then, you would have us believe that the Son, as touching His Godhead, is like to a vine, so that without a vine-dresser He is nothing, and may be neglected or even rooted up. Thus you juggle up a lie from the letter of the Scripture which says that our Lord called Himself the Vine, intending thereby the mystery of His Incarnation. Howbeit, if you are bent on it that we dispute upon the letter, I too confess, yea, I proclaim, that the Son called Himself the Vine. For woe be to me, if I deny the pledge of the salvation of His people!

160. How then do you purpose to understand the truth that the Son of God called Himself the Vine? If you interpret the saying with respect to the Substance of His Godhead, and if you suppose such a diversity of Godhead between the Father and the Son as there is of nature between a husbandman and a vine, you do double insult both to Father and to Son — to the Son, because if, as you affirm, He is, as touching His Godhead, beneath a husbandman, then must He on the same showing be esteemed lower than the Apostle Paul, forasmuch as Paul indeed called himself a husbandman, as we find it written: I have planted, Apollos has watered: but God has given the increase. 1 Corinthians 3:6 Will you have Paul, then, to be better than the Son of God?

161. Thus far the one insult. As for the other, it lies herein, that if the Son is the Vine in respect of His eternally-begotten Person, then, He having said: I am the Vine, you are the branches, John 15:5 that divinely-begotten One appears to be of one substance with us. But who is like You among the gods, O Lord? Exodus 15:11 as it

is written; and again, in the Psalms: For who is there among the clouds that shall be equal to the Lord? Or who among the sons of God shall be like God.

162. Moreover, you disparage not only the Son, but the Father also. For if the term husbandman is to comprehend in its designation all the prerogative of the Father's Sovereignty, then, seeing that Paul too is a husbandman, you set the Apostle, to whom you deny that the Son is equal, on an even footing with the Father.

163. Again, it being written, But neither he which plants is anything, nor he that waters; but God, Who gives the increase, you will rest the fullness of the Father's Majesty in a name which, as you see, stands for weakness. For if he that plants is nothing, and he that waters is nothing, but it is God, Who gives the increase [Who is all], observe what your blasphemy intends — even to expose the Father to contempt under the title of a husbandman, and to demand another God to provide the increase of the Father's labour. Wickedly, therefore, do they think to extol the Dignity of God the Father by this use of the term husbandman, in which God the Father is brought down to the level of man, as being designated by a common title.

164. Yet what wonder if, as you heretics would have it, the Father is to be exalted above a Son Whose Godhead differs not a whit from the common condition of mankind? If you suppose the Son to have been entitled the Vine with respect to His Godhead, then do ye esteem Him not only as liable to corruption and subject to changes of wind and weather, but even as partaking of manhood only, forasmuch as the Vine and its branches are of one nature, so that the Son of God appears, not to have taken upon Him our flesh, through the mystery of Incarnation, but to have altogether sprung into being from the flesh.

165. But I will indeed openly confess that His flesh, though born in a new and mysterious birth, was yet of the same nature with ours, and that this is the pledge of our salvation, not the source of the Divine Generation. He indeed is the Vine, for He bears my sufferings, whenever manhood, hitherto frail, leans on Him and so matures with plenteous fruit of renewed devotion.

166. Yet if the husbandman's power allures you, please tell me who it was that spoke in the prophet, saying: O Lord, make it known to me, that I may know; then saw I their thoughts. I was led as a harmless lamb to the slaughter and knew it not: they took counsel together against me, saying, Come, let us throw wood into his bread. Jeremiah 11:18 For if the Son here speaks of the mystery of His coming Incarnation — for it were blasphemy to suppose that the words are spoken concerning the Father — then surely it is the Son Who speaks in an earlier passage: I have planted you as a fruitful vine — how are You become bitter, and a wild vine? Jeremiah 2:21

167. And thus you see that the Son also is the husbandman — the Son, of one Name with the Father, one work, one dignity and Substance. If, then, the Son is both Vine and Husbandman, plainly we infer the meaning of the Vine with regard to the mystery of the Incarnation.

168. But not only has our Lord called Himself a Vine — He has also given Himself, by the voice of the prophet, the title of a Grape-cluster — even when Moses, at the command of the Lord, sent spies to the Valley of the Cluster. Numbers 13:24 What is that valley but the humility of the Incarnation and the fruitfulness of the Passion? I indeed think that He is called the Cluster, because that from the Vine brought out of Egypt, that is, the people of the Jews, there grew a fruit for the world's good. No man, truly, can understand the Cluster as a token of the Divine Generation — or if there be any who so understand it, they leave no conclusion open but that we should believe that Cluster to have sprung from the Vine. And thus in their folly they attribute to the Father that which they refuse to believe of the Son.

169. But if there be now left no room for doubt that the Son of God is called the Vine with respect and intention to His Incarnation, you see what hidden truth it was to which our Lord had regard in saying, The Father is greater than I. John 14:28 For after this premised, He proceeded immediately: I am the true Vine, and My Father is the Husbandman, that you might know that the Father is greater in so far as He dresses and tends our Lord's flesh, as the husbandman dresses and tends his vines. Further, our Lord's flesh is that which could increase in stature with age, and be wounded through suffering, to the end that the whole human race might rest guarded from the pestilent heat of the pleasures of this world, under the shadow of the Cross whereon Its limbs are spread.

Book V.

Prologue.

Who is a faithful and wise servant? His reward is pointed out in the case of Peter, as also in the case of Paul. Ambrose, being anxious to follow Paul's guidance, wished this book to be added to the others, for it could not be included in the preceding one. The subject for discussion is then stated, and the reason for such a discussion given. He must needs be pardoned, for usury is to be demanded from every servant for the money which has been entrusted to him. Their faithfulness is the usury desired in his own case. He will be happy if he may hope for a reward; but he does not look so much for the recompense of the saints, as for exemption from punishment. He urges all to seek to merit this.

1. Who, then, is a faithful and wise servant, whom his lord has made ruler over his household, to give them meat in due season? Blessed is that servant, whom his lord when he comes shall find so doing. Matthew 24:45-46 Not worthless is this servant: some great one ought he to be. Let us think who he may be.

2. It is Peter, chosen by the Lord Himself to feed His flock, who merits thrice to hear the words: Feed My little lambs; feed My lambs; feed My sheep. And so, by feeding well the flock of Christ with the food of faith, he effaced the sin of his former fall. For this reason is he thrice admonished to feed the flock; thrice is he asked whether he loves the Lord, in order that he may thrice confess Him, Whom he had thrice denied before His Crucifixion.

3. Blessed also is that servant who can say: I have fed you with milk and not with meat; for hitherto you were not able to bear it. 1 Corinthians 3:2 For he knew how to feed them. Who of us can do this? Who of us can truly say: To the weak became I as weak, that I might gain the weak? 1 Corinthians 9:22

4. Yet he, being so great a man, and chosen by Christ for the care of His flock, so as to strengthen the weak and to heal the sick — he, I say, rejects immediately after one admonition Titus 3:10 a heretic from the fold entrusted to him, for fear that the taint of one erring sheep might infect the whole flock with a spreading sore. He further bids that foolish questions and contentions be avoided. Titus 3:9

5. How, then, shall we act, being but ignorant dwellers set among these fresh tares in the old-standing harvest field? Matthew 13:25 If we are silent, we shall seem to be giving way; and if we contend against them, there is the fear that we too shall be held to be carnal. For it is written of matters of this sort, which beget strife: The servant of the Lord must not strive, but be gentle unto all, apt to teach, patient, with moderation instructing those that oppose themselves. 2 Timothy 2:24-25 And in another place: If any man is contentious, we have no such custom, neither the Church of God. 1 Corinthians 11:16 For this reason it was our intention to write somewhat, in order that our writings might without any din answer the impiety of heretics on our behalf.

6. And so we prepare to commence this our Fifth Book, O Emperor Augustus. For it was but right that the Fourth Book should end with our discussion on the Vine, lest otherwise we should seem to have overloaded that book with a tumultuous mass of subjects, rather than to have filled it with the fruit of the spiritual vineyard. On the other hand, it was not seemly that the gathering of the vintage of the faith should be left unfinished, while there was still all abundance of such great matters for discussion.

7. In the Fifth Book, therefore, we speak of the indivisible Godhead of the Father, the Son, and the Holy Ghost (omitting, however, a full discussion on the Holy Ghost), being urged by the teaching of the Gospel to let out on interest to human minds the five talents of the faith entrusted to these five books being as it were the principal; lest perhaps when the Lord comes, and finds His money hidden in the earth, He may say to me: Thou wicked and slothful servant, you knew that I reap where I do not sow; and gather where I have not scattered; you ought therefore to have put My money to the exchangers, that at My coming I might have received Mine Own, Matthew 25:26-27 or as it stands in another book: And I, it says, at My coming might have received it with usury. Luke 19:23

8. I pray those to pardon me, whom the boldness of such a lengthy address displeases. The thought of my office compels me to entrust to others what I have received. We are stewards of the heavenly mysteries. 1 Corinthians 4:1 We are ministers, but not all alike. But, it says, even as the Lord gave to every man, I have planted; Apollos watered; but God gave the increase. 1 Corinthians 3:5-6 Let each one then strive that be may be able to receive a reward according to his labour. For we are labourers together with God, as the Apostle said; we are God's husbandry, God's building. 1 Corinthians 3:9 Blessed therefore is he who sees such usury on his principal; blessed too is he who beholds the fruit of his work; blessed again is he who builds upon the foundation of faith, gold, silver, precious stones. 1 Corinthians 3:12

9. You who hear or read these words are all things to us. You are the usury of the money-lender — the usury on speech, not on money; you are the return given to the husbandman; you are the gold, the silver, the precious stones of the builder. In your merits lie the chief results of the labours of the priest; in your souls shines forth the fruit of a bishop's work; in your progress glitters the gold of the Lord; the silver is increased if you hold fast the divine words. The words of the Lord are pure words, as silver tried in the fire; proved on the earth, purified seven times. You therefore will make the lender rich, the husbandman to abound in produce; you will prove the master-builder to be skilful. I do not speak boastfully; for I do not desire so much my own advantage as yours.

10. Oh that I might safely say of you at that time: Lord, You gave me five talents, behold I have gained five other talents; Matthew 25:20 and that I might show the precious talents of your virtues! For we have a treasure in earthen vessels. 2 Corinthians 4:7 These are the talents which the Lord bids us spiritually to trade with, or the two coins of the New and the Old Testament, which that Samaritan in the Gospel left for the man robbed by the thieves, for the purpose of getting his wounds healed. Luke 10:35

11. Neither do I, my brethren, with greedy desires, long for this, so that I may be set over many things; the recompense I get from the fact of your advance is enough for me. Oh that I may not be found unworthy of that which I have received! Let those things which are too great for me be assigned to better men. I demand them not! Yet may Thou say, O Lord: I will give unto this last, even as unto you. Matthew 20:14 Let the man that deserves it receive authority over ten cities. Luke 19:17

12. Let him be such an one as was Moses, who wrote the Ten Words of the Law. Let him be as Joshua, the son of Nun, who subdued five kings, and brought the Gibeonites into subjection, that he might be the figure of a Man of his own name Who was to come, by Whose power all fleshly lust should be overcome, and the Gentiles should be converted, so that they might follow the faith of Jesus Christ rather than their former pursuits and desires. Let him be as David, whom the young maidens came to meet with songs, saying: Saul has triumphed over thousands, David over ten thousands. 1 Samuel 18:7

13. It is enough for me, if I am not thrust out into the outer darkness, as he was, who hid the talent entrusted to him in the earth so to speak, of his own flesh. This the ruler of the synagogue did, and the other rulers of the Jews; for they employed , the words of the Lord, which had been entrusted to them, on the ground as it were of their bodies; and, delighting in the pleasures of the flesh, sunk the heavenly trust as though into the pit of an overweening heart.

14. Let us then not keep the Lord's money buried and hidden in the flesh; nor let us hide our one talent in a napkin; Luke 19:20 but like good money-changers let us ever weigh it out with labour of mind and body, with an even and ready will, that the word may be near, even in your mouth and in your heart. Deuteronomy 30:14

15. This is the word of the Lord, this is the precious talent, whereby you are redeemed. This money must often be seen on the tables of souls, in order that by constant trading the sound of the good coins may be able to go forth into every land, by the means of which eternal life is purchased. This is eternal life, which You, Almighty Father, give freely, that we may know You the only true God, and Jesus Christ Whom You have sent. John 17:3

Chapter 1.

How impious the Arians are, in attacking that on which human happiness depends. John ever unites the Son with the Father, especially where he says: That they may know You, the only true God, etc. In that place, then, we must understand the words true God also of the Son; for it cannot be denied that He is God, and it cannot be said He is a false god, and least of all that He is God by appellation only. This last point being proved from the Apostle's words, we rightly confess that Christ is true God.

16. Wherefore let the Arians observe, how impious they are in calling in question our hope and the object of our desires. And since they are wont to cry out on this point

above all others, saying that Christ is distinct from the only and true God, let us confute their impious ideas so far as lies in our power.

17. For on this point they ought rather to understand, that this is the benefit, this the reward of perfect virtue, namely, this divine and incomparable gift, that we may know Christ together with the Father, and not separate the Son from the Father; as also the Scriptures do not separate them. For the following tells rather for the unity than for the diversity of the Divine Majesty, namely, that the knowledge of the Father and of the Son gives us the same recompense, and one and the same honour; which reward no man will have but he that has known both the Father and the Son. For as the knowledge of the Father procures eternal life, so also does the knowledge of the Son.

18. Therefore as the Evangelist immediately at the outset joined the Word with God the Father in his devout confession of faith, saying: And the Word was with God; John 1:1 and here too, in writing the words of the Lord: That they may know You, the only true God, and Jesus Christ Whom You have sent, John 17:3 he has undoubtedly, by thus connecting Them, bound together the Father and the Son, so that no one may separate Christ as true God from the majesty of the Father, for union does not dissever.

19. Therefore in saying, That they may know You, the only true God, and Jesus Christ Whom You have sent, he put an end to the Sabellians, and has also put the Jews out of court — those at any rate who heard him speak; so that the former might not suppose the Same to be the Father as the Son, which they might have done if he had not added also Christ, and that the latter might not sever the Son from the Father.

20. But, I ask, why do they not think we ought to gather and understand this from what has been already said; that as he has declared the Father to be only, true God, so we may understand Jesus Christ also to be only, true God? For it could not be expressed in any other way, for fear he might seem to be speaking of two Gods. For neither do we speak of two Gods; and yet we confess the Son to be of the same Godhead with the Father.

21. May we ask, therefore, on what grounds they think a distinction is made in the Godhead, and whether they deny Christ to be God? But they cannot deny it. Do they deny Him to be true God? But if they deny Him to be true God, let them say whether they declare Him to be a false God, or God by appellation only. For according to the Scriptures the word God is used either of the true God, or by appellation only, or of a false god. True God as the Father; God by appellation as the saints; a false god like the demons and idols. Let them say then how they will acknowledge and describe the Son of God. Do they suppose the name of God to have been falsely assumed; or was there in truth merely an indwelling of God within Him, as it were by appellation only?

22. I do not think they can say the name was falsely assumed, and so involve themselves in the open wickedness of blasphemy; lest they should betray themselves on the one hand to the demons and idols, and on the other to Christ, by insinuating that the name of God was falsely given to Him. But if they think He is called God

because He had an indwelling of the Godhead within Him — as many holy men were (for the Scripture calls them Gods to whom the word of God came), John 10:35 — they do not place Him before other men, but think He is to be compared with them; so that they consider Him to be the same as He has granted other men to be, even as He says to Moses: I have made you a god unto Pharaoh. Exodus 7:1 Wherefore it is also said in the Psalms: I have said, you are gods.

23. This idea of these blasphemers Paul puts aside; for he said: For though there be that are called gods, whether in heaven or in earth. 1 Corinthians 8:5 He said not: There be gods, but There be that are called gods. But Christ, as it is written, is the same yesterday and today. Hebrews 13:8 He is, it says; that is, not only in name but also in truth.

24. And well is it written: He is the same yesterday and today, so that the impiety of Arius might find no room to pile up its profanity. For he, in reading in the second psalm of the Father saying to the Son, You are My Son, this day have I begotten You, noted the word today, not yesterday, referring this which was spoken of the assumption of our flesh to the eternity of the divine generation; of which Paul also says in the Acts of the Apostles: And we declare unto you the promise which was made to our fathers: for God has fulfilled the same to our children, in that He has raised up the Lord Jesus Christ again, as it is written in the second psalm: You are My Son, this day have I begotten You. Acts 13:32-33 Thus the Apostle, filled with the Holy Ghost, in order that he might destroy that fierce madness of his, said: The same, yesterday, today, and forever. Yesterday on account of His eternity; today on account of His taking to Himself a human body.

25. Christ therefore is, and always is; for He, Who is, always is. And Christ always is, of Whom Moses says: He that is has sent me. Exodus 3:14 Gabriel indeed was, Raphael was, the angels were; but they who sometime have not been are by no means with equal reason said always to be. But Christ, as we read, was not it is, and, it is not, but, it is was in Him. 2 Corinthians 1:19 Wherefore it is the property of God alone to be, Who ever is.

26. Therefore if they dare not say He is God by appellation, and it is a mark of deep impiety to say He is a false god, it remains that He is true God, not unlike to the true Father, but equal to Him. And as He sanctifies and justifies whom He will, Romans 9:18 not by assuming that power from without Himself, but having within Himself the power of sanctification, how is He not true God? For the Apostle called Him indeed true God, Who according to His nature was God, as it is written: Howbeit then, when you knew not God, you serviced unto them, who by nature were not gods; Galatians 4:8 that is, who could not be true gods, for this title by no means belonged to them by nature.

Chapter 2.

Since it has been proved that the Son is true God, and in that is not inferior to the Father, it is shown that by the word **solus** *(alone) when used of the Father in the Scriptures, the Son is not excluded; nay, that this expression befits Him*

above all, and Him alone. The Trinity is alone, not amongst all, but above all.
The Son alone does what the Father does, and alone has immortality. But we
must not for this reason separate Him from the Father in our controversies.
We may, however, understand that passage of the Incarnation. Lastly the
Father is shut out from a share in the redemption of men by those who would
have the Son to be separated from Him.

27. We have fully demonstrated by passages of Scripture, in the earlier books, that
Christ is true, yea, very true God. Therefore if Christ, as it has been taught, is true
God, let us enquire why they desire to separate the Son from the Father, when they
read that the Father is the only true God.

28. If they say that the Father alone is true God, they cannot deny that God the Son
alone is the Truth; for Christ is the Truth. Is the Truth then something inferior to
Him that is true, seeing that according to the use of terms a man is called true from
the word truth, as also wise from wisdom, just from justice? We do not deem it so
between the Father and the Son. For there is nothing wanting to the Father, because
the Father is full of truth; and the Son, because He is the Truth, is equal to Him that
is true.

29. But that they may know, when they see the word alone, that the Son is in no wise
to be separated from the Father, let them remember it was said by God in the
Prophets: I stretched forth the heavens alone. Isaiah 44:24 The Father certainly did
not stretch them forth without the Son. For the Son Himself, Who is the Wisdom of
God, says: When He prepared the heavens I was present with Him. Proverbs 8:27
And Paul declares that it was said of the Son: You, Lord, in the beginning hast laid
the foundation of the earth, and the heavens are the work of Your hands. Whether
therefore the Son made the heavens, as also the Apostle would have it understood,
while He Himself certainly did not alone spread out the heavens without the Father;
or as it stands in the Book of Proverbs: The Lord in wisdom has founded the earth,
in understanding has He prepared the heavens; Proverbs 3:19 it is proved that neither
the Father made the heavens alone without the Son, nor yet the Son without the
Father. And yet He who spread out the heavens is said to be alone.

30. To show indeed how plainly we must understand the expression alone of the Son
(although we may never believe that He did anything without the knowledge of the
Father), we have here also another passage, where it is written: Which alone spreads
out the heavens, and walks as it were on a pavement over the sea. Job 9:8 For the
Gospel of the Lord has taught us that it was not the Father but the Son that walked
upon the sea, when Peter asked Him, saying, Lord, bid me come unto You.
Matthew 14:28 But even prophecy itself gives proof of this. For holy Job prophesied
of the coming of the Lord; of Whom he said in truth that He would vanquish the
great Leviathan, Job 41:8 and it was done. For that dread Leviathan that is, the devil,
He smote, and struck down, and laid low in the last times by the adorable Passion of
His own Body. Isaiah 27:1

31. The Son therefore is only and true God for this also is assigned to the Son as His
sole right. For of no created being can it be accurately said that he is alone. How can

he to whom fellowship in creation belongs be separated from the rest, as though he were alone? Thus man is seen to be a rational being among all earthly creatures, yet he is not the only rational being; for we know that the heavenly works of God also are rational, we confess that angels and archangels are rational beings. If then the angels are rational, man cannot be said to be the only rational being.

32. But they say that the sun can be said to be alone, because there is no second sun. But the sun himself has many things in common with the stars, for he travels across the heavens, he is of that ethereal and heavenly substance, he is a creature, and is reckoned among all the works of God. He serves God in union with all, blesses Him with all, praises Him with all. Therefore he cannot accurately be said to be alone, for he is not set apart from the rest.

33. Wherefore since no created being can be compared with the Godhead of the Father, the Son, and the Holy Ghost, Which is alone, not among all, but over all (our declaration concerning the Spirit being meanwhile held back); as the Father is said to be the only true God, because He has nothing in common with others; so also is the Son alone the Image of the true God, He alone is the Hand of the Father, He alone is the Virtue and Wisdom of God.

34. Thus the Son alone does what the Father does; for it is written: Whatsoever things I do, He does. John 5:19 And since the work of the Father and of the Son is one, it is well said of the Father and the Son, that God worked alone; wherefore also when we speak of the Creator, we own both the Father and the Son. For assuredly when Paul said, Who served the creature more than the Creator, Romans 1:25 he neither denied the Father to be the Creator, from Whom are all these things, nor yet the Son, through Whom are all things. Romans 11:36

35. And it does not seem out of agreement with this that it is written: Who alone has immortality. 1 Timothy 6:16 For how could He not have immortality Who has life in Himself? He has it in His nature; He has it in His essential Being; and He has it not as a temporal grace, but owing to His eternal Godhead. He has it not by way of a gift as a servant, but by peculiar right of His Generation, as the co-eternal Son. He has it, too, as has the Father. For as the Father has life in Himself, so also has He given to the Son to have life in Himself. John 5:26 As He has it, it says, so He has given it. You have learned already how He gave it, that you may not think it to be a free gift of grace, when it is a secret of His generation. Since, then, there is no divergence of life between the Father and the Son, how can it be supposed that the Father alone has immortality, while the Son has it not?

36. Wherefore let them understand that in this passage the Son is not to be separated from the Father, Who is the only true God. For they cannot prove that the Son is not the only and true God, especially as here also it may be gathered, as I have said, that Christ too is true and only God; or the passage may at least be understood partly in reference to the Godhead of the Father and the Son, and partly to the Incarnation of Christ: for knowledge is not perfect unless it confesses Jesus Christ from eternity to be only-begotten God, true Son of God, and, according to the flesh, begotten of a

Virgin. Which also this very Evangelist has taught us elsewhere, saying: Every spirit that confesses that Jesus Christ has come in the flesh, is of God. 1 John 4:2

37. Lastly, the whole of our passage teaches us that it is not improper in this verse to understand a reference to the sacrament of the Incarnation. For thus it is written: Father, the hour has come, glorify Your Son. John 17:1 When, therefore, He states that the hour has come, and prays to be glorified, how can one suppose Him to have spoken but only in accordance with the assumption of our flesh? For the Godhead has no fixed moments of time, nor does eternal light stand in need of glorification. Therefore in the only true God, Who is the Father, we also understand the only true Son of God to be in accordance with the unity of the Godhead. And in the name of Jesus Christ, which He received when born of the Virgin, we acknowledge the sacrament of the Incarnation.

38. But if they wish to separate the Son, when they read that the Father is the only true God, I suppose that when they read of the Incarnation of the Son: This is the stone which was set at naught of you builders, which has become the head of the corner; and further: There is none other name under heaven given among men, whereby we must be saved; Acts 4:11-12 then they imagine the Father is to be cut off from the benefit of imparting salvation to us. But there is neither salvation without the Father, nor eternal life without the Son.

Chapter 3.

To the objection of the Arians, that two Gods are introduced by a unity of substance, the answer is that a plurality of Gods is more likely to be inferred from diversity of substance. Further, their charge recoils upon themselves. Manifold diversity is the reason why two men cannot be said to be one man, though all men are called individually man, where a unity of nature is referred to. There is one nature alone in them, but there is wholly a unity in the Divine Persons. Therefore the Son is not to be severed from the Father, especially as they dare not deny that worship is due to Him.

39. But the Arians maintain the following: If you say that, as the Father is the only true God, so also is the Son, and confess that the Father and the Son are both of one substance, you introduce not one God, but two. For they who are of one substance seem not to be one God but two Gods. Just as two men or two sheep or more are spoken of, but a man and a sheep are not spoken of as two men or two sheep, but as one man and one sheep.

40. This is what the Arians say; and by this cunning argument they attempt to catch the more simple-minded. However if we read the divine Scriptures we shall find that plurality occurs rather among those things which are of a diverse and different substance, that is, ἑτεροούσια . We have this set forth in the books of Solomon, in that passage in which he said: There are three things impossible to understand, yea, a fourth which I know not, the track of an eagle in the air, the way of a serpent upon a rock, the path of a ship in the sea, and the way of a man in his youth. Proverbs 30:18-19 An eagle and a ship and a serpent are not of one family and nature, but of a

distinguishable and different substance, and yet they are three. On the testimony of Scripture, therefore, they learn that their arguments are against themselves.

41. Therefore, in saying that the substance of the Father and of the Son is diverse and their Godhead distinguishable, they themselves assert there are two Gods. But we, when we confess the Father and the Son, in declaring them still to be of one Godhead, say that there are not two Gods, but one God. And this we establish by the word of the Lord. For where there are several, there is a difference either of nature or of will and work. Lastly, that they may be refuted on their own witness, two men are mentioned: But though they are of one nature by right of birth, yet in time and thought and work and place, they are apart; and so one man cannot be spoken of under the signification and number of two; for there is no unity where there is diversity. But God is said to be one, and the glory and completeness of the Father, the Son, and the Holy Spirit is thus expressed.

42. Such, indeed, is the truth of unity that, when the nature alone of human birth or of human flesh is indicated, one man is the term used for the many, as it is written: The Lord is my helper, I will not fear what man can do unto me; that is, not the one person of a man, but the one flesh, the one frailty of human birth. It added also: It is better to trust in the Lord than to trust in man. Here, too, it did not denote one particular man, but a universal condition. Then, immediately after it added, speaking of many: It is better to put confidence in the Lord than to put confidence in princes. Where man is spoken of, as we have already said, there the common unity of the nature, which exists between all is indicated; but where the princes are mentioned, there is a certain distinction between their different powers.

43. Amongst men, or in men, there exists a unity in some one thing, either in love, or desire, or flesh, or devotion, or faith. But a universal unity, that embraces within itself all things agreeably to the divine glory, is the property of the Father, the Son, and the Holy Spirit alone.

44. Wherefore the Lord also, in pointing out the diversity that exists among men, who have nothing in common that can tend towards the unity of an indivisible substance, says: In your law it is written that the testimony of two men is true. John 8:17 But though He had said, The testimony of two men is true, when He came to the testimony of Himself and His Father, He said not: Our testimony is true, for it is the testimony of two Gods; but: I am One that bear witness of Myself, and the Father that sent Me bears witness of Me. John 8:18 Earlier He also says: If I judge, My judgment is true; for I am not alone, but I and the Father that sent Me. John 8:16 Thus, both in one place and the other, He indicated both the Father and the Son, but neither implied the plurality, nor severed the unity of their divine Substance.

45. It is plain, then, that whatsoever is of one substance cannot be severed, even though it be not single, but one. By singleness I mean that which the Greeks call μονοτής . Singleness has to do with a person; unity with a nature. That those things which are of a different substance are wont to be called, not one alone, but many, though already proved on the testimony of the prophet, the Apostle himself has stated in so many words, saying: For though there be that are called gods, whether in

heaven or in earth. 1 Corinthians 8:5 Do you see, then, that those who are of different substances, and not of the verity of one nature, are called gods? But the Father and the Son, being of one substance, are not two Gods, but One God, the Father, of Whom are all things, and one Lord Jesus Christ, through Whom are all things. 1 Corinthians 8:6 One God, he says, and one Lord Jesus; and above: One God, not two Gods; and then: One Lord, not two Lords. 1 Corinthians 8:4, 6

46. Plurality, therefore, is excluded, but the unity is not destroyed. But as, on the one hand, when we read of the Lord Jesus, we do not dissociate the Father, as I have already said, from the prerogative of ruling, because He has that in common with the Son; so, on the other hand, when we read of the only true God, the Father, we cannot sever the Son from the prerogative of the only true God, for He has that in common with the Father.

47. Let them say what they feel or what they think, when we read: You shall worship the Lord your God, and Him only shall you serve. Matthew 4:10 Do they think Christ should not be worshipped, and that He ought not to be served? But if that woman of Canaan who worshipped Him, Matthew 15:25 merited to gain what she asked for, and the Apostle Paul, who confessed himself to be the servant of Christ in the very outset of his letters, merited to be an Apostle not of men, neither by man, but by Jesus Christ; Galatians 1:1 let them say what they think should follow. Would they prefer to join with Arius in a league of treachery, and so show, by denying Christ to be the only true God, that they consider He should neither be worshipped nor served? Or would they sooner go in company with Paul, who in serving and worshipping Christ did not disown in word and heart the only true God, Whom he acknowledged with dutiful service?

Chapter 4.

It is objected by heretics that Christ offered worship to His Father. But instead it is shown that this must be referred to His humanity, as is clear from an examination of the passage. However, it also offers fresh witness to His Godhead, as we often see it happening in other actions that Christ did.

48. But if any one were to say that the Son worships God the Father, because it is written, You worship you know not what, we know what we worship, John 4:22 let him consider when it was said, and to whom, and to whose wishes it was in answer.

49. In the earlier verses of this chapter it was stated, not without reason, that Jesus, being weary with the journey, was sitting down, and that He asked a woman of Samaria to give Him drink; John 4:6-7 for He spoke as man; for as God He could neither be weary nor thirst.

50. So when this woman addressed Him as a Jew, and thought Him a prophet, He answers her, as a Jew who spiritually taught the mysteries of the Law: You worship you know not what, we know what we worship. We, He says; for He joined Himself with men. But how is He joined with men, but according to the flesh? And to show that He answered as being incarnate, He added: for salvation is of the Jews. John 4:22

51. But immediately after this He put aside His human feelings, saying: But the hour comes, and now is, when the true worshippers shall worship the Father. John 4:23 He said not: We shall worship. This He would certainly have said, if He had a share in our obedience.

52. And when we read that Mary worshipped Him, Matthew 28:9 we ought to learn that it is not possible for Him under the same nature both to worship as a servant, and to be worshipped as Lord; but rather that as man He is said to worship among men, and that as Lord He is worshipped by His servants.

53. Many things therefore we read and believe, in the light of the sacrament of the Incarnation. But even in the very feelings of our human nature we may behold the Divine Majesty. Jesus is wearied with His journey, that He may refresh the weary; He desires to drink, when about to give spiritual drink to the thirsty; He was hungry, when about to supply the food of salvation to the hungry; He dies, to live again; He is buried, to rise again; He hangs upon the dreadful tree, to strengthen those in dread; He veils the heaven with thick darkness, that He may give light; He makes the earth to shake, that He may make it strong; He rouses the sea, that He may calm it; He opens the tombs of the dead, that He may show they are the homes of the living; He is made of a Virgin, that men may believe He is born of God; He feigns not to know, that He may make the ignorant to know; as a Jew He is said to worship, that the Son may be worshipped as true God.

Chapter 5.

Ambrose answers those who press the words of the Lord to the mother of Zebedee's children, by saying that they were spoken out of kindness, because Christ was unwilling to cause her grief. Ample reason for such tenderness is brought forward. The Lord would rather leave the granting of that request to the Father, than declare it to be impossible. This answer of Christ's, however, is not to His detriment, as is shown both by His very words, and also by comparing them with other passages.

54. How, they say, can the Son of God be the only true God, like to the Father, when He Himself said to the sons of Zebedee: 'You shall drink indeed of My cup; but to sit on My right hand or on My left, is not Mine to give to you, but to those for whom it has been prepared of My Father?'? Matthew 20:23 This, then, is, as you desire, your proof of divine inequality; though in it you ought rather to reverence the Lord's kindness and to adore His grace; if, that is, you could but perceive the deep secrets of the virtue and wisdom of God.

55. For think of her who, with and for her sons, makes this request. It is a mother, who in her anxiety for the honour of her sons, though somewhat unrestrained in the measure of her desires, may for all that yet find pardon. It is a mother, old in years, devout in her zeal, deprived of consolation; who at that time, when she might have been helped and supported by the aid of her able bodied offspring, suffered her children to leave her, and preferred the reward her sons should receive in following

Christ to her own pleasure. For they when called by the Lord, at the first word, as we read, left their nets and their father and followed Him. Matthew 4:22

56. She then, somewhat yielding to the devotion of a mother's zeal, besought the Saviour, saying: Grant that these my two sons may sit the one on Your right hand, the other on Your left in Your kingdom. Matthew 20:21 Although it was an error, it was an error of a mother's affections; for a mother's heart knows no patience. Though eager for the object of her desires, yet her longing was pardonable, for she was not greedy for money, but for grace. Not shameless was her request, for she thought not of herself, but of her children. Contemplate the mother, reflect upon her.

57. But it is nothing wonderful if the feelings of parents for their children seem nothing to you, who think the love of the Almighty Father for His only-begotten Son a trifling matter. The Lord of heaven and earth was ashamed (to speak as accords with the assumption of our flesh and the virtues of the soul)— He was ashamed, I say, and, to use His own word, disturbed, to refuse a share even in His own seat to a mother making request for her sons. You maintain sometimes that the proper Son of the eternal God stands to give service, at other times you would have His co-session to be as that of an attendant, that is, not because there is a oneness of majesty, but because it is the order of the Father; and you deny to the Son of God, Who is true God, that which He plainly was unwilling to refuse to men.

58. For He thought of the mother's love, who solaced her old age with the thought of her sons' reward, and, though harassed with a mother's longings, endured the absence of those dearest pledges of her love.

59. Think also of the woman, that is, the weaker sex, whom the Lord had not yet strengthened by His own Passion. Think, I say, of a descendant of Eve, the first woman, sinking under the inheritance of unrestrained passion, which had been passed on to all; one, too, whom the Lord had not yet redeemed with His own Blood, and from whom He had not yet washed out in His Blood the desire implanted in the hearts of all for unbounded honour even beyond what is right. Thus the woman offended owing to an inherited tendency to wrong.

60. And what wonder if a mother should strive to win preference for her children (which is far better than if she had done it for herself), when even the Apostles themselves, as we read, strove among themselves, as to who should have the preference? Luke 22:24

61. The physician, therefore, ought not to wound a mother who has been deprived of all, nor a suffering mind, with shameful reproaches, lest when the request had been made and had been proudly denied, she should grieve over the condemnation of her petition as being unreasonable.

62. Lastly, the Lord, Who knew that a mother's affection is to be honoured, answered not the woman, but her sons, saying: Are you able to drink of the cup that I shall drink of? When they say: We are able, Jesus says to them: You shall drink indeed of

My cup; but to sit on My right hand and on My left is not Mine to give to you, but to those for whom it is prepared of My Father. Matthew 20:22-23

63. How patient and kind the Lord is; how deep is His wisdom and good His love! For wishing to show that the disciples asked for no slight thing, but one they could not obtain, He reserved His own peculiar rights for His Father's honour, not fearing to detract anything from His own rights: Who thought it not robbery to be equal with God; Philippians 2:6 and loving, too, His disciples (for He loved them, as it is written, unto the end), John 13:1 He was unwilling to seem to refuse to those whom He loved what they desired; He, I say, the good and holy Lord, Who would rather keep some of His own prerogative secret, than lay aside anything of His love. For charity suffers long, and is kind; charity envies not, and seeks not her own. 1 Corinthians 13:4

64. Lastly, that you may learn it was no sign of weakness, but rather of tenderness, that He said: It is not Mine to give to you; note that when the sons of Zebedee make the request without their mother, He said nothing about the Father; for thus it is written: It is not Mine to give to you, but those for whom it has been prepared. Mark 10:40 So the Evangelist Mark has stated it. But when the mother makes this request on her sons' behalf, as we find it in Matthew, He says: It is not Mine to give to you, but to those for whom it has been prepared of My Father. Matthew 20:23 Here He added: of My Father, for a mother's feelings demanded greater tenderness.

65. But if they think that by saying, For whom it has been prepared of My Father, He assigned greater power to His Father, or detracted anything from His own; let them say whether they think there is any detraction from the Father's power, because the Son in the Gospel says of the Father: The Father judges no man. John 5:22

66. But if we think it impious to believe that the Father has handed over all judgment to the Son in such wise that He has it not Himself — for He has it, and cannot lose what the Divine Majesty has by its very nature, — we ought to consider it equally impious to suppose that the Son cannot give what either men can merit, or any creature can receive; especially as He Himself has said: I go unto My Father, and whatsoever you shall ask of Him in My name, that will I do. John 14:12-13 For if the Son cannot give what the Father can give, the Truth has lied, and cannot do what the Father has been asked for in His name. He therefore did not say: For whom it has been prepared of My Father, in order that requests should be made only of the Father. For all things which are asked of the Father, He has declared that He will give. Lastly, He did not say: Whatsoever you shall ask of Me, that will I do; but: Whatsoever you shall ask of Him in My name, that will I do.

Chapter 6.

Wishing to answer the above-stated objection somewhat more fully, he maintains that this request, had it not been impossible in itself, would have been possible for Christ to grant; especially as the Father has given all judgment to Him; which gift we must understand to have been given without any feature of imperfection. However, he proves that the request must be reckoned amongst the impossibilities. To make it really possible, he teaches

that Christ's answer must be taken in accordance with His human nature, and shows this next by an exposition of the passage. Lastly, he once more confirms the reply he has given on the impossibility of Christ's session.

67. I ask now whether they think the request made by the wife and sons of Zebedee was possible or impossible to human circumstances, or to any created being? If it was possible, how is it that He Who made all things which were not had not the power of granting a seat to His apostles on His right hand and on His left? Or how was it that He, to Whom the Father gave all judgment, could not judge of men's merits?

68. We know well in what way He gave it; for how did the Son, who created all things out of nothing, receive it as though in want? Had He not the judgment of those whose natures He had made? The Father gave all judgment to the Son, that all men should honour the Son, even as they honour the Father. John 5:23 It is not therefore the power of the Son, but our knowledge of it, that increases; nor does what is learned by us add anything to His being, but only to our advantage; so that by knowing the Son of God, we may have eternal life.

69. As, then, in our knowledge of the Son of God His honour, but our profit, not His, is concerned; if any one thinks that the power of God is augmented by that honour, He must also believe that God the Father can receive augmentation; for He is glorified by our knowledge of Him, as is the Son: as it is written on the word of the Son: I have glorified You upon the earth. John 17:4 Therefore if that which was asked for was at all possible, it certainly was in the power of the Son to grant it.

70. Let them show, if they consider it possible, who of men or of other created beings sits either on the right hand or the left of God. For the Father says to the Son: Sit on My right hand. Therefore if any one sits on the right hand of the Son, the Son is found to be sitting (to speak in human wise) between Himself and the Father.

71. A thing impossible for man, then, was asked of Him. But He was unwilling to say that men could not sit with Him; seeing that He desired His divine glory should be veiled, and not revealed before He rose again. Matthew 17:9 For before this, when He had appeared in glory between His attendants Moses and Elias, He had warned His disciples that they should tell no man what they had seen.

72. Therefore if it was not possible for men or other created beings to merit this, the Son ought not to seem to have less power because He gave not to His apostles, what the Father has not given to men or other created beings. Or else let them say to which of them He has given it. Certainly not to the angels; of whom Scripture says that all the angels stood round about the throne. Revelation 7:11 Thus Gabriel said that he stands, as it says: I am Gabriel that stand before God. Luke 1:19

73. Not to the angels, then, has He given it, nor to the elders who worship Him that sits; for they do not sit upon the seat of majesty, but as the Scripture has said, round about the throne; for there are four and twenty other seats, as we have it in the Revelation of John: And upon the seats four and twenty elders sitting. Revelation 4:4 In the Gospel also the Lord Himself says: When the Son of Man shall sit in the

throne of His glory, you also shall sit upon twelve thrones, judging the twelve tribes of Israel. Matthew 19:28 He did not say that a share in His own throne could be given to the apostles, but that there were those other twelve thrones; which, however, we ought not to think of as referring to actual sitting down, but as showing the happy issue of spiritual grace.

74. Lastly, in the Book of the Kings, Micaiah the prophet said: I saw the Lord God of Israel sitting on His throne, and all the host of heaven standing around Him, on His right hand and on His left. 1 Kings 22:19 How then, when the angels stand on the right hand and on the left of the Lord God, when all the host of heaven stands, shall men sit on the right hand of God or on His left, to whom is promised as a reward for virtue likeness to the angels, as the Lord says: You shall be as the angels in heaven? Matthew 22:30 As the angels, He says, not more than the angels.

75. If, then, the Father has given nothing more than the Son, the Son certainly has given nothing less than the Father. Therefore the Son can in no way be less than the Father.

76. Suppose, however, that it had been possible for men to obtain what was desired; what does it mean when He says: But to sit on My right hand and on My left is not Mine to give to you? Matthew 20:23 What is Mine? Above He said: You shall drink indeed of My cup; and again He added: It is not Mine to give to you. Above He said Mine, and again lower down He said Mine. He made no change. And so the earlier passages tell us why He said Mine.

77. For being asked by a woman as man to allow her sons to sit on His right hand and His left, because she asked Him as man, the Lord also as though only man answered concerning His Passion: Are you able to drink of the cup that I shall drink of? Matthew 20:22

78. Therefore because He spoke according to the flesh of the Passion of His Body, He wished to show that according to the flesh He left behind Him an example and pattern to us of the endurance of suffering; but that according to His position as man He could not grant them fellowship in the throne above. This is the reason why He said: It is not Mine; as also in another place He says: My doctrine is not Mine. John 7:16 It is not, He says, spoken after my flesh; for the words which are divine belong not to the flesh.

79. But how plainly He showed His tenderness for His disciples, whom He loved, saying first: Will you drink of My cup? For as He could not grant what they sought, He offered them something else, so that He might mention what He would assign to them, before He denied them anything; in order that they might understand that the failure lay more in the equity of their request to Him, than in the wish of their Lord to show kindness.

80. You shall indeed drink of My cup, He says; that is, I will not refuse you the suffering, which My flesh will undergo. For all that I have taken on Myself as man, you can imitate. I have granted you the victory of suffering, the inheritance of the

cross. 'But to sit on My right hand and on My left is not Mine to give to you.' He did not say, It is not Mine to give, but: It is not Mine to give to you; meaning by this, not that He lacked the power, but that His creatures were wanting in merit.

81. Or take in another way the words: It is not Mine to give to you, that is, It is not Mine, for I came to teach humility; it is not Mine, for I came, not to be ministered unto, but to minister; it is not Mine, for I show justice, not favour.

82. Then, speaking of the Father, He added: For whom it has been prepared, to show that the Father also is not wont to give heed merely to requests, but to merits; for God is not a respecter of persons. Acts 10:34 Wherefore also the Apostle says: Whom He did foreknow, He also did predestinate. Romans 8:29 He did not predestinate them before He knew them, but He did predestinate the reward of those whose merits He foreknew.

83. Rightly then is the woman checked, who demanded what was impossible, as a special kind of privilege from Him the Lord, Who of His own free gift granted not only to two apostles, but to all the disciples, those things which He had adjudged to be given to the saints; and that too without a prayer from any one, as it is written: You shall sit upon twelve thrones, judging the twelve tribes of Israel. Matthew 19:28

84. Therefore, although we may think the demand to have been possible, there is no room for false attacks. However, when I read that the seraphim stand, Isaiah 6:2 how can I suppose that men may sit on the right hand or the left of the Son of God? The Lord sits upon the cherubim, as it says: You that sits upon the cherubim, show myself. And how shall the apostles sit upon the cherubim?

85. And I do not come to this conclusion of my own mind, but because of the utterances of our Lord's own mouth. For the Lord Himself later on, in commending the apostles to the Father, says: Father, I will that they also whom You have given Me be with Me where I am. John 17:24 But if He had thought that the Father would give the divine throne to men, He would have said: I will that where I sit, they also may sit with Me. But He says: I will that they be with Me, not that they may sit with Me; and where I am, not as I am.

86. Then follow the words: That they may see My glory. Here too He did not say: that they may have My glory, but that they may see it. For the servant sees, the Lord possesses; as David also has taught us, saying: That I may see the delight of the Lord. And the Lord Himself in the Gospel has revealed it, stating: Blessed are the pure in heart, for they shall see God. Matthew 5:8 They shall see, He says; not They shall sit with God upon the cherubim.

87. Let them therefore cease to think little of the Son of God according to His Godhead, lest they should think little also of the Father. For he who believes wrongly of the Son cannot think rightly of the Father; he who thinks wrongly of the Spirit cannot think rightly of the Son. For where there is one dignity, one glory, one love, one majesty, whatsoever you think is to be withdrawn in the case of any one of the

Three Persons, is withdrawn from all alike. For that can never have completeness which you can separate and divide into various portions.

Chapter 7.

Objection is taken to the following passage: You have loved them, as You have loved Me. To remove it, he shows first the impiety of the Arian explanation; then compares these words with others; and lastly, takes the whole passage into consideration. Hence he gathers that the mission of Christ, although it is to be received according to the flesh, is not to His detriment. When this is proved he shows how the divine mission takes place.

88. There are some, O Emperor Augustus, who in their desire to deny the unity of the divine Substance, strive to make little of the love of the Father and the Son, because it is written: You have loved them, as You have loved Me. John 17:23 But when they say this, what else do they do but adopt a likeness of comparison between the Son of God and men?

89. Can men indeed be loved by God as the Son is, in Whom the Father is well-pleased? Matthew 3:17 He is well-pleasing in Himself; we through Him. For those in whom God sees His own Son after His own likeness, He admits through His Son into the favour of sons. So that as we go through likeness unto likeness, so through the Generation of the Son are we called unto adoption. The eternal love of God's Nature is one thing, that of grace is another.

90. And if they start a debate on the words that are written: And You have loved them, as You have loved Me, and think a comparison is intended; they must think that the following also was said by way of comparison: Be merciful, as your Father Which is in heaven is merciful; Luke 6:36 and elsewhere: Be perfect, as My Father Which is in heaven is perfect. Matthew 5:48 But if He is perfect in the fullness of His glory, we are but perfect according to the growth of virtue within us. The Son also is loved by the Father according to the fullness of a love that ever abides, but in us growth in grace merits the love of God.

91. You see, then, how God has given grace to men, and do you wish to dissever the natural and indivisible love of the Father and the Son? And do you still strive to make nothing of words, where you note the mention of a unity of majesty?

92. Consider the whole of this passage, and see from what standpoint He speaks; for you hear Him saying: Father, glorify Me with the glory which I had with You before the world was. John 17:5 See how He speaks from the standpoint of the first man. For He begs for us in that request those things which, as Man, He remembered were granted in paradise before the Fall, as also He spoke of it to the thief at His Passion: Verily, verily, I say unto you, today shall you be with Me in paradise. Luke 23:43 This is the glory before the world was. But He used the word world instead men, as also you have it: Lo! The whole world goes after Him; John 12:19 and again That the world may know that You have sent Me. John 17:21

93. But that you might know the great God, even the life-giving and Almighty Son of God, He has added a proof of His majesty by saying: And all Mine are Yours, and Yours are Mine. John 17:10 He has all things, and do you turn aside the fact that He was sent, to wrong Him?

94. But if you do not accept the truth of His mission according to the flesh, as the Apostle spoke of it, Romans 8:3 and dost raise out of a mere word a decision against it, to enable you to say that inferiors are wont to be sent by superiors; what answer will you give to the fact that the Son was sent to men? For if you think that he who is sent is inferior to him by whom he is sent, you must learn also that an inferior has sent a superior, and that superiors have been sent to inferiors. For Tobias sent Raphael the archangel, Tobit 9:3 and an angel was sent to Balaam, Numbers 22:22 and the Son of God to the Jews.

95. Or was the Son of God inferior to the Jews to whom He was sent? For of Him it is written: Last of all He sent unto them His only Son, saying, They will reverence My Son. Matthew 21:37 And mark that He mentioned first the servants, then the Son, that you may know that God, the only-begotten Son according to the power of His Godhead, has neither name nor lot in common with servants. He is sent forth to be reverenced, not to be compared with the household.

96. And rightly did He add the word My, that we might believe He came, not as one of many, nor as one of a lower nature or of some inferior power, but as true from Him that is true, as the Image of the Father's Substance.

97. Suppose, however, that he who is sent is inferior to him by whom he is sent. Christ then was inferior to Pilate; for Pilate sent Him to Herod. But a word does not prejudice His power. Scripture, which says that He was sent from the Father, says that He was sent from a ruler.

98. Wherefore, if we sensibly hold to those things which be worthy of the Son of God, we ought to understand Him to have been sent in such a way that the Word of God, out of the incomprehensible and ineffable mystery of the depths of His majesty, gave Himself for comprehension to our minds, so far as we could lay hold of Him, not only when He emptied Himself, but also when He dwelt in us, as it is written: I will dwell in them. 2 Corinthians 6:16 Elsewhere also it stands that God said: Go to, let us go down and confound their language. Genesis 11:7 God, indeed, never descends from any place; for He says: I fill heaven and earth. Jeremiah 23:24 But He seems to descend when the Word of God enters our hearts, as the prophet has said: Prepare the way of the Lord, make His paths straight. Isaiah 40:3 We are to do this, so that, as He Himself promised, He may come together with the Father and make His abode with us. John 14:23 It is clear, then, how He comes.

Chapter 8.

Christ, so far as He is true Son of God, has no Lord, but only so far as He is Man; as is shown by His words in which He addressed at one time the Father, at another the Lord. How many heresies are silenced by one verse of Scripture!

We must distinguish between the things that belong to Christ as Son of God or as Son of David. For under the latter title only must we ascribe it to Him that He was a servant. Lastly, he points out that many passages cannot be taken except as referring to the Incarnation.

99. Wherefore also it is plain how He calls Him Lord, Whom He knew as Father. For He says: I confess to You, Father, Lord of heaven and earth. Matthew 11:25 First Wisdom spoke of His own Father, and then proclaimed Him Lord of creation. For this reason the Lord shows in His Gospel that no lordship is exercised where there is a true offspring, saying: What do you think of Christ? Whose Son is He? They say unto Him, The son of David. Jesus says to them, How then does David in spirit call Him Lord, saying: The Lord said to my Lord: Sit on My right hand? Then he added: If David in spirit then call Him Lord, how is He his son? And no man was able to answer Him a word. Matthew 22:42-46

100. With what care did the Lord provide for the faith in this witness because of the Arians! For He did not say: The spirit calls Him Lord, but that David spoke in spirit; in order that men might believe that as He is his, that is, David's son according to the flesh, so also He is his Lord and God according to His Godhead. You see, then, that there is a distinction between the titles that are used of relationship and of lordship.

101. And rightly did the Lord speak of His own Father, but of the Lord of heaven and earth; so that you, when you read of the Father and the Lord, may understand it is the Father of the Son, and the Lord of Creation. In the one title rests the claim of nature, in the other the authority to rule. For taking on Himself the form of a servant, He calls Him Lord, because He has submitted to service; being equal to Him in the form of God, but being a servant in the form of His body: for service is the due of the flesh, but lordship is the due of the Godhead. Wherefore also the Apostle says: The God of our Lord Jesus Christ, the Father of glory, 2 Corinthians 1:3 that is, terming Him God of the adoption of humanity but the Father of glory. Did God have two Sons, Christ and Glory? Certainly not. Therefore if there is one Son of God, even Christ, Christ is Glory. Why do you strive to belittle Him who is the glory of the Father?

102. If then the Son is glory, and the Father is glory (for the Father of glory cannot be anything else than glory), there is no separation of glories, but glory is one. Thus glory is referred to its own proper nature, but lordship to the service of the body that was assumed. For if the flesh is subject to the soul of a just man as it is written: I chastise my body and bring it into subjection; 1 Corinthians 9:27 how much more is it subject to the Godhead, of Which it is said: For all things serve You?

103. By one question the Lord has shut out both Sabellians and Photinians and Arians. For when He said that the Lord spoke to the Lord, Sabellius is set aside, who will have it that the same Person is both Father and Son. Photinus is set aside, who thinks of Him merely as man; for none could be Lord of David the King, but He Who is God, for it is written: You shall worship the Lord your God, and Him only shall you serve. Deuteronomy 6:13 Would the prophet who ruled under the Law act contrary to the Law? Arius is set aside, who hears that the Son sits on the right hand

of the Father; so that if he argues from human ways, he refutes himself, and makes the poison of his blasphemous arguments to flow back upon himself. For in interpreting the inequality of the Father and the Son by the analogy of human habits (wandering from the truth in either case), he puts Him first Whom he makes little of, confessing Him to be the First, Whom he hears to be at the right hand. The Manichæan also is set aside, for he does not deny that He is the Son of David according to the flesh, Who, at the cry of the blind men, Jesus, Son of David, have mercy on us, Matthew 20:30 was pleased at their faith and stood and healed them. But He does deny that this refers to His eternity, if He is called Son of David alone by those who are false.

104. For Son of God is against Ebion, Son of David, is against the Manichees; Son of God is against Photinus, Son of David is against Marcion; Son of God is against Paul of Samosata, Son of David is against Valentinus; Son of God is against Arius and Sabellius, the inheritors of heathen errors. Lord of David is against the Jews, who beholding the Son of God in the flesh, in impious madness believed Him to be only man.

105. But in the faith of the Church one and the same is both Son of God the Father and Son of David. For the mystery of the Incarnation of God is the salvation of the whole of creation, according to that which is written: That without God He should taste death for every man; Hebrews 2:9 that is, that every creature might be redeemed without any suffering at the price of the blood of the Lord's Divinity, as it stands elsewhere: Every creature shall be delivered from the bondage of corruption. Romans 8:21

106. It is one thing to be named Son according to the divine Substance, it is another thing to be so called according to the adoption of human flesh. For, according to the divine Generation, the Son is equal to God the Father; and, according to the adoption of a body, He is a servant to God the Father. For, it says, He took upon Him the form of a servant. Philippians 2:7 The Son is, however, one and the same. On the other hand, according to His glory, He is Lord to the holy patriarch David, but his Son in the line of actual descent, not abandoning anything of His own, but acquiring for Himself the rights that go with the adoption into our race.

107. Not only does He undergo service in the character of man by reason of His descent from David, but also by reason of His name, as it is written: I have found David My Servant; and elsewhere: Behold I will send unto you My Servant, the Orient is His name. Zechariah 3:8 And the Son Himself says: Thus says the Lord, that formed Me from the womb to be His servant, and said to Me: It is a great thing for You to be called My Servant. Behold I have set You up for a witness to My people, and a light to the Gentiles, that You may be for salvation unto the ends of the earth. Isaiah 49:5-6 To whom is this said, if not to Christ? Who being in the form of God, emptied Himself and took upon Him the form of a servant. Philippians 2:6-7 But what can be in the form of God, except that which exists in the fullness of the Godhead?

108. Learn, then, what this means: He took upon Him the form of a servant. It means that He took upon Him all the perfections of humanity in their completeness, and obedience in its completeness. And so it says in the thirtieth Psalm: You have set my feet in a large room. I am made a reproach above all mine enemies. Make Your face to shine upon Your servant. Servant means the Man in whom He was sanctified; it means the Man in whom He was anointed; it means the Man in whom He was made under the law, made of the Virgin; and, to put it briefly, it means the Man in whose person He has a mother, as it is written: O Lord, I am Your Servant, I am Your Servant, and the Son of Your hand-maid; and again: I am cast down and sore humbled.

109. Who is sore humbled, but Christ, Who came to free all through His obedience? For as by one man's disobedience many were made sinners, so by the obedience of one shall many be made righteous. Romans 5:19 Who received the cup of salvation? Christ the High Priest, or David who never held the priesthood, nor endured suffering? Who offered the sacrifice of Thanksgiving?

110. But that is insufficient; take again: Preserve My soul, for I am holy. Did David say this of himself? Nay, He says it, Who also says: You will not leave My soul in hell, neither will You allow Your Holy One to see corruption. The Same then says both of these.

111. He has added further: Save Your Servant; and, further on: Give Your strength to Your servant, and to the Son of Your handmaid; and, elsewhere, that is, in Ezekiel: And I will set up one Shepherd over them, and He shall rule them, even My Servant David. He shall feed them, and He shall be their Shepherd. And I the Lord will be their God, and My Servant David a prince among them. Ezekiel 34:23-24 Now David the Son of Jesse was already dead. Therefore he speaks of Christ, Who for our sakes was made the Son of a handmaiden in the form of man; for according to His divine Generation He has no Mother, but a Father only: nor is He the fruit of earthly desire, but the eternal Power of God.

112. And so, also, when we read that the Lord said: My time is not yet full come; John 7:8 and: Yet a little while I am with you; and: I go unto Him that sent Me; John 7:33 and: Now is the Son of Man glorified; John 13:31 we ought to refer all this to the sacrament of the Incarnation. But when we read: And God is glorified in Him, and God has glorified Him; John 13:31 what doubt is there here, where the Son is glorified by the Father, and the Father is glorified by the Son?

113. Next, to make clear the faith of the Unity, and the Union of the Trinity, He also said that He would be glorified by the Spirit, as it stands: He shall receive of Mine, and shall glorify Me. John 16:14 Therefore the Holy Spirit also glorifies the Son of God. How, then, did He say: If I glorify Myself, My glory is nothing. John 8:54 Is then the glory of the Son nothing? It is blasphemy to say so, unless we apply these words to His flesh; for the Son spoke in the character of man, for by comparison with the Godhead, there is no glory of the flesh.

114. Let them cease from their wicked objections which are but thrown back upon their own falseness. For they say, it is written: Now is the Son of Man glorified. I do not deny that it is written: The Son of Man is glorified. But let them see what follows: And God is glorified in Him. I can plead some excuse for the Son of Man, but He has none for His Father; for the Father took not flesh upon Himself. I can plead an excuse, but do not use it. He has none, and is falsely attacked. I can either understand it in its plain sense, or I can apply to the flesh what concerns the flesh. A devout mind distinguishes between the things which are spoken after the flesh or after the Godhead. An impious mind turns aside to the dishonour of the Godhead, all that is said with regard to the littleness of the flesh.

Chapter 9.

The saint meets those who in Jewish wise object to the order of the words: In the name of the Father and of the Son and of the Holy Ghost, with the retort that the Son also is often placed before the Father; though he first points out that an answer to this objection has been already given by him.

115. Why is it that the Arians, after the Jewish fashion, are such false and shameless interpreters of the divine words, going indeed so far as to say that there is one power of the Father, another of the Son, and another of the Holy Ghost, since it is written: Go, teach all nations, baptizing them in the name of the Father and of the Son and of the Holy Ghost? And why do they make a distinction of divine power owing to the mere order of words?

116. Though I have already given this very witness for a unity of majesty and name in my former books, yet if they make this the ground of debate, I can maintain on the testimony of the Scriptures that the Son is mentioned first in many places, and that the Father is spoken of after Him. Is it therefore a fact that, because the name of the Son is placed first, by the mere accident of a word, as the Arians would have it, the Father comes second to the Son? God forbid, I say, God forbid. Faith knows nothing of such order as this; it knows nothing of a divided honour of the Father and the Son. I have not read of, nor heard of, nor found any varying degree in God. Never have I read of a second, never of a third God. I have read of a first God, Isaiah 44:6 I have heard of a first and only God.

117. If we pay such excessive regard to order, then the Son ought not to sit at the right hand of the Father, nor ought He to call Himself the First and the Beginning. The Evangelist was wrong in beginning with the Word and not with God, where he says: In the beginning was the Word, and the Word was with God. John 1:1 For, according to the order of human usage, he ought to name the Father first. The Apostle also was ignorant of their order, who says: Paul the servant of Jesus Christ, called to be an Apostle, separated unto the Gospel of God; Romans 1:1 and elsewhere: The grace of our Lord Jesus Christ, and the love of God, and the communion of the Holy Ghost. 2 Corinthians 13:14 If we follow the order of the words, he has placed the Son first, and the Father second. But the order of the words is often changed; and therefore you ought not to question about order or degree, in

the case of God the Father and His Son, for there is no severance of unity in the Godhead.

Chapter 10.

The Arians openly take sides with the heathen in attacking the words: He that believes in Me, believes not in Me, etc. The true meaning of the passage is unfolded; and to prevent us from believing that the Lord forbade us to have faith in Him, it is shown how He spoke at one time as God, at another as Man. After bringing forward examples of various results of that faith, he shows that certain other passages also must be taken in the same way.

118. Last of all, to show that they are not Christians, they deny that we are to believe in Christ, saying that it is written: He that believes in Me, believes not on Me, but on Him that sent Me. John 12:44 I was awaiting this confession; why did you delude me with your quibbles? I knew I had to contend with heathens. Nay, they indeed are converted, but you are not. If they believe, that the sacrament [of Baptism] is safe; you have received it, and destroyed it, or perchance it has never been received, but was unreal from the first.

119. It is written, they say: He that believes in Me, believes not on Me, but on Him that sent Me. But see what follows, and see how the Son of God wishes to be seen; for it continues: And he that sees Me, sees Him that sent Me, John 12:45 for the Father is seen in the Son. Thus, He has explained what He had spoken earlier, that he who confesses the Father believes on the Son. For he who knows not the Son, neither knows the Father. For every one that denies the Son has not the Father, but he that confesses the Son has both the Father and the Son. 1 John 2:23

120. What, then, is the meaning of Believes not on Me? That is, not on that which you can perceive in bodily form, nor merely on the man whom you see. For He has stated that we are to believe not merely on a man, but that you may believe that Jesus Christ Himself is both God and Man. Wherefore, for both reasons He says: I came not from Myself; John 7:28 and again: I am the beginning, of which also I speak to you. John 8:25 As Man He came not from Himself; as Son of God He takes not His beginning from men; but I am, He says, Myself 'the beginning of which also I speak to you.' Neither are the words which I speak human, but divine.

121. Nor is it right to believe that He denied we were to believe in Him, since He Himself said: That whosoever believes in Me should not abide in darkness; John 12:46 and in another place again: For this is the will of My Father that sent Me, that every one that sees the Son, and believes in Him, may have eternal life; John 6:40 and again: You believe in God, believe also in Me. John 14:1

122. Let no one, therefore, receive the Son without the Father, because we read of the Son. The Son has the Father, but not in a temporal sense, nor by reason of His passion, nor owing to His conception, nor by grace. I have read of His Generation, I have not read of His Conception. And the Father says: I have begotten; He does not

say: I have created. And the Son calls not God His Creator in the eternity of His divine Generation, but Father.

123. He represents Himself also now in the character of man, now in the majesty of God; now claiming for Himself oneness of Godhead with the Father, now taking upon Him all the frailty of human flesh; now saying that He has not His own doctrine, and now that He seeks not His own will; now pointing out that His testimony is not true, and now that it is true. For He Himself has said: If I bear witness of Myself, My witness is not true. John 5:31 Later on He says: If I bear witness of Myself, My witness is true. John 7:14

124. And how is Your testimony, Lord Jesus, not true? Did not he who believed it, though he hung upon the cross, and paid the penalty for the crime he owned to, cast aside the deserts of the robber and gain the reward of the innocent? Luke 23:41

125. Was Paul deceived, who received his sight, because he believed; Acts 9:12 which sight he had lost, before he believed?

126. And did Joshua, the son of Nun, err in recognizing the leader of the heavenly host? Joshua 5:13 But after he believed, he immediately conquered, being found worthy to triumph in the battle of faith. Again, he did not lead forth his armed ranks into the fight, nor did he overthrow the ramparts of the enemy's walls, with battering rams or other engines of war, but with the sound of the seven trumpets of the priests. Thus the blare of the trumpet and the badge of the priest brought a cruel war to an end.

127. A harlot saw this; and she who in the destruction of the city lost all hope of any means of safety, because her faith had conquered, bound a scarlet thread in her window, and thus uplifted a sign of her faith and the banner of the Lord's Passion; Joshua 2:18 so that the semblance of the mystic blood, which should redeem the world, might be in memory. So, without, the name of Joshua was a sign of victory to those who fought; within, the semblance of the Lord's Passion was a sign of salvation to those in danger. Wherefore, because Rahab understood the heavenly mystery, the Lord says in the Psalm: I will be mindful of Rahab and Babylon that know Me.

128. How, then, is Your testimony not true, O Lord, except it be given in accordance with the frailty of man? For every man is a liar.

129. Lastly, to prove that He spoke as man, He says: The Father that sent Me, He bears witness of Me. John 8:18 But His testimony as God is true, as He Himself says: My record is true: for I know whence I come, and whither I go, but you know not whence I come, and whither I go. You judge after the flesh. John 8:14-15 They judge then not after the Godhead but after the manhood, who think that Christ had not the power of bearing witness.

130. Therefore, when you hear, He that believes, believes not on Me; or: The Father that sent Me, He gave Me a commandment; John 12:49 you have now learned whither you ought to refer those words. Lastly, He shows what the commandment is,

saying: I lay down My life, that I may take it again. No man takes it from Me, but I lay it down of Myself. John 10:17 You see, then, what is said so as to show He had full power to lay down or to take up His life; as He also said: I have power to lay it down, and I have power again to take it up. This commandment have I received of My Father. John 10:18

131. Whether, then, a command, or, as some Latin manuscripts have it, a direction was given, it was certainly not given to Him as God, but as incarnate man, with reference to the victory He should gain in undergoing His Passion.

Chapter 11.

We must refer the fact that Christ is said to speak nothing of Himself, to His human nature. After explaining how it is right to say that He hears and sees the Father as being God, He shows conclusively, by a large number of proofs, that the Son of God is not a creature.

132. Are we indeed to bring the Son of God to such a low estate that He may not know how to act or speak, except as He hears, and are we to suppose that a fixed measure of action or of speech is assigned to Him, because it is written: I speak not of Myself, and, further on: As the Father has said to Me, even so I speak? John 12:50 But those words have reference to the obedience of the flesh, or else to the faith in the Unity. For many learned men allow that the Son hears, and that the Father speaks to the Son through the unity of their Nature; for that which the Son, through the unity of their will, knows that the Father wills, He seems to have heard.

133. Whereby is meant no personal duty, but an indivisible sentence of co-operation. For this does not signify any actual hearing of words, but the unity of will and of power, which exists both in the Father and in the Son. He has stated that this exists also in the Holy Spirit, in another place, saying, For He shall not speak of Himself, but whatsoever He shall hear, that shall He speak, John 16:13 so that we may learn that whatsoever the Spirit says, the Son also says; and whatsoever the Son says, the Father says also; for there is one mind and one mode of working in the Trinity. For, as the Father is seen in the Son, not indeed in bodily appearance, but in the unity of the Godhead, so also the Father speaks in the Son, not with a voice of earth, not with a human sound, but in the unity of Their work. So when He had said: The Father that dwells in Me, He speaks; and the works that I do, He does; John 14:10 He added: Believe Me, that I am in the Father, and the Father in Me; or else believe Me for the very work's sake. John 14:17

134. This is what we understand according to the whole course of the holy Scriptures; but the Arians, who will not think of God the things that be right, may be put to silence by an example just suited to their deserts; that they may not believe everything in carnal fashion, since they themselves do not see the works of their father the devil with bodily eyes. So the Lord has declared of their fellows the Jews, saying: You do what you have seen your father doing; John 8:38 though they are reproved not because they saw the work of the devil, but because they did his will, since the devil

unseen works out sin in them in accordance with their own wickedness. We have written this, as the Apostle did, because of the folly of these traitors. 2 Timothy 3:9

135. But we have sufficiently proved by examples from Scripture that it is a property of the unity of the divine majesty that the Father should abide in the Son, and that the Son should seem to have heard from the Father those things which He speaks. How else can we understand the unity of majesty than by the knowledge that the same deference is paid to the Father and the Son? For what can be better put than the Apostle's saying that the Lord of glory was crucified? 1 Corinthians 2:8

136. The Son then is the God of glory and the Lord of glory, but glory is not subject to creatures; the Son therefore is not a creature.

137. The Son is the Image of the Father's Substance; Hebrews 1:3 but every creature is unlike that divine Substance, but the Son of the Father is not unlike God; therefore the Son is not a creature.

138. The Son thought it not robbery to be equal with God; Philippians 2:6 but no creature is equal with God, the Son, however, is equal; therefore the Son is not a creature.

139. Every creature is changeable; but the Son of God is not changeable; therefore the Son of God is not a creature.

140. Every creature meets with chance occurrences of good and evil after the powers of its nature, and also feels their passing away; but nothing can pass away from or bring addition to the Son of God in His Godhead; therefore the Son of God is not a creature.

141. Every work of His God will bring into judgment; Ecclesiastes 12:14 but the Son of God is not brought into judgment; for He Himself judges; therefore the Son of God is not a creature.

142. Lastly, that you may understand the unity, the Saviour in speaking of His sheep says: No man is able to pluck them out of My hand. My Father Which gave them to Me is greater than all, and no man is able to pluck them out of My Father's hand. I and My Father are one. John 10:28-30

143. So the Son gives life as does the Father. For as the Father raises up the dead and quickens them, even so the Son quickens whom He will. John 5:21 So the Son raises up as does the Father: so too the Son preserves as does the Father. He Who is not unequal in grace, how is He unequal in power? So also the Son does not destroy, as neither does the Father. Therefore lest any one should believe there were two Gods, or should imagine a diversity of power, He said that He was one with His Father. How can a creature say that? Therefore the Son of God is not a creature.

144. It is not the same thing to rule as to serve; but Christ is both a King and the Son of a King. The Son of God therefore is not a servant. Every creature, however, gives

service. But the Son of God, Who makes servants become the sons of God, does not give service. Therefore the Son of God is not a servant.

Chapter 12.

He confirms what has been already said, by the parable of the rich man who went into a far country to receive for himself a kingdom; and shows that when the Son delivers up the kingdom to the Father, we must not regard the fact that the Father is said to put all things in subjection under Him, in a disparaging way. Here we are the kingdom of Christ, and in Christ's kingdom. Hereafter we shall be in the kingdom of God, where the Trinity will reign together.

145. In divine fashion has He represented that parable of the rich man, who went to a far-off country to receive a kingdom, and to return, Luke 19:12 thus describing Himself in the substance of the Godhead, and of His Manhood. For He being rich in the fullness of His Godhead, Who was made poor for us though He was rich and an eternal King, and the Son of an eternal King; He, I say, went to a foreign country in taking on Him a body, for He entered upon the ways of men as though upon a strange journey, and came into this world to prepare for Himself a kingdom from among us.

146. Jesus therefore came to this earth to receive for Himself a kingdom from us, to whom He says: The kingdom of God is within you. John 17:21 This is the kingdom which Christ has received, this the kingdom which He has delivered to the Father. For how did He receive for Himself a kingdom, Who was a King eternal? The Son of Man therefore came to receive a kingdom and to return. The Jews were unwilling to acknowledge Him, of whom He says: They which would not that I should reign over them, bring hither and slay them. Luke 19:27

147. Let us follow the course of the Scriptures. He Who came will deliver up the kingdom to God the Father; and when He has delivered up the kingdom, then also shall He be subject to Him, Who has put all things in subjection under Him, that God may be all in all. 1 Corinthians 15:24-28 If the Son of God has received the kingdom as Son of Man, surely as Son of Man also He will deliver up what He has received. If He delivers it up as Son of Man, as Son of Man He confesses His subjection indeed under the conditions of the flesh, and not in the majesty of His Godhead.

148. And do you make objections and contemn Him, because God has put all things in subjection under Him, when you hear that the Son of Man delivers up the kingdom to God, and hast read, as we said in our earlier books: No man can come to Me, except the Father draw him; and I will raise him up at the last day? John 6:44 If we follow it literally, see rather and notice the unity of honour each gives to other: The Father has put all things in subjection under the Son, and the Son delivers the kingdom to the Father. Say now which is the greater, to deliver up, or to raise up to life? Do we not after human fashion speak of the service of delivering up, and the power of raising to life? But both the Son delivers up to the Father, and also the

Father to the Son. The Son raises to life, and the Father also raises to life. Let them create the fiction of a blasphemous division where there is a unity of power.

149. Let the Son then deliver up His kingdom to the Father. The kingdom which He delivers up is not lost to Christ, but grows. We are the kingdom, for it was said to us: The kingdom of God is within you. Luke 17:21 And we are the kingdom, first of Christ, then of the Father; as it is written: No man comes to the Father, but by Me. John 14:6 When I am on the way, I am Christ's; when I have passed through, I am the Father's; but everywhere through Christ, and everywhere under Him.

150. It is a good thing to be in the kingdom of Christ, so that Christ may be with us; as He Himself says: Lo I am with you always, even unto the end of the world. Matthew 28:20 But it is better to be with Christ: For to depart and be with Christ is far better. Philippians 1:23 Though we are under sin in this world, Christ is with us, that by the obedience of one man many may be made just. Romans 5:19 And if I escape the sin of this world, I shall begin to be with Christ. And so He says: I will come again, and receive you unto Myself; John 14:3 and further on: I will that where I am, there you may be also with Me. John 14:3

151. Therefore we are now under Christ's rule, while we are in the body, and are not yet stripped of the form of a servant, which He put upon Him, when He emptied Himself. But when we shall see His glory, which He had before the world was, we shall be in the kingdom of God, in which are the patriarchs and prophets, of whom it is written: When you shall see Abraham, Isaac, and Jacob, and all the prophets in the kingdom of God; Luke 13:28 and shall thus acquire a deeper knowledge of God.

152. But in the kingdom of the Son the Father also reigns; and in the kingdom of the Father the Son also reigns: for the Father is in the Son, and the Son in the Father; and in whomsoever the Son dwells, in him also the Father dwells; and in whomsoever the Father dwells, in him also the Son dwells, as it is written: Both I and My Father will come to Him, and make Our abode with Him. John 14:23 Thus as there is one dwelling, so also there is one kingdom. Yea, and so far is the kingdom of the Father and of the Son but one, that the Father receives what the Son delivers, and the Son does not lose what the Father receives. Thus in the one kingdom there is a unity of power. Let no one therefore sever the Godhead between the Father and the Son.

Chapter 13.

With the desire to learn what subjection to Christ means after putting forward and rejecting various ideas of subjection, he runs through the Apostle's words; and so puts an end to the blasphemous opinions of the heretics on this matter. The subjection, which is shown to be future, cannot concern the Godhead, since there has always been the greatest harmony of wills between the Father and the Son. Also to that same Son in His Godhead all things have indeed been made subject; but they are said to be not yet subject to Him in this sense, because all men do not obey His commands. But after that they have been made subject, then shall Christ also be made subject in them, and the Father's work be perfected.

153. But if the one name and right of God belong to both the Father and the Son, since the Son of God is also true God, and a King eternal, the Son of God is not made subject in His Godhead. Let us then, Emperor Augustus, think how we ought to regard His subjection.

154. How is the Son of God made subject? As the creature to vanity? But it is blasphemous to have any such idea of the Substance of the Godhead.

155. Or as every creature is to the Son of God, for it is rightly written: You have put all things in subjection under His feet? But Christ is not made subject to Himself.

156. Or as a woman to a man, as we read: Let the wives be subject to their husbands; Ephesians 5:22 and again: Let the woman learn in silence in all subjection? 1 Timothy 2:11 But it is impious to compare a man to the Father, or a woman to the Son of God.

157. Or as Peter said: Submit yourselves to every human creature? 1 Peter 2:13 But Christ was certainly not so subject.

158. Or as Paul wrote: Submitting yourselves mutually to God and the Father in the fear of Christ? Ephesians 5:21 But Christ was not subject either in His own fear, nor in the fear of another Christ. For Christ is but one. But note the force of these words, that we are subject to the Father, while we also fear Christ.

159. How, then, do we understand His subjection? Shall we review the whole chapter which the Apostle wrote, so as to give no appearance of having falsely withheld anything, or of having weakened its force with intention to deceive? If in this life only, he says, we have hope in Christ, we are of all men most miserable. But if Christ is risen from the dead, He is the first-fruits of them that sleep. 1 Corinthians 15:19-20 You see how he discusses the question of Christ's Resurrection.

160. For since by one man, he says, came death, by man came also the resurrection of the dead. For as in Adam all die, even so in Christ shall all be made alive. But each one in his own order: Christ the firstfruits; afterward they that are Christ's, who have believed in His coming. Then comes the end, when He shall have delivered up the kingdom to God, even the Father, when He shall have put down all rule and authority and power. For He must reign until He has put all enemies under His feet. The last enemy that shall be destroyed is death; for He has put all things under His feet. But when He says, all things are put under Him, it is manifest that He is excepted Which did put all things under Him. But when all things shall be subdued unto Him, then shall the Son also Himself be subject unto Him, that put all things under Him, that God may be all in all. 1 Corinthians 15:21-28 Thus also the same Apostle said to the Hebrews: But now we see not yet all things put under Him. Hebrews 2:8 We have heard the whole of the Apostle's discourse.

161. How, then, do we speak of His subjection? The Sabellians and Marcionites say that this subjection of Christ to God the Father will be in such wise that the Son will be re-absorbed into the Father. If, then, the subjection of the Word means that God

the Word is to be absorbed into the Father; then whatsoever is made subject to the Father and the Son will be absorbed into the Father and the Son, that God may be all and in all His creatures. But it is foolish to say so. There is therefore no subjection through re-absorption. For there are other things which are made subject, those, that is to say, which are created, and there is Another, to Whom that subjection is made. Let the expounders of a cruel re-absorption keep silence.

162. Would that they too were silent, who, as they cannot prove that the Word of God and Wisdom of God can be re-absorbed, attribute the weakness of subjection to His Godhead, saying that it is written: But when all things shall be subdued unto Him, then shall the Son also Himself be subject unto Him. 1 Corinthians 15:28

163. We see, then, that the Scripture states that He is not yet made subject, but that this is to come: Therefore now the Son is not made subject to God the Father. In what, then, do you say that the Son will be made subject? If in His Godhead, He is not disobedient, for He is not at variance with the Father; nor is He made subject, for He is not a servant, but the only Son of His own proper Father. Lastly, when He created heaven, and formed the earth, He exercised both power and love. There is therefore no subjection as that of a servant in the Godhead of Christ. But if there is no subjection then the will is free.

164. But if they think of this as the subjection of the Son, namely, that the Father makes all things in union with His will, let them learn that this is really a proof of inseparable power. For the unity of Their will is one that began not in time, but ever existed. But where there is a constant unity of will, there can be no weakness of temporal subjection. For if He were made subject through His nature, He would always remain in subjection; but since He is said to be made subject in time, that subjection must be part of an assumed office and not of an everlasting weakness: especially as the eternal Power of God cannot change His state for a time, neither can the right of ruling fall to the Father in time. For if the Son ever will be changed in such wise as to be made subject in His Godhead, then also must God the Father, if ever He shall gain more power, and have the Son in subjection to Himself in His Godhead, be considered now in the meantime inferior according to your explanation.

165. But what fault has the Son been guilty of, that we should believe that He could hereafter be made subject in His Godhead? Has he as man seized for Himself the right to sit at His Father's side, or has He claimed for Himself the prerogative of His Father's throne, against His Father's will? But He Himself says: For I do always those things that please Him. John 8:29 Therefore if the Son pleases the Father in all things, why should He be made subject, Who was not made subject before?

166. Let us see then that there be not a subjection of the Godhead, but rather of us in the fear of Christ, a truth so full of grace, and so full of mystery. Wherefore, again, let us weigh the Apostle's words: But when all things shall be subdued unto Him, then shall the Son also Himself be subject unto Him that put all things under Him: that God may be all in all. What then do you say? Are not all things now subject unto Him? Are not the choirs of the saints made subject? Are not the angels, who ministered to Him when on the earth? Matthew 4:11 Are not the archangels who

were sent to Mary to foretell the coming of the Lord? Are not all the heavenly hosts? Are not the cherubim and seraphim, are not thrones and dominions and powers which worship and praise Him?

167. How, then, will they be brought into subjection? In the way that the Lord Himself has said. Take My yoke upon you. Matthew 11:29 It is not the fierce that bear the yoke, but the humble and the gentle. This clearly is no base subjection for men, but a glorious one: that in the Name of Jesus every knee should bow, of things in heaven and things beneath; and that every tongue should confess that Jesus is Lord in the glory of God the Father. Philippians 2:10 But for this reason all things were not made subject before, for they had not yet received the wisdom of God, not yet did they wear the easy yoke of the Word on the neck as it were of their mind. But as many as received Him, as it is written, to them gave He power to become the sons of God. John 1:12

168. Will any one say that Christ is now made subject, because many have believed? Certainly not. For Christ's subjection lies not in a few but in all. For just as I do not seem to be brought into subjection, if the flesh in me as yet lusts against the spirit, and the spirit against the flesh, Galatians 5:17 although I am in part subdued; so because the whole Church is the one body of Christ, we divide Christ as long as the human race disagrees. Therefore Christ is not yet made subject, for His members are not yet brought into subjection. But when we have become, not many members, but one spirit, then He also will become subject, in order that through His subjection God may be all and in all.

169. But as Christ is not yet made subject, so is the work of God not yet perfected; for the Son of God said: My meat is to do the will of My Father that sent Me, and to finish His work. John 4:34 What manner of doubt is there that the subjection of the Son in me is still in the future, in whom the work of the Father is unfinished, because I myself am not yet perfect? I, who make the work of God to be unfinished, do I make the Son of God to be in subjection? But that is not a matter of wrong, it is a matter of grace. For in so far as we are made subject, it is to our profit, not to that of the Godhead, that we are made subject to the law, that we are made subject to grace. For formerly, as the Apostle himself has said, the wisdom of the flesh was at enmity with God, for it was not made subject to the law, Romans 8:7 but now it is made subject through the Passion of Christ.

Chapter 14.

He continues the discussion of the difficulty he has entered upon, and teaches that Christ is not subject but only according to the flesh. Christ, however, while in subjection in the Flesh, still gave proofs of His Godhead. He combats the idea that Christ is made subject in This. The humanity indeed, which He adopted, has been so far made subject in us, as ours has been raised in that very humanity of His. Lastly, we are taught, when that same subjection of Christ will take place.

170. However, lest anyone should cavil, see what care Scripture takes under divine inspiration. For it shows to us in what Christ is made subject to God, while it also teaches us in what He made the universe subject to Himself. And so it says: Now we see not yet all things put under Him. Hebrews 2:8 For we see Jesus made a little lower than the angels for the suffering of death. Hebrews 2:9 It shows therefore that He was made lower in taking on Him our flesh. What then hinders Him from openly showing His subjection in taking on Him our flesh, through which He subjects all things to Himself, while He Himself is made subject in it to God the Father?

171. Let us then think of His subjection. Father, He says, if You be willing, remove this cup from Me; nevertheless not My will but Yours be done. Luke 22:42 Therefore that subjection will be according to the assumption of human nature; as we read: Being found in fashion as a man, He humbled Himself, being made obedient unto death. Philippians 2:8 The subjection therefore is that of obedience; the obedience is that of death; the death is that of the assumed humanity; that subjection therefore will be the subjection of the assumed humanity. Thus in no wise is there a weakness in the Godhead, but there is such a discharge of pious duty as this.

172. See how I do not fear their intentions. They allege that He must be subject to God the Father, I say He was subject to Mary His Mother. For it is written of Joseph and Mary: He was subject unto them. Luke 2:51 But if they think so, let them say how the Deity was made subject to men.

173. Let not the fact that He is said to have been made subject work against Him, Who receives no hurt from the fact that He is called a servant, or is stated to have been crucified, or is spoken of as dead. For when He died He lived; when He was made subject He was reigning; when He was buried He revived again. He offered Himself in subjection to human power, yet at another time He declared He was the Lord of eternal glory. He was before the judge, yet claimed for Himself a throne at the right hand of God, as Judge forever. For thus it is written: Hereafter you shall see the Son of Man sitting on the right hand of the power of God, and coming in the clouds of heaven. Matthew 26:64 He was scourged by the Jews, and commanded the angels; He was born of Mary under the law; Galatians 4:4 He was before Abraham above the law. On the cross He was revered by nature; the sun fled; the earth trembled; the angels became silent. Could the elements see the Generation of Him Whose Passion they feared to see? And will they uphold the subjection of an adorable Nature in Him, in Whom they could not endure the subjection of the body?

174. But since the Father, the Son, and the Holy Spirit are of one Nature, the Father certainly will not be in subjection to Himself. And therefore the Son will not be in subjection in that in which He is one with the Father; lest it should seem that through the unity of the Godhead the Father also is in subjection to the Son. Therefore, as upon that cross it was not the fullness of the Godhead, but our weakness that was brought into subjection, so also will the Son hereafter become subject to the Father in the participation of our nature, in order that when the lusts of the flesh are brought into subjection the heart may have no care for riches, or ambition, or pleasures; but that God may be all to us, if we live after His image and likeness, as far as we can attain to it, through all.

175. The benefit has passed, then, from the individual to the community; for in His flesh He has tamed the nature of all human flesh. Thus, according to the Apostle: As we have borne the image of the earthly, so also shall we bear the image of the heavenly. 1 Corinthians 15:49 This thing certainly cannot come to pass except in the inner man. Therefore, laying aside all these, that is those things which we read of: anger, malice, blasphemy, filthy communication; Colossians 3:8 as he also says below: Let us, having put off the old man with his deeds, put on the new man, which is renewed in knowledge after the image of Him that created Him. Colossians 3:9-10

176. And that you might know that when he says: That God may be all in all, he does not separate Christ from God the Father, he also says to the Colossians: Where there is neither male nor female, Jew nor Greek, Barbarian nor Scythian, bond nor free, but Christ is all and in all. Colossians 3:11 So also saying to the Corinthians: That God may be all and in all, he comprehended in that the unity and equality of Christ with God the Father, for the Son is not separated from the Father. And in like manner as the Father works all and in all, so also Christ works all and in all. If, then, Christ also works all in all, He is not made subject in the glory of the Godhead, but in us. But how is He made subject in us, except in the way in which He was made lower than the angels, I mean in the sacrament of His body? For all things which served their Creator from their first beginning seemed not as yet to be made subject to Him in that.

177. But if you should ask how He was made subject in us, He Himself shows us, saying: I was in prison, and you came unto Me; I was sick, and you visited Me: Inasmuch as you have done it unto one of the least of these you have done it unto Me. Matthew 25:36, 40 You hear of Him as sick and weak, and art not moved. You hear of Him in subjection, and art moved, though He is sick and weak in Him in whom He is in subjection, in whom He was made sin and a curse for us.

178. As, then, He was made sin and a curse not on His own account but on ours, so He became subject in us not for His own sake but for ours, being not in subjection in His eternal Nature, nor accursed in His eternal Nature. For cursed is every one that hangs on a tree. Galatians 3:13 Cursed He was, for He bore our curses; in subjection, also, for He took upon Him our subjection, but in the assumption of the form of a servant, not in the glory of God; so that while he makes Himself a partaker of our weakness in the flesh, He makes us partakers of the divine Nature in His power. But neither in one nor the other have we any natural fellowship with the heavenly Generation of Christ, nor is there any subjection of the Godhead in Christ. But as the Apostle has said that on Him through that flesh which is the pledge of our salvation, we sit in heavenly places, Ephesians 2:6 though certainly not sitting ourselves, so also He is said to be subject in us through the assumption of our nature.

179. For who is so mad as to think, as we have said already, that a seat of honour is due to Him at the right hand of God the Father, when that is granted to Christ according to the flesh by the Father of His Generation, even a seat of a heavenly and equal power? The angels worship, and do you attempt to overthrow the throne of God with impious presumption?

180. It is written, you say, that when we were dead in sins, He has quickened us in Christ, by Whose grace you are saved, and has raised us up together, and made us sit together in heavenly places in Christ Jesus. Ephesians 2:5-6 I acknowledge that it is so written; but it is not written that God suffers men to sit on His right hand, but only to sit there in the Person of Christ. For He is the foundation of all, and is the head of the Church, Ephesians 5:23 in Whom our common nature according to the flesh has merited the right to the heavenly throne. For the flesh is honoured as having a share in Christ Who is God, and the nature of the whole human race is honoured as having a share in the flesh.

181. As we then sit in Him by fellowship in our fleshly nature, so also He, Who through the assumption of our flesh was made a curse for us (seeing that a curse could not fall upon the blessed Son of God), so, I say, He through the obedience of all will become subject in us; when the Gentile has believed, and the Jew has acknowledged Him Whom he crucified; when the Manichæan has worshipped Him, Whom he has not believed to have come in the flesh; when the Arian has confessed Him to be Almighty, Whom he has denied; when, lastly, the wisdom of God, His justice, peace, love, resurrection, is in all. Through His own works and through the manifold forms of virtues Christ will be in us in subjection to the Father. And when, with vice renounced and crime at an end, one spirit in the heart of all peoples has begun to cleave to God in all things, then will God be all and in all. 1 Corinthians 15:28

Chapter 15.

He briefly takes up again the same points of dispute, and shrewdly concludes from the unity of the divine power in the Father and the Son, that whatever is said of the subjection of the Son is to be referred to His humanity alone. He further confirms this on proof of the love, which exists alike in either.

182. Let us then shortly sum up our conclusion on the whole matter. A unity of power puts aside all idea of a degrading subjection. His giving up of power, and His victory as conqueror won over death, have not lessened His power. Obedience works out subjection. Christ has taken obedience upon Himself, obedience even to taking on Him our flesh, the cross even to gaining our salvation. Thus where the work lies, there too is the Author of the work. When therefore, all things have become subject to Christ, through Christ's obedience, so that all bend their knees in His name, then He Himself will be all in all. For now, since all do not believe, all do not seem to be in subjection. But when all have believed and done the will of God, then Christ will be all and in all. And when Christ is all and in all, then will God be all and in all; for the Father abides ever in the Son. How, then, is He shown to be weak, Who redeemed the weak?

183. And lest you should by chance attribute to the weakness of the Son, that it is written, that God has put all things in subjection under Him; learn that He has Himself brought all things into subjection to Himself, for it is written: Our conversation is in heaven, from whence also we look for the Saviour, the Lord Jesus, Who shall change our vile body that it may be fashioned like His glorious body

according to the working, whereby He is able to subdue all things unto Himself. Philippians 3:20-21 You have learned, therefore, that He can subdue all things unto Himself according to the working of His Godhead.

184. Learn now how He receives all things in subjection according to the flesh, as it is written: Who wrought in Christ, raising Him from the dead, and setting Him at His own right hand in the heavenly places, above principality and power and might and dominion and every name that is named not only in this world, but also in that which is to come; and has put all things under His feet. Ephesians 1:20-21 According to the flesh then all things are given to Him in subjection; according to which also He was raised from the dead, both in His human soul and His rational subjection.

185. Many nobly interpret that which is written: Truly my soul will be in subjection to God; He said soul not Godhead, soul not glory. And that we might know that the Lord has spoken through the prophet of the adoption of our human nature, He added: How long will you cast yourselves upon a man? As also He says in the Gospel: Why do you seek to kill Me, a man? John 8:40 And He added again: Nevertheless they desired to refuse My price, they ran in thirst, they blessed with their mouth, and cursed with their heart. For the Jews, when Judas brought back the price, Matthew 27:4 would not receive it, running on in the thirst of madness, for they refused the grace of a spiritual draught.

186. This is the reverent interpretation of subjection, for since this is the office of the Lord's Passion, He will be subject in us in that in which He suffered. Do we ask wherefore? That neither angels, nor powers, nor height, nor depth, nor things present, nor things to come, nor any other creature may separate us from the love of God, which is in Christ Jesus. Romans 8:38-39 We see then, from what has been said, that no creature is excepted; but that every one, of whatever kind it may be, is enumerated among those he mentioned above.

187. At the same time, we must also think of the words which, after first saying Who shall separate us from the love of Christ? Romans 8:35 he wrote next: Neither death, nor life, nor any other creature can separate us from the love of God, which is in Christ Jesus. We see, then, that the love of God is the same as the love of Christ. Thus it was not without reason that he wrote of the love of God, which is in Christ Jesus, lest otherwise you might imagine that the love of God and of Christ was divided. But there is nothing that love divides, nothing that the eternal Godhead cannot do, nothing that is unknown to the Truth, or deceives Justice, or escapes the notice of Wisdom.

Chapter 16.

The Arians are condemned by the Holy Spirit through the mouth of David: for they dare to limit Christ's knowledge. The passage cited by them in proof of this is by no means free from suspicion of having been corrupted. But to set this right, we must mark the word Son. For knowledge cannot fail Christ as Son of God, since He is Wisdom; nor the recognition of any part, for He created all things. It is not possible that He, who made the ages, cannot know

the future, much less the day of judgment. Such knowledge, whether it concerns anything great or small, may not be denied to the Son, nor yet to the Holy Spirit. Lastly, various proofs are given from which we can gather that this knowledge exists in Christ.

188. Wherefore we ought to know that they who make such statements are accursed and condemned by the Holy Spirit. For whom else but the Arians in chief does the prophet condemn, seeing that they say that the Son of God knows neither times nor years. For there is nothing which God is ignorant of; and Christ, yea the most high Christ, is God, for He is God over all. Romans 9:5

189. See how horrified holy David is at such men, in limiting the knowledge of the Son of God. For thus it is written: They are not in the troubles of other men, neither will they be scourged with men; therefore their pride has laid hold on them; they are covered with their wickedness and blasphemy; their iniquity has stood forth as it were with fatness; they have passed on to the thoughts of their heart. Truly he condemns those who think that divine things are to be regarded in the light of the thoughts of the heart. For God is not subject to arrangement or order; seeing that we do not perceive even those very things, which are common among men and often occur in the history of the human race, to turn out always after the arrangement of some stated rule, but often to happen suddenly in some secret and mysterious manner.

190. They have thought, he says, and have spoken wickedness. They have spoken wickedness against the Most High. They have set their mouth against heaven. We see then that he condemns, as guilty of wicked blasphemy, those who claim for themselves the right to arrange the heavenly secrets after the semblance of our human nature.

191. And they have said: How has God known? And is there knowledge in the Most High? Do not the Arians echo this daily, saying that all knowledge cannot exist in Christ? For He, they say, stated that He knew not the day nor hour. Do they not say, how did He know, while they maintain that He could not know anything but what He heard and saw, and apply by a blasphemous interpretation that which concerns the unity of the divine Nature to weaken His power?

192. It is written, they say: But of that day and that hour knows no man, no, not the angels which are in heaven, neither the Son, but the Father only. Mark 13:32 First of all the ancient Greek manuscripts do not contain the words, neither the Son. But it is not to be wondered at if they who have corrupted the sacred Scriptures, have also falsified this passage. The reason for which it seems to have been inserted is perfectly plain, so long as it is applied to unfold such blasphemy.

193. Suppose however that the Evangelist wrote thus. The name of Son embraces both natures. For He is also called Son of Man, so that in the ignorance attached to the assumption of our nature, He seems not to have known the day of the judgment to come. For how could the Son of God be ignorant of the day, seeing that the treasures of the wisdom and knowledge of God are hidden in Him? Colossians 2:3

194. I ask then, whether He had this knowledge by reason of His Being, or by chance? For all knowledge comes to us either through nature, or by learning. It is supplied by nature, as for instance to a horse to enable it to run, or to a fish to enable it to swim. For they do this without learning. On the other hand, it is by learning that a man is enabled to swim. For he could not do so unless he had learned. Since therefore nature enables dumb animals to do and to know what they have not learned, why should you give an opinion on the Son of God, and say whether He has knowledge by instruction or by nature? If by instruction, then He was not begotten as Wisdom, and gradually began to be perfect, but was not always so. But if He has knowledge by nature, then He was perfect in the beginning, He came forth perfect from the Father; and so needed no foreknowledge of the future.

195. He therefore was not ignorant of the days; for it does not fall to the lot of the Wisdom of God to know in part and in part to be ignorant. For how can He who made all things be ignorant of a part, since it is a less thing to know than to make. For we know many things which we cannot make, neither do we all know things in the same way but we know them in part. For a countryman knows the force of the wind and the courses of the stars in one way — the inhabitant of a city knows them in another way — and a pilot in yet a third way. But although all do not know all things, they are said to know them; but He alone knows all things in full, Who made all things. The pilot knows for how many watches Arcturus continues, what sort of a rising of Orion he will discover, but he knows nothing of the connection of the Vergiliæ and of the other stars, or of their number or names, as does He Who numbers the multitude of stars, and calls them all by their names; Whom indeed the power of His work cannot escape.

196. How then do you wish the Son of God to have made these things? Like a signet ring which does not feel the impression it makes? But the Father made all things in wisdom, that is, He made all things through the Son, who is the Virtue and Wisdom of God. 1 Corinthians 1:24 But it befits such Wisdom as that to know both the powers and the causes of His own works. Thus the Creator of all things could not be ignorant of what He did — or be without knowledge of what He had Himself given. Therefore He knew the day which He made.

197. But you say that He knows the present and does not know the future. Though this is a foolish suggestion, yet that I may satisfy you on Scriptural grounds, learn that He made not only what is past, but also what is future, as it is written: Who made things to come. Isaiah 45:11 Elsewhere too Scripture says: By whom also He made the ages, who is the brightness of His glory and the express Image of His Person. Hebrews 1:2-3 Now the ages are past and present and future. How then were those made which are future, unless it is that His active power and knowledge contains within itself the number of all the ages? For just as He calls the things that are not as though they were, Romans 4:17 so has He made things future as though they were. It cannot come to pass that they should not be. Those things which He has directed to be, necessarily will be. Therefore He who has made the things that are to be, knows them in the way in which they will be.

198. If we are to believe this about the ages, much more must we believe it about the day of judgment, on the ground that the Son of God has knowledge of it, as being already made by Him. For it is written: According to Your ordinance the day will continue. He did not merely say the day continues, but even will continue, so that the things which are to come might be governed by His ordinance. Does He not know what He ordered? He who planted the ear, shall He not hear? He that formed the eye shall He not see?

199. Let us however see if by chance there may be some great thing, which could be beyond the knowledge of its Creator; or at least let them choose whether they will think of something great and superior to other things, or something very little and mean. If it is very little and mean, it is no loss, to speak after our fashion, to know nothing of worthless and petty things. For as it is a sign of power to know the greatest things, it seems rather to be a sign of inferior work to look upon what is worth less. Thus He is freed from fastidiousness, yet is not deprived of His power.

200. But if they think it a great and important thing to know the day of judgment: Let them say what is greater or better than God the Father. He knows God the Father, as He Himself says: No man knows the Father but the Son and he to whomsoever the Son will reveal Him. Matthew 11:27 I say, does He know the Father and yet not know the day? So then you believe that He reveals the Father, and yet cannot reveal the day?

201. Next because you make certain grades, so as to put the Father before the Son, and the Son before the Holy Spirit, tell me whether the Holy Spirit knew the day of judgment. For no thing is written of Him in this place. You deny it entirely. But what if I show you He knew it? For it is written: But God has revealed them to us by His Spirit, for the Spirit searches all things, yea the deep things of God.
1 Corinthians 2:10 Wherefore, because He searches the deep things of God, since God knows the day of judgment, the Spirit also knows it. For He knows all that God knows, as also the Apostle states, saying: For what man knows the things of a man, save the spirit of man which is in him, even so the things of God knows no man, but the Spirit of God. 1 Corinthians 2:11 Take heed therefore lest either by denying that the Holy Spirit knows, you should deny that the Father knows; (For the things of God, the Spirit of God also knows, but the things which the Spirit of God does not know, are not the things of God). Or by confessing that the Spirit of God knows, what you deny that the Son of God knows, you should put the Spirit before the Son in opposition to your own declaration. But to hesitate on this point is not only blasphemous but also foolish.

202. Now consider how knowledge is acquired, and let us show that the Son Himself proved that He knew the day. For what we know we make clear either by mention of time or place or signs or persons, or by giving their order. How then did He not know the day of judgment Who described both the hour and the place of judgment, and the signs and the cases?

203. And so you have it: In that hour he which shall be on the housetop let him not come down to take his goods out of his house, and he that is in the field, let him

likewise not return back. Luke 17:31 To such a point in the future did He know the issues of dangers, that He even showed the means of safety to those in danger.

204. Could the Lord be ignorant of a day Who Himself said of Himself that the Son of Man is Lord of the Sabbath? Matthew 12:8

205. He has also elsewhere marked out a place, when He said to His disciples who were showing Him the building of the temple, Do you see all these things? Verily I say unto you, there shall not be left one stone upon another which shall not be thrown down. Matthew 24:2

206. When questioned also about a sign by His disciples, He answered: Take heed that you be not deceived. For many shall come in My name, saying I am Christ; Luke 21:8 and further on He says: and great earthquakes shall be in various places, and famines, and pestilences, and terrors from heaven, and there shall be great signs. Luke 21:11 Thus He has described both persons and signs.

207. In what manner He tells that the armies will surround Jerusalem, or that the times of the Gentiles are to be fulfilled, and in what order — all this is disclosed to us by the witness of the Gospel words. Therefore He knew all things.

Chapter 17.

Christ acted for our advantage in being unwilling to reveal the day of judgment. This is made plain by other words of our Lord and by a not dissimilar passage from Paul's writings. Other passages in which the same ignorance seems to be attributed to the Father are brought forward to meet those who are anxious to know why Christ answered His disciples, as though He did not know. From these Ambrose argues against them that if they admit ignorance and inability in the Father, they must admit that the same Substance exists in the Son as in the Father; unless they prefer to accuse the Son of falsehood; since it belongs neither to Him nor to the Father to deceive, but the unity of both is pointed out in the passage named.

208. But we ask for what reason He was unwilling to state the time. If we ask it, we shall not find it is owing to ignorance, but to wisdom. For it was not to our advantage to know; in order that we being ignorant of the actual moments of judgment to come, might ever be as it were on guard, and set on the watchtower of virtue, and so avoid the habits of sin; lest the day of the Lord should come upon us in the midst of our wickedness. For it is not to our advantage to know but rather to fear the future; for it is written: Be not high-minded but fear. Romans 11:20

209. For if He had distinctly stated the day, he would seem to have laid down a rule of life for that one age which was nearest to the judgment, and the just man in the earlier times would be more negligent, and the sinner more free from care. For the adulterer cannot cease from the desire of committing adultery unless he fears punishment day by day, nor can the robber forsake the hiding places in the woods

where he dwells, unless he knows punishment is hanging over him day by day. For impurity generally spurs them on, but fear is irksome to the end.

210. Therefore I have said that it was not to our advantage to know; nay, it is to our advantage to be ignorant, that through ignorance we might fear, through watchfulness be corrected, as He Himself said: Be ready, for you know not at what hour the Son of Man comes. Matthew 24:44 For the soldier does not know how to watch in the camp unless he knows that war is at hand.

211. Wherefore at another time also the Lord Himself when asked by his Apostles (Yes, for they did not understand it as Arius did, but believed that the Son of God knew the future. For unless they had believed this, they would never have asked the question.)— the Lord, I say, when asked when He would restore the kingdom to Israel, did not say that He did not know, but says: It is not for you to know the times or years, which the Father has put in His own power. Acts 1:7 Mark what He said: It is not for you to know! Read again, It is not for you. For you, He said, not for Me, for now He spoke not according to His own perfection but as was profitable to the human body and our soul. For you therefore He said, not for Me.

212. Which example the Apostle also followed: But of the times and seasons, brethren, he says, you have no need that I write unto you. 1 Thessalonians 5:1 Thus not even the Apostle himself, the servant of Christ, said that he knew not the seasons, but that there was no need for the people to be taught; for they ought ever to be armed with spiritual armour, that the virtue of Christ may stand forth in each one. But when the Lord says: Of the times which the Father has put in His own power, Acts 1:7 He certainly cannot be without a share in His Father's knowledge, in whose power He is by no means without a share. For power grows out of wisdom and virtue; and Christ is both of these.

213. But you ask, why did He not refuse His disciples as one who knew, but would not say; and, why did He state instead that neither the angels nor the Son knew? Mark 13:32 I too will ask you why God says in Genesis: I will go down now, and see whether they have done altogether according to the cry that has come unto Me. And if not, that I may know. Genesis 18:21 Why does Scripture also say of God: And the Lord came down to see the city and the tower, which the sons of men built. Genesis 11:5 Why also does the prophet say in the Book of the Psalms: The Lord looked down upon the children of men, to see if there were any that did understand, and that did seek God? Just as though in one place, if God had not descended, and in the other, if He had not looked down, He would have been ignorant either of men's work or of their merits.

214. But in the Gospel of Luke also you have the same, for the Father says: What shall I do? I will send My beloved Son; it may be that they will reverence Him. Luke 20:13 In Matthew and in Mark you have: But He sent His only Son, saying: they will reverence My Son; Matthew 21:37 In one book He says: It may be that they will reverence My Son; Mark 12:6 and is in doubt as though He does not know; for this is the language of one in doubt. But in the two other books He says: They will reverence My Son; that is, He declares that reverence will be shown.

215. But God can neither be in doubt, nor can He be deceived. For he only is in doubt, who is ignorant of the future; and he is deceived, who has predicted one thing, while another has happened. Yet what is plainer than the fact that Scripture states the Father to have said one thing of the Son, and that the same Scripture proves another think to have taken place? The Son was beaten, He was mocked, was crucified, and died. He suffered much worse things in the flesh than those servants who had been appointed before. Was the Father deceived, or was He ignorant of it, or was He unable to give help? But He that is true cannot make a mistake; for it is written: God is faithful Who does not lie. Titus 1:2 How was He ignorant, Who knows all? What could He not do, Who could do all?

216. Yet if either He was ignorant, or had not power (for you would sooner agree to say that the Father did not know than own that the Son knows), you see from this very fact that the Son is of one Substance with the Father; seeing that the Son like the Father (to speak in accordance with your foolish ideas) does not know all things, and cannot do all things. For I am not so eager or rash in giving praise to the Son as to dare to say that the Son can do more than the Father; for I make no distinction of power between the Father and the Son.

217. But perhaps you say that the Father did not say so, but that the Son erred about the Father. So now you convict the Son not only of weakness, but also of blasphemy and lying. However if you do not believe the Son with regard to the Father, neither may you believe Him with regard to that. For if He wished to deceive us in saying that the Father was in doubt as though He knew not what would take place, He wished also to deceive us about Himself in saying that He did not know the future. It would be far more endurable for Him to stretch the veil of ignorance in front of that which He does of His own accord, than that He should seem to be deluded by a result contrary to what He had foretold in the things He had declared of His Father.

218. But neither is the Father deceived, not does the Son deceive. It is the custom of the holy Scriptures to speak thus, as the examples I have already given, and many others testify, so that God feigns not to know what He does know. In this then a unity of Godhead, and a unity of character is proved to exist in the Father and in the Son; seeing that, as God the Father hides what is known to Him, so also the Son, Who is the image of God in this respect, hides what is known to Him.

Chapter 18.

Wishing to give a reason for the Lord's answer to the apostles, he assigns the one received to Christ's tenderness. Then when another reason is supplied by others he confesses that it is true; for the Lord spoke it by reason of His human feelings. Hence he gathers that the knowledge of the Father and the Son is equal, and that the Son is not inferior to the Father. After having set beside the text, in which He is said to be inferior, another whereby He is declared to be equal, he censures the rashness of the Arians in judging about the Son, and shows that while they wickedly make Him to be inferior, He is rightly called a Stone by Himself.

219. We have been taught therefore that the Son of God is not ignorant of the future. If they confess this, I too — that I may now answer why He declared that neither angels, nor the Son, but only the Father knows— call to mind His wonted love for His disciples also in this passage, and His grace, which by its very frequency ought to have been known to all. For the Lord, filled with deep love for His disciples, when they asked from Him what He thought unprofitable for them to know, prefers to seem ignorant of what He knows, rather than to refuse an answer. He loves rather to provide what is useful for us, than to show His own power.

220. There are, however, some not so faint-hearted as I. For I would rather fear the deep things of God, than be wise. There are some, however, relying on the words: And Jesus increased in age and in wisdom and in favour with God and man, Luke 2:52 who boldly say, that according to His Godhead indeed He could not be ignorant of the future, but that in His assumption of our human state He said that He as Son of Man was in ignorance before His crucifixion. For when He speaks of the Son, He does not speak as it were of another; for He Himself is our Lord the Son of God and the Son of a Virgin. But by a word which embraces both, He guides our mind, so that He as Son of Man according to His adoption of our ignorance and growth of knowledge, might be believed as yet not fully to have known all things. For it is not for us to know the future. Thus He seems to be ignorant in that state in which He makes progress. For how does He progress according to His Godhead, in Whom the fullness of the Godhead dwells? Colossians 2:9 Or what is there which the Son of God does not know, Who said: Why do you think evil in your hearts? Matthew 9:4 How does He not know, of Whom Scripture says: But Jesus knew their thoughts? Luke 6:8

221. This is what others say, but I— to return to my former point, where I stated it was written of the Father: It may be they will reverence My Son, — I think indeed this was written in order that the Father, as He was speaking of men, might also seem to have spoken with human feelings. But still more am I inclined to think that the Son Who went about with men, and lived the life of man, and took upon Him our flesh, assumed also our feelings; so that after our ignorance He might say He knew not, though there was not anything He did not know. For though He seemed to be a man in the reality of His body, yet was He Life, and Light, and virtue came out of Him, Luke 6:19 to heal the wounds of the injured by the power of His Majesty.

222. You see then that this matter has been solved for you, since the saying of the Son is referred to the assumption of our state in its fullness, and it was thus written concerning the Father, in order that you might cease to cavil at the Son.

223. There was nothing then of which the Son of God was ignorant, for there was nothing of which the Father was ignorant. But if the Son was ignorant of nothing, as we now conclude, let them say in what respect they wish Him to seem to be inferior. If God has begotten a Son inferior to Himself, He has granted Him less. If He has granted Him less, He either wished to give less, or could only give less. But the Father is neither weak nor envious, seeing that there was neither will nor power before the Son. For wherein is He inferior, Who has all things even as the Father has them? He

has received all things from the Father by right of His Generation, John 16:15 and has shown forth the Father wholly by the glory of His Majesty.

224. It is written, they say: For the Father is greater than I. John 14:28 It is also written: He thought it not robbery to be equal with God. Philippians 2:6 It is written again that the Jews wished to kill Him, because He said He was the Son of God, making Himself equal with God. John 5:18 It is written: I and My Father are one. John 10:30 They read one, they do not read many. Can He then be both inferior and equal in the same Nature? Nay, the one refers to His Godhead, the other to His flesh.

225. They say He is inferior: I ask who has measured it, who is of so overweening a heart, as to place the Father and the Son before his judgment seat to decide upon which is the greater? My heart is not haughty nor are my eyes raised unto vanity, says David. King David feared to raise his heart in pride in human affairs, but we raise ours even in opposition to the divine secrets. Who shall decide about the Son of God? Thrones, dominions, angels, powers? But archangels give attendance and serve Him, cherubim and seraphim minister to Him and praise Him. Who then decides about the Son of God, on reading that the Father Himself knows the Son, but will not judge Him. For no man knows the Son, but the Father. Matthew 11:27 Knows it says, not judges. It is one thing to know, another to judge. The Father has knowledge in Himself. The Son has no power superior to Himself. And again: No man knows the Father, but the Son; and He Himself knows the Father, as the Father knows Him.

226. But you say that He said He was inferior, He said also He was a Stone. You say more and yet you impiously attack Him. I say less and with reverence add to His honour. You say He is inferior and confess Him to be above the angels. I say He is less than the angels, yet do not take from His honour; for I do not refute His Godhead, but I do proclaim His pity

Chapter 19.

The Saint having turned to God the Father, explains why he does not deride that the Son is inferior to the Father, then he declares it is not for him to measure the Son of God, since it was given to an angel — nay, perhaps even to Christ as man — to measure merely Jerusalem. Arius, he says, has shown himself to be an imitator of Satan. It is a rash thing to hold discussions on the divine Generation. Since so great a sign of human generation has been given by Isaiah, we ought not to make comparisons in divine things. Lastly he shows how carefully we ought to avoid the pride of Arius, by putting before us various examples of Scriptures.

227. To You now, Almighty Father, do I direct my words with tears. I indeed have readily called You inapproachable, incomprehensible, inestimable; but I dared not say Your Son was inferior to Yourself. For when I read that He is the Brightness of Your glory, and the Image of Your Person, Hebrews 1:3 I fear lest, in saying that the Image of Your Person is inferior, I should seem to say that Your Person is inferior, of which the Son is the Image; for the fullness of Your Godhead is wholly in the Son. I have often read, I freely believe, that You and Your Son and the Holy Spirit are boundless,

unmeasurable, inestimable, ineffable. And therefore I cannot appraise You so as to weigh You.

228. But be it so, that I desired with a daring and rash spirit to measure You? From whence, I ask, shall I measure You? The prophet saw a line of flax with which the angel measured Jerusalem. An angel was measuring, not Arius. And he was measuring Jerusalem, not God. And perchance even an angel could not measure Jerusalem, for it was a man. Thus it is written: I raised my eyes and saw and beheld a man, and in his hand there was a line of flax. Ezekiel 40:3 He was a man, for a type of the body that was to be assumed was thus shown. He was a man, of whom it was said: There comes a man after me, Whose shoe's latchet I am not worthy to unloose. John 1:27 Therefore Christ in a type measures Jerusalem. Arius measures God.

229. Even Satan transforms himself into an angel of light; 2 Corinthians 11:14 what wonder then if Arius imitates his Author in taking upon himself what is forbidden? Though his father the devil did it not in his own case, that man with intolerable blasphemy assumes to himself the knowledge of divine secrets and the mysteries of the heavenly Generation. For the devil confessed the true Son of God, Arius denies Him.

230. If, then, I cannot measure You, Almighty Father, can I without blasphemy discuss the secrets of Your Generation? Can I say there is anything more or less between You and Your Son when He Himself Who was begotten of You, says: All things which the Father has are Mine. John 16:15 Who has made Me a judge and a divider of human affairs? This the Son says, Luke 12:14 and do we claim to make a division and to give judgment between the Father and the Son? A right feeling of duty avoids arbiters even in the division of an inheritance. And shall we become arbiters, to divide between You and Your Son the glory of the uncreated Substance?

231. This generation, it says, is an evil generation. It seeks a sign, and there shall no sign be given it, but the sign of Jonas the prophet. Luke 11:29 A sign of the Godhead then is not given, but only of the Incarnation. Thus when about to speak of the Incarnation the prophet says: Ask you a sign. And when the king had said: I will not ask, neither will I tempt the Lord, the answer was: Behold a Virgin shall conceive. Therefore we cannot see a sign of the Godhead, and do we seek a measure of it? Alas! Woe is me! We impiously dare to discuss Him, to Whom we cannot worthily pray!

232. Let the Arians see to what they do. I have unlawfully compared You, O Father, with Your works in saying that You are greater than all. If greater than Your Son, as Arius maintains, I have judged wickedly. Concerning You first will that judgment be. For no choice can be made except by comparison, nor can anyone be put before another without a decision being first given on Himself.

233. It is not lawful for us to swear by heaven, but it is lawful to judge about God. Yet You have given to Your Son alone judgment over all.

234. John feared to baptize the flesh of the Lord, John forbade Him, saying: I have need to be baptized by You, and You come to me? Matthew 3:4 And shall I bring Christ under my judgment?

235. Moses excuses himself from the Priesthood, Peter is for avoiding the obedience demanded in the Ministry; and does Arius examine even the deep things of God? But Arius is not the Holy Spirit. Nay, it was said even to Arius and to all men: Seek not that which is too deep for you. Sirach 3:22

236. Moses is prevented from seeing the face of God; Exodus 33:23 Arius merited to see it in secret. Moses and Aaron among His Priests. Moses who appeared with the Lord in glory, that Moses then saw only the back parts of God in appearance; Arius beholds God wholly face to face! But no one, it says, can see My face and live.

237. Paul also speaks of inferior beings: We know in part and we prophesy in part. 1 Corinthians 13:9 Arius says: I know God altogether and not in part. Thus Paul is inferior to Arius, and the vessel of election knows in part, but the vessel of perdition knows wholly. I know, he says, a man, whether in the body or out of the body, I cannot tell, God knows, how he was caught up into Paradise and heard unspeakable words. 2 Corinthians 13:3-4 Paul carried up to the third heaven, knew not himself; Arius rolling in filth, knows God. Paul says of himself: God knows; Arius says of God: I know.

238. But Arius was not caught up to heaven, although he followed him who with accursed boastfulness presumed on what was divine, saying: I will set my throne upon the clouds; I will be like the Most High. Isaiah 14:14 For as he said: I will be like the Most High, so too Arius wishes the Most High Son of God to seem like himself, Whom he does not worship in the eternal glory of His Godhead, but measures by the weakness of the flesh.

www.ingramcontent.com/pod-product-compliance
Lightning Source LLC
Chambersburg PA
CBHW071403120626

46546CB00002B/799